HOME FARM

ONE FAMILY'S LIFE ON THE LAND

HOME FARM

MICHAEL WEBSTER
CAMDEN HOUSE

CAMDEN
•HOUSE•

PUBLISHING © Copyright 1989 by Camden House Publishing

Canadian Cataloguing in Publication Data

Webster, Michael
    Home farm

ISBN 0-920656-17-X

1. Moreland family.   2. Dairy farming – Ontario.
3. Farm life – Ontario.   4. Dairy farmers – Ontario
– Biography.   I. Title.

SF229.7.A1W42 1989   338.1'762142'0922
                                               C89-094332-X

Trade distribution by
Firefly Books
250 Sparks Avenue
Willowdale, Ontario
Canada M2H 2S4

Printed in Canada for
Camden House Publishing
(a division of Telemedia Publishing Inc.)
7 Queen Victoria Road
Camden East, Ontario
K0K 1J0

Design by
Linda J. Menyes

Cover illustration
by David Craig

Colour separations by
Superior Engravers Limited, Hamilton, Ontario
and Hadwen Graphics Limited, Ottawa, Ontario

Printed and bound in Canada by
D.W. Friesen & Sons
Altona, Manitoba

CONTENTS

For Debbie,
who sustains me.

FOREWORD

This book chronicles the life of one farm family through a complete growing season—from spring fence-mending to fall ploughing. It would not have been possible without the wholehearted cooperation of Bill and Eileen Moreland, their employees and their neighbours. All were friendly and completely open with their lives in the way that people who live in the country usually are—and none more than Bill and Eileen, who fed me, put me up, let me share their private moments and answered my questions with more patience than I could have mustered had our roles been reversed. They asked only one thing in return.

"Let me get this straight," Bill said when I first approached them about the project. "This book will let people know what it's like to be a dairy farmer?"

"Yes."

He and Eileen exchanged a glance. "Sure," he said.

As much as possible, then, this is their book—a diary of the summer of 1987, a forum for their views, a snapshot of their lives. In the time I spent at Rustowil Farm with Bill and Eileen, they became my friends, and I am happy to give them a chance to have their say.

My role at the farm was primarily that of an observer, and not wanting to become a character in the book, I made an effort to avoid upsetting the dynamics of Bill and Eileen's family and community relationships. I was, I think, fairly successful; certainly, I became intensely involved in their personal lives, but for the most part, I kept my opinions to myself. I was much less scrupulous about the dynamics of farm chores. I planted grain, baled hay, fixed fences, shovelled manure, ferried wagons and handled far more bales of hay and straw than I wanted to. In the barn, I helped feed, doctor and milk the cows, and in the process, I came to know most of them as individuals. Still, my contribution to the running of the farm was relatively minor, and I have identified myself as a participant only on those rare instances when not doing so would leave a gap in the narrative.

I would like to acknowledge the contribution to this book of my editor, Wayne Grady, and the rest of the people who were instrumental in its production: Tracy C. Read, Charlotte DuChene, Linda J. Menyes, Ellen Brooks Mortfield, Patricia Denard-Hinch, Marta Scythes, Marg Pearce-Wilson, Catherine DeLury, Eileen Whitney, Lois Casselman, Frank B. Edwards and Mirielle Keeling. I also thank Jennifer Bennett, Merilyn Mohr and the rest of my co-workers who were inconvenienced by my absences, both physical and mental. In addition, a wide circle of family and friends offered support, patience, understanding and an occasional swift kick when it was needed. And, of course, I need to mention my children, Stephen and Colleen, who will delight in repaying me for two years of inconsistent parenting by heaping abuse on my writing.

Finally, readers will note that the people in the book slip back and forth between metric and imperial measurements. Cows produce both gallons and kilograms of milk; Bill plants his seed at so many kilograms to the acre, then harvests his crops in either tonnes or bushels. Such is Canadian farm life in the late 20th century. I apologize to those who find it confusing, but I trust that most readers will understand the measurements as readily as the Morelands do.

BOOK I

FENCE-MENDING

The most noticeable thing about Bill Moreland is his hands. The rest of him is unremarkable: medium height, medium build, glasses, clean-shaven features that are pleasant but, well, unremarkable. He is 42 years old, and the first hints of the grey to come can be seen in his dark hair. Still, his face is largely unlined, and his trim, fit body could belong to a man 10 years younger. His hands, though, appear to have been cut off someone else's arms and stuck into Bill's sleeves. They are red and swollen; scarred, dry and cracked. His fingernails are thick and horny, white instead of pink, more flat than curved. They look as if they belong to a man in his 60s. They are the hands of a farmer.

This morning, as every morning, Bill opens the aluminum door to the milk house at ten to five and fumbles for the light switch. He lifts his hat – a red baseball cap advertising a brand of corn – rubs his hair and yawns loudly, blinking in the sudden light. He has been awake for less than five minutes, just long enough to get dressed and walk out to the barn. It will be three hours before he eats breakfast, and he has not even had a cup of coffee, although, in truth, his taste for coffee is the same as for alcohol – he drinks it if it is given to him, but he never bothers to ask for it. Next, he grabs a rechargeable flashlight from its holder on the wall, flips a switch on a stainless steel box that will give the milking equipment a final rinse, turns on the lights in the barn and steps through a glass door.

There are 75 black-and-white cows in Bill's barn, all of them purebred Holsteins, the most productive breed of dairy cow in the world, and they lie with their hind legs cocked over milk-swollen udders. Lining the sides of the long, narrow barn like cars in a parking garage, the two rows of cows are arranged nose in, tails facing a wide centre aisle that runs the 200-foot length of the barn. A pair of narrower aisles along each wall are just wide enough to allow a feed cart to pass in front of the cows. As Bill steps into the centre aisle from the short passage leading from the milk house, the younger cows get to their feet like insolent recruits. The older ones, knowing they have time, stay put. At the far end of the barn are 27 heifers (young cows not yet in production); in the end nearest the milk house, 48 adults wait to be milked.

Bill walks up and down the centre aisle, briefly flicking the flashlight beam at the vagina of each cow. He is looking for abnormalities – a swollen vulva or a bloody or mucous discharge – that would indicate the onset of estrus or abortion. This twice-daily examination is one of the many attentions to detail that have earned Bill a reputation for being a good farmer. Satisfied, he puts the flashlight back in the milk house, then pulls a spiral notebook from a drawer below the plywood shelf that serves as a desk. "April 7/87, a.m. Oneida, CD," he writes. Oneida, a reliable cow born on the farm seven years ago, has a clear discharge, an early sign of estrus. As he puts away the notebook, a pickup truck swings into the barnyard, its lights still on high beam, and parks beside the milk house. Five o'clock. Bill's employees – hired man Tom MacFarlane and herdsperson Jean Scott – have arrived.

Tom is a boyish 24, with the muscular build and easy grace of a welterweight boxer. He lacks an athlete's intensity, however, preferring measured, efficient movements to the quickness he is capable of. In big-toed leather work boots, jeans held up with red suspenders, a plaid shirt and striped engineer's cap from which shocks of straight brown hair protrude, he is the picture of a country boy, an impression strengthened by his unguarded expression and slow, shy smile. Tom is aware of this impression, and while he doesn't actually cultivate it, he doesn't plough it under either. Raised on a farm in Quebec, working on a farm in Ontario, he is proud of his rural upbringing and attitudes – he would not trade them for a cynical urban sophistication any more than he would exchange his duties here for the higher wages and benefits of a factory or office job.

Jean is Bill's sister, a year younger at 41. She is short and, since the birth of a son four years ago, inclined to a bosomy stoutness. Her upper lip shows the scars, now faint, of several childhood operations to correct a harelip, but her speech is unaffected, and if the experience made her childhood difficult, she does not admit to it. She has lively blue eyes, a good smile and an abiding, unquestioning love for animals – especially for "my girls," as she calls the cows – and an only slightly more discriminating love for her fellow humans. Her duties as herdsperson include keeping the breeding and registration records up to date, selecting sires and doing some buying and selling. She knows the cows better than Bill does, knows by heart each one's production record, its parents and grandparents, its offspring, even the name of the next calf it will bear.

She also knows the fate of each cow shipped off the farm; some have gone to buyers in the United States, Europe and South America. "Why, we even sent one to the zoo here in Gananoque," she likes to tell visitors, referring to a local wild-animal park. "When Komet – that's Oneida's mother – got too old and infirm to milk any longer, we called the zoo and they sent out a truck." She pauses for an exquisitely timed silence. "They were really good. We walked her out of the barn, and they shot her so she fell right in the back of the truck. Then they took her and cut her up to feed to the lions and the tigers. So we like to say we have one of our cows at the zoo."

At ten after six, Bill's father comes into the barn. Russell Moreland bought the 100-acre lot on which the barn now stands – what the Morelands now call the home farm – in 1931 with a loan from his father and money he had saved working on a Great Lakes freighter. He married Ruth Makin the following year. During the Depression, which Russell always calls "The Dirty Thirties," the capital letters clear in his voice, he worked the land with horses, Ruth kept hens and turkeys, and the two of them milked 25 cows by hand. One bitterly cold night in February 1943, the barn caught fire, and everything – barn, crops, cows, horses, tractor, even their dog – was lost. Russell worked the rest of that winter cutting firewood for pay, and when they rebuilt the barn in the spring, his neighbours donated a few cows to get them started again. They raised five children and bought more land, and when Bill, after graduating from college, declared he wanted more say in how the farm was run, Russell and Ruth gratefully retired.

He is now 80 years old but has more agility, energy and enthusiasm for life than many men a quarter of a century younger. Eight years ago, he had a tumour removed from his stomach, along with a good chunk of his digestive tract. His doctor has since told him that all the other patients on whom he performed that operation suffered severe side effects and died within five years. Russell has not even changed his eating habits and, as he has for 56 years, helps with chores every morning. Ruth, too, used to come to the barn every morning, but two years ago, she fell and broke her hip. She has not been in the barn since.

Russell's job is to empty the night's accumulation of manure from the narrow gutter behind the cows. He does so by walking to the far end of the barn and pushing the red button on an electrical box labelled "stable cleaner." This engages a 425-foot loop of heavy chain fitted at 16-inch intervals with paddles that scrape the gutter clean, up one side and down the other, pulling the manure through a hole in the wall and dumping it onto a concrete pad behind the barn. Russell oversees the 15-minute operation, opening the tap on a barrel positioned to drip lubricating oil onto the chain. When the stable cleaner has made a complete circuit, he shuts everything off and forks clean straw into the bottom of the gutter. Later, Bill checks the oil tap. "Sometimes," he says, "Father forgets to turn it off."

14

Bill breaks open six or eight bales of straw under the cows and into the manure gutter every day. "Some people say we use too much straw," he says, "but we have it here anyway, and boy, we sure get a lot of organic matter this way. Straw is carbon, and when it soaks up all the urine, it makes nitrogen. It does a lot of good for the soil." Every fall, Bill digs into the pile behind the barn and spreads it on his fields. The newest way to handle manure is to turn it into a liquid – keep the straw out of it, water it down to a slurry and pump it into a storage tank. "Everyone got excited about liquid systems a while back, but they're expensive, and when you have trouble with them, you really have trouble. Now it seems like this is the cheapest system, and we get all that organic matter too. Looks like we're smarter than we thought." He grins. "We're so far behind we're ahead of our time."

Also behind the times is Bill's milking equipment, known as a pipe-line system (everything in agriculture these days is a system – manure handling system, milking system, baling system, feeding system) because of the two-inch-diameter glass pipe that loops around the barn above the cows' heads. Bill, Tom and Jean share five milkers, leap-frogging their way up the double row of cows. Frothy white milk fills the pipeline, which carries it to a sealed stainless steel tank in the milk house. From udder to tank (and thence to dairy and supermarket shelf), it is never exposed to the air. In older systems, the milk from each cow was pumped into a pail, then carried to the milk house and poured through a filter into the tank – more sanitary, certainly, than hand milk-ing into an open pail but not as clean as a pipeline. In newer systems, the cows are milked in a special milking parlour, where they come to the equipment in shifts of 6 to 12 animals. The milkers work in a sunken area with the udders presented to them at waist level. The parlour can be kept cleaner than the barn, so there is some increase in sanitation, but the system's real advantage over a pipeline is in the labour it saves. Milking parlours are expensive, though, and are usu-ally found on farms with herds larger than Bill's.

Attached to most milking parlours is a loafing barn, a come-and-go-as-you-please arrangement in which the cows have the run of the place and can lie down wherever they want. Most farmers appreciate the extra freedom and exercise this affords the cows, but along with the freedom come concerns about injuries, cleanliness and an increase in mastitis – an infectious inflammation of the udder. Bill's cows are kept in "tie stalls," so called because the cows are tied to a steel bar with a short length of chain attached to a collar they wear around their necks. Some of Bill's cows wear old-fashioned leather collars, some chain. The ties have a swivel snap to prevent them from twisting and are about 18 inches long – short enough to keep the cows from backing out of their stalls, long enough to allow them to reach up with their heads when they are standing, to lay their heads on the floor when they are lying down and to curl their heads back on their flanks when they are sleeping. They can reach far enough ahead to steal a little grain or hay from their neighbours and far enough back to groom themselves or scratch an itch with their tongues. Since the cows spend more than 20 hours a day in their stalls in winter, this degree of comfort is a welcome improvement over the old-fashioned stanchions, which held the cow's neck between a pair of vertical wooden slats or steel bars.

"One time," Bill says, "I heard an old veterinarian say, 'The farmer is a stress remover,' and I never forgot that. It's true. We remove the stress of weather by providing a nice warm barn. We remove the stress of bad feed, dirty water, disease, crowding, all that. Taking away all that stress allows the cow to produce, and that's what it's all about." He moves to the next cow. "I saw a sign in a farmer's barn once that says it all: 'Every cow is a mother. Treat her like one.'"

Farmers also put some stress on their cows, pushing the limits of physiology by breeding for special traits and feeding them high-protein, high-energy diets. Bill has five cows that each produce more than 100 pounds of milk a day. That's about five gallons morning and night from each of them, 45 one-litre waxed cartons every day. One of Bill's top five cows produces enough milk in a week to keep a family of three in milk and ice cream for a year. That's a lot of milk, and to maintain that production, he feeds them a lot of grain – 45 pounds every day. "I don't feed as much grain as some farmers, though. A guy up the road feeds 60 pounds a day, and his cows are just bones. They eat all that grain, but they don't gain any weight – they put everything into their udders. It all goes into production." Genetic potential, farmers call it, the ability to eat like a horse, stay skinny and put everything into the mammaries. If they could bottle it and sell it, the farm-debt crisis would be over tomorrow. "I think cows ought to have more forage than that," Bill continues. "It's not as hard on their digestive systems, and it keeps them healthier. Cows ought to turn grass into milk. That's what they're for."

Nevertheless, Bill's cows eat very little green grass, partly because of the climate in which they live and partly because of his need to control their diet. The modern Canadian Holstein cow is a highly bred

16

creature, the paragon of her species, but she needs a carefully formulated ration to reach her full potential. For producers like Bill, fresh pasture is an inconsistent food source: it is available only three or four months of the year; its palatability and nutrition are inconsistent; and it is impossible to measure or control how much of it the cows eat. He prefers to serve pantry goods, foodstuff he has grown and stored on the farm. "When I was in agricultural college, I decided that the way to get ahead in this business was to grow your own feed. I've tried to do that, and so far, it's worked out all right."

Bill feeds his cows baled hay, haylage (alfalfa hay stored in an airtight silo), corn and barley, all of which he grows on the farm, plus a few purchased items, such as protein and mineral supplements. His feed bills are low – at least they are if his crops are good – but the investment in machinery, time and labour is heavy. And if the weather turns bad or insects or diseases reduce the crop substantially, he must still pay for his machinery, seed and fertilizer – and then buy his feed. Every spring, Bill lays his profits for the year on a 450-acre crap table and waits for the dice to stop bouncing. Too much rain, too little rain, the right amount of rain at the wrong time, too hot, too cool, late spring, early fall: these are the rolls on which the house wins. Bill watches the weather closely. He always knows what the forecast is, but he never forgets that the meteorology office is 25 miles away at the Kingston airport – the weather there is not necessarily the weather on his farm. He reads his own thermometer, measures the water in his own rain gauge and glances at his own sky every time he steps out a door.

It is almost 8:30 before morning chores are done and he can leave the barn. He's been up for 3½ hours now, but this is his first chance to consider the day. He is not happy with what he sees. March came in rather lamblike this year, with rain instead of snow, but it went out more kitten than lion, with a few flurries interspersed with more rain. There was a hard rain on the weekend, but now, in the second week of April, the sun is out, the breeze is decidedly warm, and the forecast is for more sun and even warmer temperatures. People in the city are digging light jackets out of their closets and leaving their winter coats at home. They are smiling at each other and calling this the first real day of spring.

Bill is not immune to the sheer pleasure of the day, but it is beginning to look like a hot, dry spring, and it is making him nervous. He stops beside a puddle in the driveway and puts his hands on his hips.

"Well, I know there's a lot of people who think this weather is really great," he says. "I don't want to disappoint them, but I don't like it." He looks around. The remaining snow is in ragtag drifts that follow the fencerows and reach into the fields, gripping the soil with decaying fingers. Where the ploughed ground lies exposed, clods of dirt are thawing and drying in the sun.

"Ideally," he says, "you should have nice, soft rain for a couple of weeks and the temperature come up real slow. That way, the frost goes out of the ground evenly, and the moisture gets down into the soil instead of running off into the ditches." Abrupt changes in the weather are as detrimental to the soil that will nurture Bill's crops as they are to the plants themselves. This year, his worries have started early. "These hard rains and then this" – he makes a whooshing sound and raises his arms – "sudden warming." He shakes his head and lets his arms fall. "I don't know, we'll just have to see what happens."

———

In the house, Bill's wife Eileen and their 4-year-old son Mark have breakfast ready and are waiting for "the men." Eileen is a few weeks older than Bill, petite and attractive in a girl-next-door sort of way. She wears large-framed glasses, keeps her brown hair short and uses little or no makeup, even when she and Bill go out. Her personality is bright and friendly; she usually hums her way through the day, absently singing "la-la-la-la" to a song she has forgotten the words to. Like Bill, Eileen has a strong Christian faith; unlike him, she has the gift – at times the curse – of empathy. Always willing to share the emotions of others, she finds that tears of happiness or sorrow come easily to her. "Oh, I'm always crying," she says. "I cry at weddings and funerals. I don't know why. I just seem to put myself in the other person's place. It used to embarrass me, but now I don't worry about it."

Bill and Eileen were married in 1975, when they were both 30. They share an immense practicality, and they have created a comfortable, practical marriage. Both are capable of snappishness at times, but they communicate well enough to avoid shouting matches. Neither insists on physical demonstrations of affection, and though they hug and kiss in private, public displays are minimal; instead, they show their affection in glances and in the quiet, private jokes they share. Bill is the more single-minded of the two and can usually impose his will on Eileen. Often, though, if he knows she cares about an issue, he backs off.

Mark is a thoughtful child, as curious and imperious as any 4-year-old, but he demands an independence and respect that is beyond his years. If Eileen speaks sharply to him, he is likely to respond, "Mommy, please don't yell at me. I don't like it when you do that." He is not above using tears and tantrums to get what he wants, a ploy that works better with Eileen than with Bill. Mark is adopted, a Children's Aid Society ward who came with breathtaking suddenness after they had been waiting for a year and a half. "They called on Friday and said they were bringing a baby out on Sunday," Eileen recalls. "Well, we didn't have *anything*. We had to tear into town and buy a crib and some clothes and diapers. I was so excited, I even forgot to ask if it was a boy or a girl. I didn't care. The only thing I remember thinking was, 'I hope it doesn't have red hair.' " She laughs in embarrassment. "I don't know why I thought that mattered."

Eileen was born and raised near Sharbot Lake, about an hour's drive from her present home. She was the fourth of eight children, the third of five girls, and she remembers a happy childhood. "With eight of us, our backyard was just like a playground. We had a lot of happy times, and we're still really close." She attended a one-room schoolhouse – "Well, two rooms, really" – and enjoyed the experience. "It was kind of neat. Grades six, seven and eight would dictate lessons to the younger grades, and I really enjoyed that. I decided then to be a teacher, and I never changed my mind." She flushes and drops her eyes, suddenly self-conscious. "It was always my dream."

After high school – "It was so big, I couldn't find my way around for the longest time" – and two years of teachers college in Ottawa, she realized her dream in 1965 with a grade-one class. "Oh, I think grade one is the best year to teach. The children are so enthusiastic. They believe what the teacher says – not like the older grades, when they think they already know everything. The younger children come in like open books. You can just teach them so much."

During that time, she shared an apartment with two other teachers, but not before spending a year in a boarding house best remembered for its meatloaf. "I hated it. We would have meatloaf for supper, and I just knew I would get a cold meatloaf sandwich for lunch the next day. I used to dump it in the garbage, but you know, I never said anything." She smiles. "I wouldn't do that now."

In 1970, Eileen found what she thought would be her life's work. In those days, it was called a "readiness" class. "The first year, there were 14 children who were not ready for grade one but who couldn't be held back in kindergarten. Every child in that class was different – some had auditory problems, and I remember one girl with a spatial-relationship problem who used to walk into doors. She improved the equivalent of 3½ years in one year. I really enjoyed that time." The children in that class needed a lot of attention and affection, a lot of what Eileen calls "mothering," and she was just the person to give it to them.

In January 1973, she found herself working at a treatment centre for emotionally disturbed children in Kingston. "I taught only four or five children at a time – but that was plenty," she recalls. "Boy, the language those kids used. They sure broadened my vocabulary. I remember in the first week or so of school, I had to leave the room for a minute, and when I came back, someone had written 'eff off' on the blackboard, only they spelled it right out in big letters. They wanted to see if it bothered me, to see if they could get me that way. When I came back into the room, I looked at it but I didn't say anything. I just left it on the board and went on with the lesson. After a while, one of the children came up and offered to clean the board for me. I said, 'No, it's all right. I don't need the board for anything. The janitor can clean it off.'

"That didn't stop them from swearing, but after a couple of months, I took them aside, one at a time, sat them on my lap and said, 'Look, it doesn't bother me if you swear, but you don't hear me talking like that, do you? I don't think it sounds very nice, so why don't you stop? It'll be more pleasant for everybody.' And after a while, they did." Worried that the summer holidays were causing the children to lose some of the gains made during the school year, she helped initiate a summer school programme and soon found herself supervising it.

At the time, she was sharing an apartment with a girlfriend and had become friends with Oakley and Shirley Clow. Oakley owns the John Deere dealership around the corner from Rustowil Farm. One afternoon, Eileen and Shirley got the giggles and hauled out a high school yearbook to look over the single men in the neighbourhood. When they got down to a short list, Shirley roped Oakley into passing judgement. "I believe," he said after some thought, "the man best suited for you is Bill Moreland."

In the early autumn of 1973, Bill Moreland had just turned 28 and was every inch a farm boy. Except for a stint at agricultural college, he had lived at home all his life. His mother cooked all his meals for him, did his laundry, picked up his socks. If he wanted to go somewhere by himself, he drove the farm truck, and if he had a date, he borrowed his father's car. Dates were rare, though – most Saturdays,

Bill stayed home to watch the hockey game on television, and the rest of his energies went into farming and playing pickup hockey at a local arena. He seldom touched alcohol, had tried cigarettes and cigars but had found them unappealing, and wouldn't have experimented with drugs even if he had known where to find them.

"We were worried about Bill," Russell recalls. "He wasn't interested in girls for the longest time, and we thought he was never going to get married."

"Yes," says Ruth. "I used to think, 'What will happen to Bill when we're gone?' "

They needn't have been concerned. At Shirley's urging, Oakley concocted an excuse to call Bill over to the shop, and Bill, unaware he was to be paraded before a prospective spouse, drove over on the tractor. By 1973, the '60s had arrived in rural eastern Ontario – Bill had sideburns, and his hair covered most of his ears, a style that did not suit him. He was wearing a ragged jacket and bell-bottom jeans that had been patched by his younger sister Emmy with a flamboyant paisley material. Between giggles, Eileen and Shirley peeked through the curtains and sized him up. "That first day I saw him, Bill was wearing his patched pants, and he looked pretty disreputable," Eileen says. "But I didn't let that deter me."

Bill never stood a chance. A week later, Shirley met him at a dance and made him leave his date to dance with her. Eileen continues the story: "They were dancing together, and Shirley asked Bill, 'Are you interested in meeting a girl with wife-like qualities?' I'll never forget that phrase, 'wife-like qualities.' Bill didn't faint, and the next time I saw Shirley, she said, 'I've got a date for you.' Bill picked me up for our first date at Shirley and Oakley's, and that's the story." She grins. "Shirley and Oakley lived happily ever after."

On Bill's next birthday, the Clows invited Bill and Eileen for dinner, and the two women spent the afternoon making and decorating a cake. "We made it in the shape of a farmer and put a straw hat on it and gave it a pitchfork and a patch on one knee. We spent so much time on the cake that dinner was late. Afterwards, Bill took me aside and said, 'You know, on a farm you have to have meals ready on time.' Can you imagine? Bill saying *that*? He's never been on time for a meal in his life." Six months later, in March 1975, they were married. "I remember when I was a little girl, I bet my grandmother $10 that I would never marry a farmer because I couldn't imagine anything worse. But I never paid her."

They moved in with Russell and Ruth, but the elder Morelands started work on their bungalow as soon as the frost was out of the ground and moved into it in August, leaving the old house to the young couple. Well, not entirely – Bill and Eileen still shared it with the hired man, who lived on the main floor. In fact, they did not have the house to themselves until after Tom started working on the farm in 1986 – and he stayed with them for his first month on the job. "I'll never forget the first day I came into the house after Tom moved out," says Eileen. "It felt so empty. It was so wonderful, I just put my arms out and danced from one room to the next."

A March wedding, followed by a two-week honeymoon in Jamaica – Bill's first trip anywhere – then back to the farm. Eileen finished the school year, supervised summer school and taught again in the fall. But at the Christmas break, she quit her job and walked away from teaching. The reasons were complex. The drive to Kingston and back added an hour and a half to each working day in good weather, and with winter coming, the time spent on the road could only increase. Suburbanites living near large cities might be glad of a 45-minute trip to work, but farming communities are usually more restrained in their travel, and a trip to Kingston is still a major expedition for the Morelands – something to be planned for, not undertaken on the spur of the moment.

In addition, Eileen was feeling some burnout. She had been caring for emotionally disturbed children for three years without a break. She remembers one child whose attention span, she says, was zilch – he demanded a new activity every minute of the day. As much as she enjoyed the challenge and rewards of the job, she felt its stresses too. And Bill put some pressure on her as well. After 30 years of living with his mother, he was ill-equipped to be a househusband: he had no energy, patience or time for a share of the household duties, and no skill in preparing his own meals. In fairness, Bill is now, a dozen years later, more sensitive to women's issues. Still, although he picks up after himself better than he used to, his contribution to household chores is largely restricted to setting and clearing the table or filling and emptying the dishwasher. If Eileen is away at lunchtime, he demonstrates no culinary skills beyond serving cold cereal, toast and ice cream.

"Really, though," Eileen says, "it was just more beneficial for me to be at home." With morning chores lasting from 5 till 8:30, it was inconvenient to have snow cleared out of the driveway so Eileen could get to work at 8. More important, she could look after the domestic chores and take over the bookkeeping too, freeing Bill to concentrate on the actual farming. The farm comes first, and like an ailing and cantankerous old dowager, it tends to suck up any extra time or energy. To Eileen's credit, she has resisted the farm's powerful suction and has not allowed herself to be drawn into a spiral of increasing farm responsibility. She helps with the milking during busy times, a contribution she usually enjoys, but she avoids planting, harvesting and other fieldwork. She claims to be happy and to find her life full and rewarding, and except for a trace of wistfulness when she talks about her teaching years, there is no reason to doubt her.

Perhaps the transition from career woman to farm wife would have been easier if children had been forthcoming. After a dozen years of trying, however, there has been no success. "We've both been through the tests," she says. "There's no apparent reason for us not to have children, but nothing happens. Otherwise, the house would be full." It is easy to read in her unguarded eyes that this is a far greater disappointment than any regrets she may have over giving up her career as a teacher. "It seems so unfair sometimes, when you read about these abandoned babies and all these women who are having abortions." Having already received one child for adoption, their chances of getting a second are slim. "We put our name in, but it's pretty hopeless. The waiting list is so long, they don't even do a home check anymore – they just take your phone number. But we haven't given up. I believe there are a couple more children out there for us. And we could still have one of our own, even though I *am* in my 40s. I'm not worried about that."

Eileen's hopes may seem to border on the miraculous, but for her, that does not put them beyond what is possible. "I believe that things that happened a long time ago can still happen today. I remember once, a young boy from around here was taken to emergency with a respiratory problem, and about seven or eight of us sat down and prayed for him. The doctor said he was amazed that he pulled through. People look at you as if you have six heads and are developing a seventh if you say it, but I believe prayer helped him." As for her prayers to bear a child, Eileen says, "I believe God answers prayers, but I know that sometimes the answer is no."

As much as he would prefer April showers to a spell of premature summer, today is Bill's first day of spring too, the first day of outside work devoted to preparing for the coming season of growth and hope. After breakfast – porridge, toast with butter (not margarine) and jam, juice and milk – he and Tom head across the road to check the fence around a section of rough pasture. Between them, they carry a partial roll of barbed wire, some black wire (a pliable wire used to attach fences to steel posts and to join just about everything else around the farm), wire cutters, a hammer, a sharp axe and a honey can full of nails and fence staples. They walk across a double set of railroad tracks – the main Toronto-Montreal CN line – and open the gate to a 50-acre plot of land the Morelands call "the Quarry" for the obvious reason that it contains an abandoned granite pit.

When this area was first settled in the 1790s, the making of inexpensive wire was a fledgling industry and cattle were kept in with fences made of wooden rails, the zigzagging snake-rail and upright patent fences that can still be seen in various states of disrepair throughout eastern Canada. It was more than 100 years later that wire fences became common in this region, and now, virtually every farm is enclosed with a woven- or paige-wire fence – seven or eight horizontal strands four feet high, held in place at 16- or 18-inch intervals by vertical stays. Most of the paige-wire around this pasture is 20 years old or more, and it is rusted, sagging and broken. The whole fence has been propped up or wired together at least once, and in the worst places, newer wire – put in a decade ago – fortifies the old.

In short, the barrier is a parody of the fence builder's axiom, "Horse high, bull strong and pig tight." This is a fence that a reasonably long-legged horse could step over and a pig would hardly notice. As for the bull, well, sometimes there is one on the other side of the fence, so Bill avoids the grief of unwanted pregnancies by pasturing only bred heifers on this side. New paige-wire costs about 35¢ a foot, plus the fenceposts and labour to string it, and this parcel of land has a 1½-mile-long perimeter, so Bill is content to patch and repatch what is there, doing the minimum required to keep the heifers in. Indicating the rocks and trees on the other side of the fence, he says, "There's nothing over there for them anyway, and we don't push them very hard here. Not hard enough, really. They waste a lot." He means that he won't put cattle in here until June, when the grass will be up to their knees. This will give them plenty to eat, but much of the grass will turn an unappetizing brown in the summer heat. "Besides," he adds, "we feed them a little grain every day, so they don't go far." In fact, the cows stay close to the grain trough up by the tracks and do not go through the fence all summer.

Bill and Tom head south, away from the house, clambering over boulders and slithering down rain-sodden slopes, constantly checking the fence as they go. Paige-wire, says Bill, deteriorates in a definite pattern. "The uprights go first, then the middle strands. The top and bottom are always the last to go. They must put more steel in them." They pick up branches that have fallen across the fence, prop up sagging wires, rewire broken ones and brace wobbly posts. They carefully straighten and reuse rusty staples pulled from useless posts and salvage bits of black wire from previous patch jobs. The savings from a day of this tedious recycling would not buy a cup of coffee, but Bill's sense of thrift is deeply ingrained. Occasionally, they sharpen the end of a fallen sapling and drive it into the rocky ground to serve as a new fencepost. "We should have brought the tractor and auger," says Bill as Tom tries unsuccessfully to jab a stake into the ground. Tom smiles at the joke, for the spot is inaccessible to tractors and the ground impervious to even a tractor-driven posthole auger. "I think I got lucky," he grunts. With every thrust, the earth around the hole quivers and rocks can be heard rubbing together underground, but Tom has found a seam, and the post goes in a foot or more. Good enough. They wire on a few strands of fence.

Leaving the rocky land, they cross a couple of grassy meadows, hop over a small creek and climb up a wooded slope. Here, suddenly, the rest of the world seems remote. Cars and trucks are presumably roaring down Highway 401 a couple of miles to the south, but here, the only sound is last year's leaves rustling in the breeze. Overhead, a pair of mallards beat their way north, and in the woods, heard but unseen, a ruffed grouse slaps its wings together in hurried flight. Tom, who loves to hunt and camp and tramp through the woods, is much more of an outdoorsman than Bill, who defers to his knowledge.

"What kind of tracks are these, Tom?" he asks. "Groundhog?"

"Yeah, I think so." Tom is more taciturn than usual, perhaps playing up his role as frontiersman.

"What do you think made this, Tom?"

"Fox. They like to go along in places like this."

Close to the top of the hill, Tom kneels to examine a patch of mud. "Deer tracks," he declares, and Bill, leaning over his shoulder for a look, is pleased. "It's nice to know they're around. I'm not much for hunting or fishing," he says and grins. "Not much of a killer, I guess. Still, I'd like to be a good shot, and I like to shoot groundhogs. Nothing personal, just because of what they do to my fields."

He straightens up and looks around. Through a break in the leafless trees, he can see the tops of his silos, but they are half a mile away, and time and responsibility are holding their breath among the trees. The woodlot opens one's pores to the surrounding quiet – the gurgle of spring runoff, the chorus of peepers at the foot of the hill and, for the first time in months, the smell of the earth. Here, the senses are seduced, not assaulted. "We don't go to the city often," Bill says quietly. "I just don't enjoy it. You always have to watch you don't get run over or something. I prefer the quiet out here." The city he is talking about is Kingston, a modest community of 60,000 people and hardly a beehive of hit-and-run drivers.

They reach the back corner of the property and turn west. When they come to a dead stump riddled with large woodpecker holes, Tom sets down the axe and asks, "Did you hear the one about the Texan woodpecker and the Quebec woodpecker?" Bill turns and waits.

"Well, the Texan woodpecker comes up to Quebec and he sees the Quebec woodpecker working away at an old tree, and the Quebec woodpecker's beak is all bent and he's not getting anywhere. Well, the Texan woodpecker thinks, 'I better see what's going on here,' so he says, 'Mind if I give it a try?' The Quebec woodpecker says, 'Sure, go ahead.' So he gives it a try, and pretty soon the old chips are just a-flying. So the Quebec woodpecker says to himself, 'This is really something. I better go down to Texas and see what kind of trees they have down there.' So he flies down there and finds a woodpecker working on a tree, and his beak is all bent and he's not getting anywhere. So he says, 'Mind if I have a try?' and pretty soon the old chips are just a-flying." Tom pauses. "Know what the moral of the story is? The farther you are away from home, the harder your pecker is."

The hillside soon drops off into a swampy area, and Bill and Tom encounter their first big problem. Until now, the damage to the fence has been minor and the patching quick and practised, with little discussion necessary. But here, a dead pine tree – 30 feet tall and 18 inches thick – has blown down on the fence. It is far too big to lift off, and the two men set down their loads, put their hands on their hips and stare at it. They appear to be trying to levitate the tree trunk.

Bill is the first to speak. "I guess we have to go back and get the chain saw," he says. Tom does not answer, and Bill makes no move to leave. Then, "I suppose it would only take us 15 or 20 minutes to chop through the thing with the axe, and it might take us an hour to walk back and get the saw."

Tom sighs and nods. "Yeah, and use it for about 30 seconds."

Throughout this exchange, Bill and Tom continue to look at the tree trunk, not at each other. Bill plainly does not want to waste an hour going for the saw, then lugging it back home again. Obviously, he is the boss, able to order Tom to cut the tree with the axe but aware that some people might think it unreasonable to be asked to do such a job with a hand tool. He has felt around the subject, as he might feel around a cut for signs of infection, and has found no tenderness. Finally, he looks over at Tom and says, "Well, see what it's like, Tom. Is it hard or what?" Tom takes a preliminary hack at it, and the first couple of inches are punky. They raise eyebrows at each other and nod. In the end, it takes 12 minutes to chop through the trunk – three turns each – and although they have their jackets off by the time they are done, neither man is puffing. As they pick up the fallen fence and retighten it, Tom grins at a sudden thought. "Just our luck there'll be another one around the corner."

In fact, there is – a fallen elm nearly two feet in diameter and hard as bone. They both laugh when they come to it, and Bill tells Tom to bring the saw over tomorrow morning. They are heading north again now, back to the house and barn, climbing out of the swamp and back down the wooded hillside. On the other side of the fence, the landowner has opened up the woodlot by cutting down a lot of ironwoods – slow-growing trees that rarely get bigger than six inches in diameter – to give the valuable oaks and maples more room to grow. The ironwoods have been lying scattered across a rocky, hard-to-reach slope for three years, and every year, the sight of them offends Bill. "That's good wood," he complains. "I could heat my house all winter with that, and it's just going to waste. In another year or so, it won't be any good."

Finally, heading back to the house for a late lunch and already thinking of the 100-acre pasture they will walk this afternoon, they pass the backside of the Quarry – twin buttocks of bald, round granite rising 50 feet out of the pasture and separated by a 150-foot-wide fissure 500 feet long. Before it stopped operations in the late 1920s, a Toronto-based company removed thousands of cubic yards of granite from the site, most of it for cobblestones. "They tell me there's a street in Toronto that still has them," Russell says later, "the cobblestones made here. I don't know, but that's what they tell me." From the top of the rock, it's easy to see how the work was done. U-bolts, big enough for a man to stick his boot under, remain embedded in the rock where they once grounded cables for massive timbers that would lift and swing the slabs of rock while engines running the winches rumbled in nearby buildings. The squared-off ledges of exposed rock are still measured out at eight-inch intervals by half-round drill holes. After the fire in 1943, Russell pushed the remains of his barn and the carcasses of his cattle and horses over the steep sides of this hole, and the Morelands have been dumping old fences and other debris into the Quarry for half a century, but they have not yet broken the surface of the scummy water that now covers its bottom.

In its heyday, the Quarry employed 100 men, housing them in a bunkhouse next to the railroad tracks. Many of them worked in an open shed, where they used hammers and chisels to break the slabs of unyielding granite into 4-by-8-by-4-inch cobblestones. Brutal work it was, and strong, tough men they must have been to do it, sweating in the summer heat and calling to each other above the rhythmic ringing of steel on stone. A railroad siding that once curved off the main line is now a tractor path, and all that remains of the shed are a few piles of stone chips and the echoes of long-silenced hammers.

The land came up for sale soon after Russell bought the farm across the road. "I remember Dad said to me, 'Russ, don't let anyone else get in there.' That was back in The Dirty Thirties, and I didn't have the money to buy it, so Dad came down and lent it to me." He paid $500 for the 50-acre lot. "It was quite a bit of money at the time, but we've taken thousands of dollars' worth of wood out of there." The slope is rich in hardwoods: oak, ash and – uncommon in this area – hickory. "Great wood for whiffletrees and wagon tongues," says Russell. "Oh, you can't beat hickory for that. Yes sir, there's some good wood up in there, but it's hard to get. When you had the horses, of course, you were all right, but you're kind of licked with your tractors." He shakes his head. "Too bad. That wood is just going to waste."

BOOK II

PLANTING BARLEY

The weather continues unseasonably warm and dry for the next two weeks, peaking at 27 degrees C on April 20, Ruth Moreland's birthday. "The day Ruth was born," Russell says the next morning, "her father walked across the ice on the canal to get the doctor." He shakes his head. "It just shows you how things can change."

The unexpected hot spell has Bill and most of the other farmers in the area scrambling to get their spring planting done. Each year, Bill grows about 120 acres of barley, feeding most of it to his cattle, selling a tonne or two if he has it to spare and if the price is high enough. Barley is a useful crop for dairy farmers: fairly easy to grow, nutritious (slightly higher in protein and lower in carbohydrates than corn) and inexpensive to store. A modified grass, barley was first domesticated in Ethiopia or Turkey but is now grown in almost every country in the world, from the tropics to the subarctic. Although it is occasionally found floating around in soups and stews, most of the barley we consume is in the form of beer, whisky and, most often, meat — it plays an important part in the rations of cattle, swine and poultry. Canadian farmers harvest 14 million tonnes of barley a year: 6 million are exported, and most of the rest is fed to livestock.

As different from Kentucky bluegrass as a grey wolf is from a poodle, barley is still a grass, and like any suburban lawn, it grows best in cool weather. Fertilizing the land and keeping down the weeds are important to the success of the crop, but the most direct influence on crop yields is the time that it's planted. In Canada, with its cold winters, rapid warming and hot summers, timing is crucial — every week of delay in spring planting results in a measurable reduction in the harvest. To take full advantage of cool-weather growth, farmers must plant barley on well-drained land that was ploughed in the fall, and they must be ready at a moment's notice to pull out onto the fields with their tillage equipment. In the third week of April, when the fields are often covered with snow or, more likely, soaked by a steady drizzle, Bill and the other farmers up and down the concession are caught by the hot, dry weather. He hurriedly phones the Co-op to order seed and supplies.

As important as it is to get the barley in, Bill does not want to "get on the land," as farmers say, too early. As anyone who has shovelled mud can appreciate, wet soil is too sticky to be worked. Worse, driving heavy tractors on wet land compacts the soil, making it impervious to the spread of roots and, later, to life-giving rains. Each morning, Bill kicks the drying crust off the ploughed land near the barn, digs out a handful of black dirt and squeezes it, forming a ball that he tosses lightly into the air. "It should be dry enough to fall apart when you catch it a few times."

At least in the abstract, planting a field of barley is no different from planting a vegetable garden. Farmer and gardener both wait until the earth is workable before they mix it up, incorporating last year's remains and breaking up this year's clumps. Then they smooth the surface of the dirt, place the seed at the correct depth, cover it and pat the soil firmly around the seed to be sure it gets enough moisture. The difference is in the square footage and therefore in the tools: tractors and cultivators replace the spade to break up the soil, a harrow is a 16-foot-wide garden rake, and a seed drill and packer do the work of many hands.

Farming is done on such a large scale these days — a single field on a modern farm is larger than the growing area that once supplied a whole village — it is easy to forget that a tractor is simply a mechanical ox, that the massive pieces of tillage equipment it pulls are just glorified shovels, hoes and rakes, that a combine does more quickly but no better what many people in the world still do by hand. In the centuries since Central American natives first planted corn, squash and bean seeds in earth mounded over a buried fish head, agriculture in this hemisphere has seen many technological advances — in plant and animal breeding, chemistry, mechanization and international trade — that have profoundly affected farming. But they have not changed it. The miracles of growth from seed, of photosynthesis and of ripening remain the same. The unending cycle of humans being nourished by animals that are nourished by plants that are nourished from the soil to which they all return continues. Farming has been enlarged, quickened and intensified, but it has not been altered in any of its elements.

It is tempting to accept the vision of early agriculture given to us in public school — bas-relief Egyptians bringing an order to the wonderful fertility of the Nile floodplain. Recently, though, archaeologists have determined what common sense should have told us all along: the Garden of Eden does not need a gardener, and those who live surrounded by an abundance of food will not bother to invent new systems to grow it. Almost certainly, agriculture developed in the highlands, in the dry and infertile areas where food was scarce and a steady supply of it was worth creating — those places where the collective work of land clearing and irrigation and planting and weeding and harvesting and storing food was more rewarding than going out to gather it.

And so Bill waits for sun and wind to dry the soil, and he measures its progress not by an electronic digital readout but by the feel of the cool earth in his bare hands. While waiting, he sets out to make a few modifications to the new seed drill he bought last year. The drill, which cost him $8,500, is not much different in design or function from the prototype offered by pioneering English agriculturist Jethro Tull in 1730. It consists of a wide, shallow hopper for the seeds of grain, 18 revolving wheels with tiny notches that take one seed at a time and deposit them at timed intervals in one of 18 pipes that direct the seed into a shallow trench opened (then closed behind the seed) by 18 pairs of metal discs set seven inches apart. A modern addition to this clever machine is the "grass box," a second hopper that sprinkles alfalfa or other grass seeds on the ground behind the discs. Bill wants to attach the remnants of a spring-tooth harrow – three rows of lightweight sprung-steel tines that do little more than scrape the earth – behind the drill so that he can lightly cover the grass seed without making an extra trip around the field.

SEED DRILL

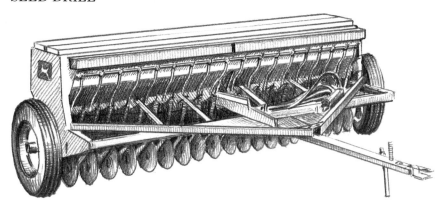

He spends most of Wednesday morning scratching his head and figuring out the best way to rejoin the harrow pieces and attach them to the drill, while Tom tightens or replaces loose or worn teeth on a cultivator. This work – like all of Bill's repairs – is done at the machine shop of his brother Tom. Tom Moreland, at 51, is nine years older than Bill, and although they are about the same height, Tom is heavier, with longer legs and a shorter back. He is more inclined to swear than Bill and has a looser, if more sardonic, sense of humour. He is also one of those people gifted with mechanical aptitude, the kind of person whose mere presence will make an engine run more smoothly. He is an auto mechanic, a welder and a machinist – a man who can never quite get his fingernails clean no matter how hard he scrubs. "Tom was always crazy about cars," his mother remembers. "Even at the table, he was always pushing his fork around the plate like a car." He built and raced stock cars for many years and now operates a make-anything, fix-anything repair shop in a large, cluttered building behind his house. A sign over the workbench reads: "An ounce of enterprise is worth a pound of government aid."

Tom tried farming once, and for a while, he and Bill formed a partnership with their father. Rustowil Farm, they called it (Russ-Tom-William), and the name has stayed, emblazoned in foot-high letters on the barn, although the partnership has long since dissolved. Tom was good at the fieldwork and wonderful with the machinery, but he lacked the special kind of patience needed around the barn. Cows did not run better in his presence. After three years, he let Bill buy him out. About that time, a farm up the road was auctioned off, and using prices from that sale, the three men set the value of Rustowil Farm at $50,000 and agreed on a split. That was in 1970. A dozen years later, Bill approached Russell about reworking the deal.

As Russell remembers it, "Bill came to me and said, 'I don't think we used Tom right.' I said, 'Well, he's satisfied,' and Bill said, 'Yes, but things have changed.' " Indeed they had. Land prices skyrocketed in the 1970s – Bill had just paid $80,000 for a run-down farm on the next concession that needed $40,000 worth of tile drainage installed – and Rustowil was worth many times what it had been in 1970.

"Well," Russell continues, "Tom had borrowed some money through Farm Credit, and he still owed about $15,000, and Bill said to me, 'I want to take that over. You tell Tom.' So I went to Tom, and he said not to worry, he had agreed to the original deal and he was doing fine financially. Then I told him, 'This is something Bill wants to do,' and he said okay.

"You know, there's a lot of families that don't get along, and it's nice to see two boys that do. Bill, he never wanted to be a millionaire, but just the same, that was a pretty decent thing to do." For his part, Bill has free access to the tools and equipment in Tom's shop, and although he pays as much as anyone else for Tom's welding or mechanical skills, he is usually put to the head of the line. So when Bill asks Tom to weld the spring harrow onto the seed drill and rig up some kind of a hook to hold it off the ground when travelling from one field to another, the work is done that afternoon.

Bill and Tom MacFarlane (when there is any chance of confusion between Tom the brother and Tom the hired man, Bill and Eileen use the last name, rather than the relationship) get back to the house for lunch at about 1 o'clock. Bill thinks of noon as lunchtime but seldom gets to the house before 12:30. Eileen usually plans the meal for 10 to 20 minutes after 12, and on the rare occasions when Bill is in before the meal is ready, he is irritated that lunch was not prepared "on time." Bill always has more chores than he has time, and he does not like to wait. Today, of course, he doesn't have to wait, but before they sit down, he spots a tow truck hauling a pickup down the road.

"Here, Tom, you should have a look. It'll be good for you to see this – a GM product being towed." Bill is a loyal Ford man; Tom takes pride in his GM half-ton.

"Hmph," Tom says. "Probably got sideswiped by some guy in a Ford."

They sit down and join hands around the table in the Quaker style, while Bill, then Eileen, say a short, unprepared grace. During the meal – meat, mashed potatoes and corn – Bill asks Eileen if she will feed the calves and help with the afternoon milking, since it is Jean's day off. "I guess so," says Eileen, who has been expecting to anyway. Then she adds, "If I'm needed." Bill groans. It is an old ritual, begun in the early years of their marriage, when a local newspaper ran a short feature on their farm. The reporter asked Bill if Eileen did much work on the farm, and Bill, not wanting to look as though he worked his young wife too hard, replied, "Oh, yes, if she's needed." Eileen, who actually does less farm work than some women but nevertheless handles all the finances and spends part of almost every day in the barn, was miffed for not getting the credit she deserved. The phrase has entered their store of private jokes.

When Eileen gets up to clear the table for dessert, she sees the Co-op truck pull into their driveway. It stops, then backs out and continues down the road. "Oh, Bill, you really have to get that mailbox changed." The Morelands have a nice black "summer" mailbox set in an old-fashioned stainless steel milk can, but they replace it every winter with a rusty old box with "Russell Moreland" still stencilled on the side. Bill faithfully puts out the old one every Halloween day – rowdies occasionally play mailbox baseball that night, bashing them from the back of a pickup truck with baseball bats – but he is less conscientious about getting the new one out in spring. The driver of the Co-op truck has apparently been confused by finding the wrong mailbox at what he thought was the right laneway.

The truck returns just as Bill and Tom are tucking into a plate of carrot cake (with icing *and* ice cream), and Eileen calls out the window that the men are still having their dinner and will be out in five minutes. The truck has a tonne of fertilizer, some alfalfa seed and herbicides – worth $1,600 altogether – and Bill wants to store it in an old 40-foot truck trailer he bought for a few hundred dollars and set on blocks between two sheds. It makes an inexpensive building that is weather- and rodent-proof. Bill wonders out loud if the Co-op truck can pull into a muddy spot and back up to the trailer doors without getting stuck.

" 'Course it can," Tom deadpans. "It's a GM."

After finishing his cake and slipping on his boots, Bill takes the invoice from the driver and introduces himself. "Hi. I'm Bill Moreland. I don't believe I know you." The driver, a thick-chested man with wire-rimmed glasses, close-cropped blond hair and forearms like Popeye, gives his name as George. "Farm boy, are you?" Bill inquires.

"Yeah, my dad was in dairy till a couple of years ago. He just keeps a few beef now." George doesn't say why his father made the change, but it is an old joke among dairy farmers that most of them quit for health reasons – they get sick of milking cows.

Bill owns about 450 acres of land – some of it rough pasture and bush like the Quarry, some of it a fairly light loam, some of it as good and productive a clay loam as any in the county – and he rents another 100 acres. By Prairie standards, where one farm can stretch over several sections of land, that is not large, but in eastern Ontario, Bill is considered to have a big medium-sized farm. Russell started in 1931 with what he calls the home farm, the 100-acre lot that includes the barn and the house where Bill and Eileen now live. He added the Quarry across the road in 1936 and, in 1944, a long, 50-acre parcel adjoining the east boundary of the home farm. Tom Moreland and his wife Betsy live in a bungalow on that land, as do Russell and Ruth, and though the fences between the two parcels of land have long since been removed, that 50 acres is known as Tom's place. This is what the farm looks like:

A long, U-shaped driveway enters the home farm from the road, travels north for about 100 yards to Bill and Eileen's house, turns right and continues east past the barn and outbuildings, then over onto

FARM LAYOUT

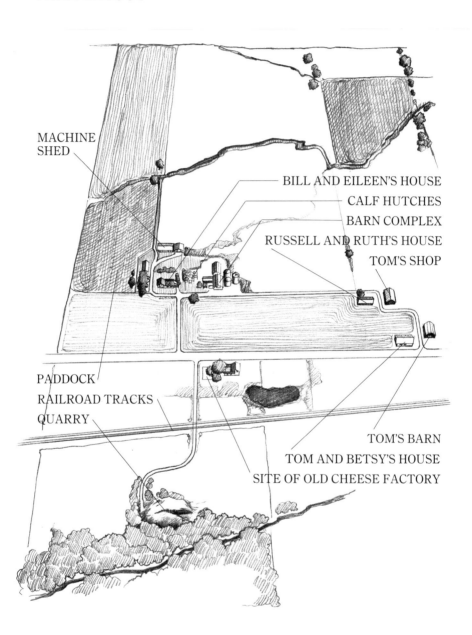

MACHINE
SHED

BILL AND EILEEN'S HOUSE

CALF HUTCHES

BARN COMPLEX

RUSSELL AND RUTH'S HOUSE

TOM'S SHOP

PADDOCK

RAILROAD TRACKS

QUARRY

TOM'S BARN

TOM AND BETSY'S HOUSE

SITE OF OLD CHEESE FACTORY

Tom's place, where it jogs between Tom's shop and Russell and Ruth's house, then turns south and meets the paved road again at Tom and Betsy's. A drainage ditch cuts across the farm from east to west, marking a clear front and back.

This year, the back of the farm and the field in the southwest corner – about 90 acres – are all in hay; the rest, about 20 acres on Tom's place and 24 acres on the home farm, was ploughed last fall for barley. The other 16 acres are either in permanent pasture or used up by buildings, exercise yards, laneways and ditches. Russell gets on the land with a cultivator on Thursday morning; by Saturday morning, it is tilled and smoothed and ready to plant.

Next year, Bill wants to take hay off the 24 acres on the home farm, so he uses a planting technique known as "seeding down": he plants alfalfa seed and barley at the same time. If everything works right, both crops will sprout, but the alfalfa, which is a slow-starting plant, will limp along while the barley shoots up with vigorous abandon. When the barley is harvested in late July or early August, the alfalfa will have a month or two of unimpeded growth to prepare for winter. Bill ensures that his alfalfa gets enough light and room to grow by blocking off every second run in the seed drill. Instead of planting 1½ bushels of barley per acre in rows 7 inches apart, he plants 1 bushel at 14 inches. Barley is a bushy plant that tends to grow in clumps, and Bill says this technique does not reduce the barley yield very much but adds significantly to the survival rate of the alfalfa. The alfalfa seed costs $50 an acre, and Bill is counting on it to give him three years of hay crops before it needs to be replanted, so there is a lot riding on the success of this seeding.

The 20-acre field on Tom's place will be used for barley again next year, so it is not seeded down, although he does sprinkle grass seed on it. This time, however, the barley is seeded at the full rate and the grass is red clover, a low-growing, short-lived plant sown as a green-manure crop; Bill will simply plough it under in the fall for the nutrition it will pass on to the soil. Clover, like alfalfa, is a legume, so it has the ability to feed on nitrogen that its roots remove from air pockets between the soil particles. (Strictly speaking, it's not the roots that remove the nitrogen but a bacteria that has a symbiotic relationship with special nodes on the roots – the important thing is the plant feeds on soil *and* air.) This means that the plant can be richer in nitrogen than the soil in which it grows: when the plant is incorporated into the soil, it enriches it, becoming a sort of fertilizer – a green manure.

It costs Bill only $7 an acre for the red-clover seed, and it will allow him to reduce his nitrogen application next spring by about 100 pounds an acre – this year, Bill is paying about $25 for 100 pounds of nitrogen. Despite these figures, though, Bill and other farmers who plant green manures are in the minority. At a time when expenses are mounting into the thousands of dollars, an extra few hundred spent on clover seed can make a big difference, especially when the results are uncertain. Bad weather or bad luck can nullify the whole investment. Also, the clover ties up nutrients and removes water from the soil as it grows, enough in a dry year to affect the current grain crop.

Still, Bill feels it is worth the risk. "Besides," he says, "it's more than just the fertilizer value. You're adding organic matter or humus or whatever you want to call it to the soil, and you just can't put a dollar value on that." Organic matter makes the heavy soil on Bill's farm more friable and more resistant to erosion, drought and heavy rains.

On Saturday morning, Bill fills the grain hopper and grass box with barley and red-clover seed and drives over to Tom's place. This is a big moment on the farm calendar, this first burying of seed in the ground – an act of faith in the ever fragile miracle of renewed life. There is no record, of course, of the first people who placed a seed in the sun-warmed ground and returned after several phases of the moon to pick the fruit of the resulting plant. But imagine the leap of intuition it must have taken to understand the connection between the release of seeds in fall and the growth of a new plant the following spring. The men and women who first struggled to follow this shadowy, distant logic must have reeled at the concept. And then they grasped the corollary of the new idea: that this berry, this fruit, this vegetable, which is only found over there, can now be made to grow here.

As a feat of connective reasoning, it equals the discovery of the relationship between sex and childbirth. As a formative step in the concept of controlling one's environment – and therefore in the evolution of humankind's sense of identity – it rivals the taming of fire. Agriculture was invented where it was needed – that is, where food was not plentiful – and it must have taken enormous strength of character to keep a hoard of seeds through the lean season and then to abandon them in the ground. Little wonder that spirits were said to live in the seeds, the soil, the rain, the sun; that the still mysterious success or failure of the crop was attributed to the whims of the gods; that sacrifices and fasting and dancing and festivals accompanied the planting of the seeds. And it is difficult not to believe that the cycle of life,

38

death and renewal so evident in the practice of agriculture influenced the progress of religious thought. There exists no better model for faith in life after death than the planting of a seed.

For today, though, Bill is more concerned with good works than with faith. Germination and growth may be miracles, but they are also botany, and he is going to do everything in his power to make sure the miracles happen. He doesn't have time for sacrifices or even rituals. Bill is too practical for that – "too much of a farmer," he often says – and indeed, he so lacks any sense of occasion that he cannot even remember the date of his wedding anniversary. Bill has been taking part in the process of spring planting for 30 years, and like a pilot going through a preflight checklist, he is too aware of the science of it to appreciate the magic. He parks the tractor next to the east boundary of the 20-acre field on Tom's place, calibrates the seed drill to apply 1½ bushels of barley and 5 pounds of clover to the acre, then hops on the tractor and, without pausing long enough to take a deep breath, lets out the clutch and begins to plant.

He marks out the field in long, north-south rows, working his way toward the barn one 12-foot drill width at a time, except that the wheels of the drill are outside the seed runs, so he must overlap each wheel track enough to keep the 7-inch row spacing uniform. This works well looking over his left shoulder as he comes south; going north and looking over his right shoulder, however, he finds that the harrow installed by his brother sticks out a bit too far on that side and all but eradicates the wheel mark he is using as a guide. Bill, who has promised Eileen they can visit some friends in the evening, does not want to take the time to stop and fix it, but he frets about leaving some bare spots. "If I'm not right on, I'd rather be too close than too far away. If I miss a strip, Father will really give me the gears about it." He works across Tom's place – the boundary between it and the home farm is still marked by a few trees – then changes to alfalfa seed in the grass box, closes alternate seed runs and begins working the home farm toward the barn.

As Bill changes fields, Tom pulls out onto the seeded portion with another tractor and the cultipacker, a 12-foot-wide roller with scalloped ridges that firm the seedbed to ensure good seed-to-soil contact. It will also mark the surface of the field in a pattern of grooves and punctures that traps rainwater and limits erosion. He starts at the far end, working in short, east-west rows perpendicular to the lines scratched in the soil by the spring-tooth harrow on the back of the seed drill. It would be easier and quicker to work the field the long way, but Bill feels this does a better job. "If you go behind the drill, the cultipacker can kind of ride along on top, but if you go crossways, it falls into each groove and packs the soil down where the seeds are. But it's rougher going." Indeed it is. The tractor bounces over the ridges, and the cultipacker slams down into the grooves with a rhythmic, metallic *clack-clack, clack-clack*. It sounds like a passing freight train. In addition, the roar of the tractor, which is at about three-quarter throttle, is loud enough that Tom has to shout to make himself heard. Both he and Bill use hearing protectors, the earmuff type worn by airport workers.

The work is not particularly hard, given a basic familiarity with farm machinery, although the seeding requires more care and concentration than the cultipacking. In many ways, it is pleasant—a spring breeze sweeps fluffy clouds out of a sunny sky, a flock of geese spearheads the spring migration, gulls wheel in lazy spirals, and the bare soil smells of sweet promise. But it is also taxing: the unseasonably warm temperature is compounded by the heat of the tractor; the bumpy ride is jarring (modern tractors have padded seats, but the frames of the machines do not have springs, so what you ride over is what you feel); the noise, even with the earmuffs, is numbing; and the tractor is always at the centre of its own dust storm. "It gets pretty boring," says Tom. "Sometimes I think I'm going to forget to turn when I get to the end and just go right through the fence. So every once in a while, I take the earmuffs off, and the noise kind of wakes me up."

Tom starts working the field in a back-and-forth pattern, but the tight 180-degree turn at each end means he has to slow down enough to shift gears, so he switches to doing it in a series of loops that reduces each corner to 90 degrees, like this:

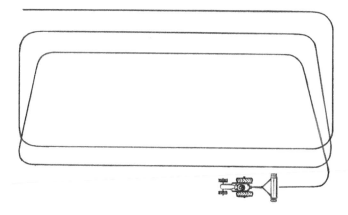

Still, he says, "you can't turn too tight, because the front tires dig into the ground and they might turn up a few seeds." There are about a million barley seeds buried in a patch of ground the size of a shopping-mall parking lot, and almost 30 million clover seeds; and Tom, who has no personal stake in the success of this crop, is concerned about a handful of seeds that may be lost by his turning too sharply. This is a gardener's attitude, this sense of caring for each individual seed, and it denotes a pride of workmanship that makes Tom a valuable employee. "Tom's a good man," says Russell. "We're lucky to have him. Damn lucky."

———

"I thought you told me those Montreal Canadiens could play hockey." It's the last week of April, and the second round of the Stanley Cup play-offs has just begun. Montreal lost its first game against Quebec last night, 7 to 5. Russell is a die-hard Montreal fan, and he is concerned about the quality of their play. Bill, who went to bed after the first period, commiserates. He is driving Russell and Tom to a farm he rents on the next concession, a mile and a half away. By the time he pulls into the lane, they have decided that Montreal will rebound and take the series.

The farm belongs to Ed Johnston, who is out in the yard when Bill arrives. Ed is a tall, brawny man in his 70s, white-haired and balding but still active, though his joints are getting stiff and he tends to lean against whatever he can for support. He has a loud voice, the kind of voice that carries, and when he laughs, as he does often, he throws his head back and booms it out – "Haw, haw, haw" – in a deep-throated rumble that rattles windowpanes. On every syllable, he raises his shoulders and lets them drop. He is wearing a silver hard hat, and chewing tobacco from a round can he keeps in his shirt pocket.

Ed and his wife raised three daughters in the same house he grew up in. "He inherited what used to be a pretty good little farm here," says Bill. "His father and mother ran it, and they had a nice little herd of dairy cows. Ed was always good to work, but when he took over the farm, it just seemed to go downhill. He was always doing one thing or another, and he just didn't seem to have the time for the farm." He bought a truck and a tractor with a loader and opened up a gravel pit on the back of the farm. He delivered a lot of gravel to area farms and covered expenses, but he didn't charge enough to make any money at it. "We never knew the price of gravel till we had to get it from someone else," says Russell. "No one would have minded if he'd charged what it was worth," adds Bill, "but it was as if Ed had the attitude he was doing people a favour." When construction began on nearby Highway 15, Ed sold a lot more gravel to the company that built the roadbed. "He should have had a nice little nest egg out of that," says Bill, "but he didn't." Bill likes Ed – everybody likes Ed – but he disapproves of this lost opportunity, and it shows in the corners of his mouth. Ultimately, though, he accepts Ed as he is. "You couldn't ask for a better neighbour."

Eventually, Ed took a job with the provincial government, working on a highway maintenance crew. "He worked at that for years," remembers Bill, "worked at it like it was his own business." Then, about 20 years ago, he got into a jam. He was in debt and strapped for cash, so he asked other farmers in the area to rent his farmland from him. Several offered to buy the land, but none would rent it. Ed felt they wanted him to go broke so that he would have to sell out and they could buy his farm. Finally, he went to see Russell, who lent him enough money – no strings attached – to get over the hump. Ever since, Ed has rented the land to the Morelands for the nominal sum of $600 a year, paid in monthly installments. For their part, Russell and Bill have farmed Ed's place with the same care they show to their own land.

Ed is retired now and finally has time for the farm. He takes justifiable pride in a large vegetable garden and putters around with a trio of ancient tractors, cleaning up rock piles and digging drainage ditches. The cows have been gone for years, and the barn is looking rickety, but other than that, Ed's farm – his father's farm – is looking neater and more productive than it has in years. This year, Bill is going to plant barley in three of Ed's fields, each separated by no more than a line of trees: 20 acres up by the road, 12 acres at the back and 8 acres in the middle. The land here is higher and sandier than at the home farm, but it is not tile-drained, so he is seeding it down to inexpensive nonlegumes – mostly timothy and ryegrass, species that can withstand wet soil conditions. Bill calls the hay that will come from these fields next year grass hay, to distinguish it from the more nutritious alfalfa hay, and he will feed it to his heifers and other cows that are not being milked.

But first, he has to get this year's crop in the ground, and even before that, he must tackle what is surely every farmer's least liked chore – picking rocks. There is an endless store of rocks under the surface of this alluvial land – hence Ed's gravel pit – and as the dirt heaves and groans through the annual freeze-thaw cycle, it squeezes a few of them closer to the surface, where they are caught and exposed by the plough. Bill has picked rocks out of these fields every spring for a couple of decades, and every year, there is a new crop. Rock-pickers—machines to harvest this crop—are too expensive to be justified by the few hours it takes to pick each field by hand. "It's not too bad," Bill shrugs, "if you keep at it every year."

In fact, it is hard, dirty work. Bill and Tom walk one on each side of Ed, who is pulling a small trailer with a rusty tractor that looks as if it were made in the previous century. Indeed, it is old enough that Ed climbs onto the seat from the rear of the machine, a feature designed to make farmers used to horses feel more comfortable with the newfangled machines. Bill and Tom throw any rocks fist-sized or larger into the trailer. They must walk quickly to keep up to the tractor. The job is made worse by the breeze, which blows dust into their eyes, and by the condition of the field, which is littered with clods that are indistinguishable from dirty rocks. Bill is tense today, worried about the lack of rain, but the sun and shirtsleeves weather have even him in good spirits. Working on the right side of the tractor, Bill calls instructions to Ed. "Big ones on the left, little ones on the right." Tom and Ed smile but hold their peace until, half an hour later, Ed winks at Tom and drives to the left of the largest rock they've seen all day. It is almost the size of a breadbox, but Bill pries it out of the ground and heaves it into the trailer without a word. The other two burst out laughing. "The left side," Bill says, grinning. "Big ones on the left."

Later, he pretends to be concerned about Ed's stamina and offers to trade jobs. "D'you want me to drive for a while, Ed?"

"Haw, haw, haw." Ed shakes his shoulders and shows his tobacco-dappled dentures.

A farmer's fields are exposed to the eyes of the world, and like all farmers, Bill is a keen observer of how his neighbours conduct their business. Many of them don't bother to pick rocks, especially on rented land. Driving down the road, Bill notices the boulders and bits of brush that clutter some fields. He has a saying for farmers who don't clean their fields. "If they can't drive over it," he says, "they drive around it." He will do neither: he will stop and move it out of the way. "Look at that," he says later in the spring, pointing to a boulder the size of a trash can in a nearby field. The young grain parts around it like flowing water, and in the eddy, a patch of weeds and brush is growing that will spread even farther into the field. "The guy who farms that land has a loader for his tractor that could push that into a fencerow in a few minutes, but instead, he's been driving around it for years. I don't understand it." Bill sets high standards for himself, but he feels no aggrandizement if others do not meet them. Rather, it irritates him—if he can farm that well, anybody can, and should.

Russell, who has been cultivating in the front field, pulls into the middle field where the others are picking rocks. He is driving a blue Ford tractor, model 7700. It is a big tractor, with back wheels as tall as a man and, in front of each, a ladder with three steps to climb up into the cab. The cab is sealed to keep out the noise and dust—the doors are as tight-fitting as those on an old Volkswagen beetle, the kind that used to float in swimming pools—and it is equipped with a heater, an air conditioner and an AM-FM radio. He is pulling the cultivator, its curved tines ripping up the soil and breaking down the clods that look like rocks. Behind the cultivator is a harrow, a kind of flexible chain mesh fitted with short prongs that further break up the clods and level the field. Bill sets his hands on his hips, in the way he does when he is thinking, and watches his father. "You know, I paid $23,000 for that tractor, $3,000 for the cultivator and another, oh I don't know, about $1,000 for the chain harrow. $27,000." He shakes his head, and the expression on his face is identical to that of someone in a supermarket who has just seen a week's groceries total $150.

Russell finishes cultivating shortly after the rocks are picked, and although the clods have been reduced only to the size of golf balls, Bill declares the field ready for planting. Certainly, no gardener would consider it suitable to accept seeds, and Bill readily admits to having somewhat unconventional views on seedbed preparation. "Some guys like to dig up the soil to a depth of six or eight inches, but the way I figure it, the seed is only planted about an inch deep, so what's the point? I set the cultivator so the teeth go down about three inches. It used to be, when fuel was cheap, you could get a great big tractor and really bore through it, and that was a lot of fun. But we never did that. Too cheap, I guess. Most guys like a finer seedbed than this, but I figure I'm going to go over it three more times—with the drill, the spring-tooth harrow and the cultipacker. That's three more operations; they may be minor ones, but they'll make a difference. I figure that what you've got after you're done is what you call the seedbed."

Back at the house for another late lunch, Bill finds Eileen waiting with several messages: the vet is coming at 4:30 to look at Emy Q's udder; the milk tester will be here tonight; and the hoof trimmer is coming on Friday. All these people are going to require some of Bill's time, and he is getting irritable about it. The forecast is calling for rain. "Great," he says, scowling. Even after two weeks of worrying about the unusual lack of rain, Bill can still complain about the interruption in his planting schedule that rain will cause.

Filling the drill with barley and grass seed after lunch, he is still fretting. "I have to get my time better organized. I should have been out in the field an hour ago, instead of doing this now." He could have been too, if he had left the rock picking to Tom and Ed. Russell points this out to him later in the day, reproving him for wasting his time, and Bill squirms like a child home late for dinner. "Yeah, I know," he says lamely, "but I hate to take off and leave the boys to do the hard work."

With Tom, Jean, Russell and Eileen, Bill has a substantial labour pool at his disposal, but it means he is responsible for keeping them all busy. It gives him a manager's status – and a manager's headaches. Much of his effort goes into making sure that jobs and equipment and supplies are lined up so everyone always has something to do, and much of his time is spent worrying about who is going to do what and when. But Bill is a doer, and the managerial cloak is often an uncomfortable fit. "Sometimes I wish I was just doing the work. I don't like all this running around. It used to be I didn't have to worry about anybody else, and I could just look over my shoulder and see what I'd gotten done. I like that feeling. I like seeing the results of my work like that – the immediate reward. I don't get that feeling much anymore."

Yet planning is vitally important at a time like this – when conditions are perfect for planting and any delay represents a potential drop in yield and therefore in income. And every passing day brings the possibility of bad weather that may close up the fields for weeks. This is all the more true for a dairy farmer, whose workday, in an odd way, is short. Bill rises before 5 a.m. and works until after dusk, but barn chores mean he cannot start his fieldwork until after 9, and he has to quit for milking at 4:30. It is a 14-, 15-, sometimes 16-hour workday that leaves only banker's hours for doing any work – the rest is used up by milking and feeding the cows. But, of course, milking is the *raison d'être* of the whole operation – it cannot be ignored. Nothing is done on Bill's farm unless it makes milking more productive, more cost-effective or more efficient.

The short workday and the unknowable weather make the manager's role even more important. Bill has helpers working in different fields, even on different farms, and he can never quite give himself over to the pleasure and immediate reward of doing his own job.

Russell, who managed a smaller farm in a simpler time, has no patience for it. When Bill drives his tractor over to Russell's in the next field, Russell invariably says, "What are you doing, just driving around? You might better take the car, it's more comfortable." He smiles when he says it, but he always says it. And when Bill carefully explains the intricacies of the new drill to Tom at some length, Russell mutters, "Bill always likes to talk. He's never doing anything, just talking about it. I wish he'd been around when my father was alive. Dad would just go over and tell Tom what to do, and that would be it. Yes sir, he got things done, my dad."

Bill is aware of his father's attitude. "Dad can't stand all this time spent getting ready to do something. He just kind of wades in and starts ripping and tearing. But things have changed since he ran things. His way, I think, there's a lot of stuff that gets started before it should. You can save a lot of time in the long run by taking a little time to understand something in the beginning." As the week wears on and one tousled field after another is combed smooth and parted and patted into place, Bill becomes increasingly tense, increasingly animated. He works after milking each night until dark gathers at 8:30, then comes home to eat dinner. Afterwards, weary but never quite satisfied, he falls asleep on the couch. "He's all in an uproar," says Jean. Russell is more blunt: "He's bounding around like a fart in a mitten."

———

Friday is hoof-trimming day; the day, Jean says, that "her girls" are going to get a manicure. Bill and Tom are already on the land when a truck and trailer arrive and are backed in front of the door to the exercise yard. A hand-lettered sign on the back of the trailer says:

Twin L Hoof Trimming
Owned by Phylis Lanoue
Operated by Cliff Lanoue

Phylis is a short, stout woman with salt-and-pepper hair and a friendly smile. She is clearly the brains of the outfit. Her husband Cliff does the actual trimming. He is short and wiry, with a full beard and the air of a man who has worked hard all his life. He will be stooped when he is old, if he lives that long—he has heart trouble and was once told he should have surgery or he would never work again. He refused, went back to work three days later and, he says, has missed only four days of work in the years since.

Cliff transforms the trailer into a combination squeeze chute and tilt table; that is, a sort of narrow, plywood-sided stall that can tip a cow on her side. Then, under Jean's direction, Cliff slips a rope halter on each of the cows in turn, leads them out of the barn and into the chute. He walks out the other end of the chute but closes the head gate (a pair of bars) on the cow's neck as she comes through, holding her head in place. He then slips a pair of eight-inch-wide belts under her chest and belly and tightens them with a ratchet, while Phylis operates a lever that hydraulically tips the whole chute, lifting the cow until she is lying on her side with her feet sticking out. Phylis then folds out a hinged board, which serves as a pillow for the cow, grabs a shovel and cleans off the plywood when the cow shits – and they all do. Meanwhile, Cliff ties down the cow's feet and begins to trim the hooves.

Cows, like deer, moose, buffalo, pigs and camels, have cloven hooves and dewclaws just above them on the back of each leg. Cliff trims the dewclaws with a pair of nippers that look like a cross between pliers and heavy-duty toenail clippers. For the hooves, he uses a larger version of the same tool with two-foot-long wooden handles, first clipping off the point of the toe, then working around the edge before taking some off the bottom of the foot. When the hooves are trimmed, Cliff touches them up with a cow-sized emery board – a hand-held electric grinder. Like any domestic animal that walks on its toenails, cows can become uncomfortable – even go lame – if their feet are not trimmed regularly. Nevertheless, many farmers neglect this area of health care. "Some farmers let their hooves get too long," says Cliff. "Then you can only cut off so much because the blood goes out farther too." Always the stress remover, Bill has his cows' hooves trimmed once a year. "These cows have the best feet I've seen this year," says Cliff.

He can trim a cow in less than 10 minutes, which earns him $18, but he says his arms ache at night if he has to cut hooves longer than eight hours a day. He would like to work only five days a week too, but he often puts in longer hours, and he almost always works on Saturdays. Word travels fast along the concession roads of rural Ontario, and when Twin L Hoof Trimming arrives in a community, it tends to pick up a lot of extra jobs. Phylis, who records their appointments in a spiral notebook, says they are already booked up for the summer – not bad for a business just entering its third year. Cliff worked as a dairyman for 27 years, most recently on a farm in Alberta, where he helped milk 250 cows twice a day. "I just got tired of working for other people," he says. He and Phylis invested $5,000 in building the trailer, and they have never looked back.

When it is Lulu's turn to have her hooves trimmed, Jean calls Mark from the house. Mark has asked to be present because Lulu is his favourite cow and he feels responsible for her. He often visits her in the barn, standing in front of her stall, second from the door to the milk house. He talks softly to her, sharing his 4-year-old's secrets and gazing with his wide brown eyes into hers. Lulu is a good listener, a matronly great-grandmother born on the farm 10 years ago. In her lifetime, Lulu has given more than 65,000 kilograms (14,000 gallons) of milk, and she continues to produce 72 pounds of milk each day, almost twice the national average. Three of her daughters and two granddaughters are being milked now, and two of her great-granddaughters will come into production next year. Lulu – unless he works at it, Mark says "Oolu" – is now well into old age, and gravity has become the dominant factor in her appearance. Her once magnificent udder now hangs pendulously and sways alarmingly as she walks, her topline droops toward the ground, and her feet and joints have taken on a size and heaviness they did not have in her youth. But her eyes remain clear and, if not intelligent, at least observant. She is placid, imperturbable and patient by nature – quiet enough to let Mark sit on her back – and she lets Cliff lead her into the chute without baulking.

Mark sits on Jean's knee, and when Phylis tips Lulu on her side, he is worried. "She looks scared," he says.

"No, sweetie," says Jean, "I think she just looks surprised." Indeed she does. For all her years of experience, Lulu seems to have forgotten about tilt tables – her eyes are bulging, and the expression on her face could only be disbelief. One teat has been caught under the sling, and Cliff carefully frees it, getting sprayed with milk as he does. Like all the other cows, Lulu shits, then relaxes and lays her head on the plywood pillow. Mark soon loses interest and wanders off.

————

On the last Saturday in April, Bill and Eileen get a babysitter for Mark, put on their good clothes and take themselves out for the night. The occasion is an appreciation night for Bert Wilson, the local veterinarian who is retiring. Bert Wilson has had a practice in the area for 37 years, and except for Brian Willows, a young partner taken on eight years ago, he has been the only veterinarian many area farmers have known. Last year, Bert started getting chest pains. His doctor told him to take an extended vacation, and he did, bringing a young married couple – both vets – into the practice. At first, Bert said he would keep his hand in, but this spring, he officially handed over the practice to his young partners.

Tonight, Bert thinks he is attending the 30th wedding anniversary of a close friend, and it has been the job of his wife Marion to sustain the deception. Amazingly, considering the weeks of preparation and the number of people aware of the evening's real purpose, she seems to have succeeded. She arranges for them to arrive after the guests are in their seats, and Bert — a tall, elegant man with white hair and a dapper moustache — seems genuinely astonished at the applause that greets his arrival. There are nearly 200 people crammed into the hall above the Seeley's Bay Fire Hall, almost all of them dairy farmers. Like the cows tied in their barns, the men all bear a superficial resemblance to each other: necks tanned, cheeks and noses red from the sun, foreheads winter-white from hiding under caps that say Co-op or John Deere or Pioneer Seeds. The lines of their oversized hands are written in dirt that soap cannot reach.

Bill and Eileen share a table with Russell, who has come with them; Jim and Karen Abrams, a quiet couple who live not far away; Bob and Brigid Pyke, who farm 50 miles away on Wolfe Island in partnership with Bob's brother and his wife and who also own a farm just north of Gananoque, a few miles east of the Morelands; and Phil and Connie Dyer, who manage the Gananoque farm for the Pykes. Brigid was born a city girl — her father was a lawyer in London, Ontario — but she is all farmer now and has earned the respect of those born to the land. She recently became the first woman elected president of the Ontario Federation of Agriculture (OFA), a group representing 20,000 farmers in Ontario, and she won the vote by promising to give farmers a stronger voice in provincial politics. She is an attractive, determined 42-year-old, and when she speaks on an issue she cares about, the words come out of her mouth with square edges, as hard and irresistible as bricks.

Perhaps because she is at the table, the conversation covers a range of issues that swing on the hinge between agriculture and politics. They start with free trade, but so little is known about what is happening in the early rounds of negotiations that there is little to discuss. "We've got [Minister of Agriculture John] Wise saying that marketing boards are untouchable and [Canadian trade negotiator Simon] Reisman saying that everything is on the table," declares Brigid. "All we can do is keep plugging away at them, telling them our concerns."

The couples at the table have all travelled in parts of the United States where the growing season is long enough for farmers to plant and harvest two crops instead of one, and they know they cannot compete against such an advantage. The marketing and processing of dairy products is tightly regulated in Canada, and these dairy farmers like that – they feel the controls have given the public a product with unimpeachable quality and have given the farmers a structured and stable market in which to sell it. They fear the loss of these controls under free trade, claiming that imports of low-cost, low-quality milk from the United States will downgrade their product and ruin their market. "If I knew for sure that free trade was coming," says Bill, "I'd sell my farm tomorrow while it's still worth something."

They talk about tobacco. Bob Pyke reports that another tobacco farmer in southwestern Ontario committed suicide this week, the third to do so this year. Tobacco is a valuable crop that requires a lot of care, and as a result, tobacco farms are characteristically small and unsuited for most other crops. Health concerns and government restrictions are drastically reducing tobacco sales; unable to diversify or to sell their quota, their specialized equipment or even their land, tobacco farmers watch helplessly as their homes and businesses sink into a quicksand of debt. None of the dairy farmers at the table smoke, and they don't want their children to, but they instinctively come to the farmers' defence. "Last year," says Brigid, "the government collected millions of dollars in tax revenue from the sale of tobacco products. And they spent millions more on a public education programme to tell people that smoking is bad for their health . . . "

"And God knows how much they spent on cancer research and health care for people dying of lung cancer," Bob interjects.

". . . but here we have a significant number of people who are obviously in need of help, and they won't do anything for them," she continues. "I mean, these farmers have contributed to the economy of this country in a big way for a lot of years, producing a product that was in demand and that the government was willing to make a lot of money on. Now these people are in trouble – and they're suffering, really suffering – and the government says, 'Sorry, we haven't got any money to help them.' I think that's pretty hypocritical."

She is interrupted by the call for dinner, which is served buffet style. As they stand in line to heap their plates with roast beef, mashed potatoes, gravy, salad, vegetables and rolls with butter, someone mentions electric fencing. "Shh," says Bill. "Don't let Vicki Miller hear about *that*." Electric fences contain livestock by administering painful electric shocks; Miller is an outspoken animal rights activist who made headlines by gaining the presidency of the Toronto Humane Society. She is concerned not only with animal welfare – the prevention of cruelty to animals and the establishment of codes of practice that ensure their humane treatment – but with animal rights, the belief that human rights do not extend to using animals for our own purposes. She is a vegetarian and opposes all aspects of livestock farming, including dairy farming.

As recently as a couple of decades ago, Miller would have been dismissed as a crank, but things have changed. People with similar beliefs have shut down the harp seal hunt on the ice of the St. Lawrence River, only a few hundred miles downstream from this very hall. They have committed acts of violence and vandalism at university laboratories where research includes experiments on animals – in Canada, the best-known example is the taking of a baboon from a laboratory at the University of Western Ontario, in London. European advertising campaigns that graphically connect those who wear furs with the grisly murder of innocent animals have cut deeply into the livelihoods of Canadian fur trappers. Now, they are turning their attention to farms. In Britain, where the movement is strongest, there have already been farm-gate confrontations and talk of raids to "liberate" animals kept "in bondage."

In Canada, there has been more talk than action, but thoughtful farmers know they should mount a preemptive publicity strike to help an urban population understand what an animal farm is really like. Most farmers like their animals and are proud of the way they treat them. They know that an uncomfortable or unhappy animal cannot reach its potential level of production, and they often say that even if they didn't like their animals, they would keep them happy because contented animals make more money. They believe that if they could demonstrate this simple logic to people in the city, the Vicki Millers of the world would never be heard. But they also know that city people tend to go "Aww" when they see pictures of pigs in pens or chickens in cages or cows tied by the neck, and don't look closely enough to see the expensive heating system that keeps the animals warm in winter or the carefully designed ventilators that circulate fresh air without drafts. They are not there to see the concern on the farmer's face when illness strikes or the endless fiddling with vents and fans and feeding programmes to make everything just right. The average North American farm animal is better fed, better housed and better cared for than most humans on this planet.

Farmers are aware, too, that their record for successful publicity campaigns is dismal. Individually, farmers are too reticent and practical to take the aggressive, catchy, emotional approach that is needed; as a group, they are too independent and fragmented to let anyone do it for them. Brigid has just completed a series of public debates with Vicki Miller, who, in this company, she need only describe as "really something." In the last of the debates, Miller silenced her usually voluble opponent with the contention that yes, plants also have rights. The debates were widely attended by farmers, who were personally affronted by what they heard. Brigid tells about a pig farmer who confronted Miller after a meeting. "He was just shaking – his veins were all sticking out, and he was practically purple in the face. I thought he was going to have a heart attack. He was so angry, he couldn't even talk at first – he just kind of sputtered. Finally, he leaned over the table and practically screamed at her, 'Have you ever laid down on your back in a pigpen?' She didn't know what to say. Anyway, it turns out that this guy has a problem with drafts in his barn, and the only way he can be sure his pigs aren't getting a draft is to lie down on the floor at pig level and feel for them."

"Now *that's* dedication," says Bill.

The feeling at the table is one of community – a closeness born of shared experiences and attitudes – and it is clear that these are people who are where they want to be and are doing with their lives what they want to do. But there is also an undercurrent of isolation, an awareness that belonging to this community excludes them from belonging to others. Not just isolated – under attack. They are the ancient castle at the top of the hill, and the multitudes are laying siege. We want farmers to provide us with food, and lots of it – pure, clean, fresh, unadulterated food. But cheap. We want our food to be so cheap that we won't notice the money we spend on it, so cheap that farmers cannot make a living unless they produce more and more of it. But stay small – don't change, we say to farmers, don't crowd your animals in barns, don't use those labour-saving chemicals, don't incorporate your businesses, don't protect yourselves with marketing boards. And don't raise your prices, or we will import food from climates where it can be grown more cheaply.

If the farming community is a castle on a hill, then the castle is crumbling. There are fewer than a quarter of a million farmers in Canada, barely 1 percent of the population. In Russell's day, there were three times as many, and they accounted for 6 percent of the population. Bill's land incorporates what used to be three separate farms, and in that, he is typical of the trend in agrarian demographics. One-third the number of farmers now cultivate the same area of land as was under the plough before World War II. In 1962, a bushel of barley and a barrel of oil both sold for $2.50; now, 25 years later, the bushel of barley still sells for $2.50, and to pay his bills, each farmer grows four times as many bushels.

None of this is mentioned at the table, and there is no paranoia or bitterness, but it is a context for their discussion, a shared understanding of the world in which they live. When the dishes are cleared and the coffee is poured, even this passes. What remains is community, not that which separates them from others but that which brings them together. The master of ceremonies is Jack Conner, a trim, white-haired man who, with his wife Virginia, is a good friend of Bert and Marion. The Conners are tragic figures in this community. They and their two sons, Eldon and Ted, once owned one of the largest and most prosperous farms in the area, a 400-acre farm on which they milked 100 cows. Ten years ago this fall, they were filling a 75-foot-high silo with corn silage. They reached the 40-foot level, and Ted – then 31 years old – climbed into the silo to level the heap of silage. He knew that fermenting corn silage releases silo gas, a combination of lethal gases that can asphyxiate a person in seconds, so he had started a tractor-operated blower before he went up the silo. He would be working in a current of fresh air. But the tractor stalled, and Ted collapsed in the silo. Within minutes, Bill Carr, a 47-year-old neighbour who had worked for the Conners since he was 17, climbed into the silo and tried to rescue him. He, too, collapsed. The other Conner boy, Eldon, went in after his brother and friend. All three died. Jack did not go into the silo after his sons, and one can only imagine the agony of the decision that kept him out. He and Virginia soon put the farm up for sale, and it is now the Gananoque-area farm owned by Bob and Brigid Pyke.

At the time of his death, Eldon Conner was engaged to be married to Jean Moreland. But it was Bill, driving past the farm soon after the accident, who first learned of the tragedy. When he got home, Jean was in the barn alone.

"Jean, there's been an accident at Conners'."

"Oh, no," she said. "Not Eldon."

"Yes."

Although that was a decade ago, Jack and Virginia are still pointed out to visitors as "the ones who lost their sons in that silo accident." People still look at them and think, "What a terrible thing to have happened to them," and then, in an echo so quiet they won't admit they heard themselves think it, "I'm so glad it didn't happen to me." For the Conners, time has had its effect, and they can laugh again and plan an evening of fun for their friends. Virginia makes a brief presentation to Marion Wilson, saying let's not forget who really ran the show and listing her duties: Bert's wife, mother to his children, housekeeper, secretary, bookkeeper, receptionist, telephone answering service, short-order cook, surgical assistant and nurse. Jack follows with a speech in which he points out that although Bert is a good veterinarian, he's a lousy euchre player and an even worse fisherman. Jack says that if Bert is going to stop being a veterinarian, he had bloody well better try to become a better fisherman. He unveils an electric boat motor of the kind used for trolling and says that he hopes this will help Bert achieve his new goal.

He is replaced at the front of the hall by Brian Willows, the oldest of the younger vets taking over Bert's practice. Brian talks about first coming to work for Bert, playing a pretty credible James Herriot to Bert's Siegfried. He recalls the many times Bert chewed him out for forgetting tools and equipment at various farms, but, he continues, when taking an inventory in order to turn over the business, he found that Bert, too, had left things behind in his travels. "Fortunately, we were able to phone around and find them. For the sake of convenience, I've asked the ladies who found these items to bring them along tonight, and I wonder if they would hand them in now." At this, there is a great clanking of stainless steel, and a dozen women bring forward a variety of bulky antique medical instruments, which they heap on the table in front of Bert. When they are seated again and the applause has died, Brian continues. "What we didn't realize was how many articles of clothing Bert had left behind. And I don't know why – maybe Marion can explain it – but it always seemed to be the women who knew where the clothing was." At this, the women return with hats, coveralls, a shirt and – delivered with a flourish and greeted with a roar of approval – an oversized pair of purple boxer shorts.

The next speaker, an elderly man with a cane and an emphysemic rasp, declares that it is all right to say what a great fellow Bert was, but it's also true that he made some terrible mistakes. He warms up with the obligatory story about a heifer that delivered a calf a few weeks after Bert declared it was not pregnant, then launches into a story about a fine colt he once had. "We couldn't leave it because the kids were still quite young, so I called Bert." He means the high-spirited stallion might have hurt the children, so he arranged for Bert to geld it. "Well, Bert said it looked like about a 5-minute job, and he came down to the barn to do it, but after about 20 minutes, he went out to the car and got a tranquillizer. I held the bag while he put the tranquillizer in the horse's neck, and he got the job done all right, but the next day, the horse's neck and the whole side of his face was all swollen up. In the end, he lost one eye, and it ruined the horse. France wanted horse meat that year, so we sold him." He stops, and there is some uncomfortable shuffling of feet. This is not the lighthearted story people expected. Bert, behind the pile of stainless steel and purple shorts, has put his hands over his face. "But there was a happy ending, after all," the man continues. "We made enough on the sale of the horse to pay the vet bill." This produces a roar of laughter and applause, partly in relief that there was a punch line after all, and even Bert throws his head back and laughs.

Finally, Bert rises to speak. He is obviously unprepared, but he reminisces about his first days in practice in 1950, touring the back roads of the area in a 1935 car that had no brakes. He recalls that the roads were not ploughed then and that he was often ferried to the barn in the back of a manure spreader, the only conveyance with enough clearance to get through the snowdrifts. He talks about the changes he has seen in his 37 years of practice ("most of them for the better") and the many advances in veterinary medicine. He pauses, then says in a strong, steady voice, "I've had two great loves in my life. My family . . . " His voice cracks, and he turns his back on the room for a few moments. There is a scattering of applause in approval of his sentiment. He faces the room again and continues, ". . . and the practice of veterinary medicine."

He apologizes to his children for not having had the time to spend with them and thanks his wife for putting up with him. He recalls with a smile that she would take phone messages for him in the early days of his practice and that many of the farmers—especially the older ones—did not want to talk to a woman about the symptoms of their cows' digestive or reproductive malfunctions. They would say only that a cow was sick and please send the vet. The vet, of course, wanted to know what to take with him when he went, and he encouraged his wife to ask what the problem was. One time, a farmer was obviously reluctant to give out any details, but Marion kept after him until the poor man finally blurted out, "She can't shit!"

Bert commends the young vets on their abilities and says he is happy to leave his business in their hands. Setting up another story, he reminds people that one of the new hormonal drugs available to vets will induce labour in a recalcitrant pregnant cow. "I went to one farm, and we were walking down the line, and the farmer pointed to a cow and said, 'That turned out all right.' I didn't know the situation because it had been Brian who came out, so I asked what he meant. 'Well,' the farmer said, 'the young vet came out. He seduced the cow, and she had the calf just fine.' "

When the laughter dies down, Bert seems ready to conclude. "I've dedicated my life to the care of the black-and-white cow," he says. "And I'd do the same thing all over again if I had the chance."

———————

"It's a good thing the boss isn't here," says Bill, meaning his father. He is fiddling with a new hydraulic auger, making sure the bolts are tight and everything is set up properly. It's the sort of time-consuming preparatory work that Russell has no patience for. "When I get something new like this and I know it's going to take a little adjustment, I always like to get him doing something else so he's not around to give me a hard time about it." Russell is cultivating a field on the next farm.

A hydraulic auger is a tool Bill uses to load granular fertilizer into his fertilizer spreader from a wagon fitted with a gravity box, a kind of miniature boxcar that self-empties because its bottom slopes steeply to a hatch door on one side. The auger, powered by the hydraulic system of a tractor, is something Bill has wanted for years, but the $750 price tag has, until now, seemed just a little too much to pay for convenience. Previously, he pailed the fertilizer into the spreader by hand, but Bill is in his 40s now and suffers from occasional lower back pain – what he calls "farmer's back." Last year, he got a new fertilizer spreader with a one-tonne capacity, and he pailed it full without checking the bolts on the new machine. "Afterwards," he says, "we found out that somebody at the factory had bolted a clamp on upside down. Anyway, when I drove away, the hopper tipped up like a dump truck and spilled the whole load." He reversed the clamp, pailed it full again from the pile on the ground and ordered a hydraulic auger.

Now he has the spreader, which looks and works like an overgrown lawn fertilizer, and the auger, hanging from a gravity box full of fertilizer, parked in Ed Johnston's backyard. Ed, wearing his silver hard hat and spitting tobacco juice, has come out to see what's going on.

Satisfied that everything is in order, Bill backs the spreader under the spout of the auger but finds he cannot close the mechanism in the

CORN WAGON WITH HYDRAULIC-POWERED AUGER

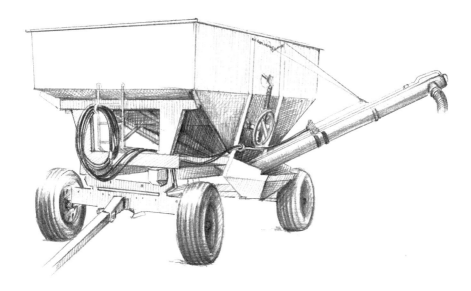

bottom of the hopper that shuts off the flow of fertilizer. Somehow, a piece of metal has been bent. "It must be Monday," Bill grimaces. Ed gets a pair of channel-lock pliers, and Bill dives into the spreader hopper, which is about the size of a two-person hot tub. There, he assumes a three-point stance on his knees and forehead, and he tries to twist the metal back into shape.

"Must be pretty tough stuff," hollers Ed in a voice that could be heard on the next concession.

"Not really," grunts Bill.

"Well, you're pulling on it pretty hard."

"Oh, I don't know. I'm gritting my teeth a lot, but I'm not getting too far. I think my days of getting stronger are over, Ed. I'm over the hill now, all worn out."

"Ah, shi-i-it," drawls Ed, cackling to himself.

Bill gets the closing mechanism straightened, then connects the hydraulic hoses to the tractor, opens the unloading door on the gravity box, starts the tractor, flips a lever and looks expectantly at the flexible black pipe leading from the auger to the spreader. The auger rumbles and shivers, but nothing comes out the end of the pipe. Muttering to himself, Bill disconnects the hoses and inserts them in the opposite sockets. This time, the auger pumps fertilizer into the spreader – at least it does until the black pipe, which Bill has neglected to tighten, falls off on Ed's head.

"Judas Priest!" Bill exclaims, quickly shutting off the auger. Except when driven to the occasional "hell" or "damn" by bureaucratic stupidity, this is as close as he ever gets to profanity.

Ed lets out a bellow of surprise loud enough to rattle windows, but he is unaffected by the mishap, aside from getting a little fertilizer down the back of his shirt. He laughs and shakes his shoulders. "Haw, haw, haw. That's why I wear this hard hat." He is grinning hugely, pleased to be in the middle of the action.

Finally, Bill gets the auger working properly, but he has time to spread only one load before it is time to check on Russell and Tom, both of whom are working in different fields. He hardly gets to the end of the driveway when the other two arrive from different directions. The two younger men get off their tractors and approach Russell, who, predictably, says, "What are you driving around for? You got no work to do?" He shakes his head. "Say, did you hear about the fellow who went to the proctologist?" Bill and Tom exchange a smile. "The doctor is putting on one of these rubber gloves, and the fellow says, 'Hey, Doc, do you think you could use two fingers instead of one?' And the doctor says, 'Yeah, I suppose so, but why would I want to?' 'Well,' the guy says, 'I was hoping to get a second opinion.' "

Bill passes on new instructions, shuffling tractors and equipment between the remaining fields. In the first week of planting, the three men have seeded 75 acres, leaving 45 acres divided among four separate fields. Each field must be cultivated at least twice, fertilized, harrowed, picked over for rocks, planted and cultipacked. It means a lot of juggling of tractors and equipment, the kind of managerial decision making Bill would rather not have to do. It also means a lot of big equipment in small places, a practice that offends Bill's sense of propriety. "It's too bad we haven't got something smaller for these little fields. Maybe we should have saved some of the old horse-drawn stuff," he says, not meaning it. "You know, when you look at that old equipment, you wonder how they ever got anything done in those days. I mean, those dinky little cultivators were only about 6 feet wide, compared to, what, 16 feet for mine. And their seed drills were only about half as wide. Everything done with horses, and you had to stop and rest them every hour or so. It took them weeks to get anything done.

"Of course, they didn't get started till later, and they didn't get their crop in till later, either. Nowadays, we have more production. We can get the crop in a lot earlier, and we get a bigger crop because of it. They're talking about getting 70, 80, maybe 90 bushels to the acre soon. That's really something." Crop yields like that are impressive, especially compared with the average of 22 bushels per acre in the 1860s and even with 40 bushels per acre as recently as 1965. Some European farmers, using intensive techniques more familiar to green-house operators than to farmers, are claiming yields of more than 100 bushels to the acre.

But Bill rarely states one side of an argument without at least hint-ing at the other side. "The problem is, we're producing ourselves out of business. I don't know, sometimes you wonder why you bother." As impressive as such yields are, the world is already drowning in grain. The stock of unused feed grains will grow to 224 million tonnes this year, and that excess will push prices lower by as much as 5 per-cent. For an individual farmer, the choice is clear – accept the loss or grow 5 percent more grain just to stay even. In Canada, as in most of the world, few farmers could afford to take the loss even if they wanted to, and this year's crop once again promises to be larger than last year's, boosting stocks, driving prices farther down. It's a nasty, frustrating cycle – farmers around the world choking on the very bounty they hope will save them – and it is made all the more bitter by the knowledge that a continent's worth of people who cannot afford to buy the sur-plus are going hungry.

Bill plants the last of his barley in the last week of April, a remark-able turn of events. Depending on the spring weather conditions, grain planting sometimes drags on into the middle of May. This year, though, April has been exceptionally warm and dry – with less than an inch of rain since planting began and a mean temperature 3.4 Cel-sius degrees warmer than average. A few degrees may not seem to matter much, but in this part of the country, the mean temperature (the midpoint between the day's high and low temperatures) often hovers around the 5 degree mark in April. For most plants, this is the on/off switch, the point at which they start or stop growing. Poten-tial plant growth over a given period of time is measured in units called growing degree-days, defined as the number of degrees by which the mean temperature on a given day exceeds 5 degrees C. Thus, for the record-setting highs on Ruth Moreland's birthday, the high was 27.2 and the low 8.0, for a mean temperature of 17.6: 12.6 growing degree-days. In Bill's area, the norm for April is 52.3 growing degree-days. This year, there were 131.6.

The trend carries on into May, with temperatures above normal—246 growing degree-days against a norm of 200—and rainfall below normal. Well below—scattered showers are forecast for several days, but although dark clouds gather and the wind blows, nothing stronger than a sprinkle falls on Bill's farm during the whole month of May. It constitutes a minor drought and confirms Bill's earlier fears about a sudden spring. Still, it is not without some benefit. "In a way, it's nice that it worked out like this," says Bill. "We're not all jammed up trying to get our corn planted at the same time as the barley. It gives us kind of a break, a chance to get some wood cut and catch up on a few other things."

It also means that the hay crop does not grow as rapidly as Bill expected it to. As May progresses, he starts to worry that he will not have enough hay to meet his needs for the following winter. This fear is aggravated by a high alfalfa winterkill. Though rich in protein and other nutrients, alfalfa is a delicate crop, sensitive to ice or extreme cold in the winter and to wet soil in the growing season. This past winter brought a heavy snow cover, which offered protection from the cold, until a warm spell followed by a cold snap in early March left many fields covered with ice for several days. Not long, but long enough to damage the alfalfa. At best, alfalfa is a three-year crop—each year, it is less dense, and the grass takes over the hayfield. After walking through his fields one evening, Bill says, "Last year's seeding doesn't look too bad, but the two-year-old stuff looks like three-year-old, and the three-year-old looks like grass." He scurries around the neighbourhood and arranges to rent some extra hay land for the summer.

Meanwhile, one field at a time, the barley is sprouting. Resurrected after lying in the ground for three days, it first appears as a green haze that gradually resolves into tentative spikes, a 5 o'clock shadow on the jowls of the earth. After another three days, the rows are discernible, and suddenly, the focus changes—the eye is drawn down the length of the row. What was a field of individual plants forcing their separate ways out of the close earth, like dreamers struggling to rouse themselves from sleep, is now a single unit, a crop.

Planted early and out of the ground as promptly as the arrival of a tax notice, the barley has a good start. It is a promising beginning, and if it gets some rain soon (but not too much) and if it isn't attacked by insects or diseases or overcome by weeds, the crop may flourish. If it gets some rain.

BOOK III

PLANTING CORN

The Morelands have a strong sense of family tradition. Russell was the third of six children, the middle of five boys. His two older brothers, Paul and Les, were given their uncles' names; the two younger ones, Reid and Arthur, their mother's and grandmother's maiden names. Bill has his grandfather's name, and many of his cousins, nieces and nephews bear names repeatedly drawn from the family's genealogy: William, Thomas, Paul, James, Margaret, Anne, Elizabeth and May.

A brief history of the Moreland family starts in Ireland, with the marriage of James and Margaret (Peggy) Reid in 1831, a century before their great-grandson bought his 100-acre farm near Joyceville, Ontario. The Reids lived in County Antrim, Ulster, a couple of miles down the road from the home of another future immigrant to Canada, Timothy Eaton. James was a gardener by trade, a Presbyterian and an Orangeman; Peggy bore him four children, three of whom – Jane, Paul and John – lived beyond infancy. No doubt, the young family anticipated a life as uneventful as that of their parents and grandparents, but their generation saw more change than any since the beginning of British rule in 1625 and more horror than any since the Norse raids a millennium earlier.

For reasons still debated by historians, the British Isles, particularly Ireland, experienced a population explosion of unparalleled proportions in the latter part of the 18th and the first half of the 19th centuries. Reliable – or at least undisputed – figures are not available, but it would be reasonable to say that the population doubled in that time, and the pressures this created on land, food and jobs sparked one of history's great diasporas. From 1825 to 1845, about 1.3 million people left the British Isles, drawn by promises of land and opportunity to British North America, the United States, Australia and New Zealand. Of these, nearly half a million were Irish who immigrated to British North America. In fact, from the end of the Napoleonic Wars until the mid-1850s, annual immigration to this country from Ireland almost always exceeded that from England, Scotland and Wales combined, and it was not until the 1891 census that Canada's population contained more English-born persons than Irish-born. Many of the Irish immigrants settled in Upper Canada – of the half-million residents there in 1842, one-quarter of them were born either in Ireland or in Canada to Irish-born parents, twice as many as from anywhere else.

These figures represent only the first wave of 19th-century Irish immigration, the one brought on by the pressures of rising population; and indeed, the area least affected by this was County Antrim, home of the young Reid family. The second wave was inspired by the great potato famine, when a potato blight virtually wiped out the country's largest agricultural export and its most basic food staple. Between 1845 and 1850, nearly a million people died of starvation and related causes in Ireland, and another million fled the country. During the next 20 years, two million more emigrated, and in the 20 years after that, another million – four million people in 45 years. By 1891, 4 out of every 10 people born in Ireland were living in another country. The population decline continued right up to the modern postwar era. Ireland must surely be the only country in the world in which the current population (three million) is only half what it was in 1840.

Of those emigrants who fled their homeland in the last half of the 1840s, about a quarter came to British North America. Of these, almost half – 104,000, including James and Peggy Reid and their three children – arrived in the year 1847. A.B. Hawke, the chief immigration agent for Canada West (later called Ontario), noted that fully three-quarters of the immigrants under his charge that year were Irish, and he described them as "diseased in body and belonging to the lowest class of unskilled labourers." The latter slur is a little unfair. In general, the unskilled labourers who left Ireland in those days could afford to get no farther than Liverpool, and often only as stowaways. Those who came to Canada were mostly skilled workers, like the Reids, or tenant farmers. In our day, we describe boatloads of such people as "economic refugees." Because they have no money or job prospects and because they will not die in their homeland for overtly political reasons, we say they should be turned away.

Certainly, though, Hawke's "diseased in body" description was accurate. Many of those who arrived in Canada had already been weakened by hunger and disease when they left Ireland. Added to this was the fear of the unknown, the homesickness of people who had never before been more than a day's horseback ride from the birthplace of their grandparents, and the hardships of the month-long sea voyage. And according to a report received by a select committee of the British House of Lords (and noted in *The Irish in Ontario* by Donald Harman Akenson, a neighbour of the Morelands), conditions in steerage were hard indeed: "Hundreds of poor people, huddled together without light, without air, wallowing in filth and breathing a fetid atmosphere; sick in body, dispirited in heart; the fever patients lying between the sound in sleeping places so narrow as to deny them the natural restlessness of the disease." They died by the thousands on the ships, in quarantine and in the ports where they disembarked. Among the deaths, a personal tragedy made remote by time and repetition, was that of James Reid. Bound for a job in Toronto, he was buried near the shore of Lake Ontario, in Kingston (the grave has since been relocated to allow construction of a hospital on the site). His widow and children settled on nearby Amherst Island.

Peggy, then 37, never remarried, and took comfort in smoking a pipe. Her eldest child, Jane, married an Irish sailor named James Moreland on Valentine's Day, 1853. She was 20 years old. James had apprenticed at sea at the age of 13 and had worked the north Atlantic until 1845, when he settled in Canada. At the time of his marriage, he was 32 and was dividing his time between sailing the Great Lakes and, after freeze-up, cutting and splitting wood. James soon earned his captain's papers and, despite long absences, managed to father six children in the next decade. In the spring of 1865, the Moreland family had outgrown their house on Amherst Island, and Captain James was thinking about farming, a booming industry then, partly because of new markets opened during the Civil War in the United States. He purchased 300 acres near Sunbury, 11 miles north of Kingston, where Jane bore five more children, the last at the age of 44.

The farm at Sunbury was – and is – a beautiful site, encompassing a high, wooded hill and fertile bottomland. Captain James built a magnificent brick house on the brow of the hill overlooking two small lakes at each end of a mile-wide valley. In an area characterized by rocky outcroppings and steep pastures, the lush farmland in this valley is an anomaly, a bit of the Emerald Isle in what can be a bleak area of eastern Ontario. The land is still farmed by Morelands, who still live in the brick house overlooking the valley. The house – large, two-storeyed, standing resolute behind stately maple shade trees – is decidedly Victorian: body modestly clothed in verandahs, steeply pitched bosom ruffled with gingerbread trim. The wooden shingles on the roof are covered with green moss, but so grand is the house and its setting that passersby are reminded of copper-roofed palaces.

In the tradition of the day, James and Jane's eldest sons left home for farms or careers of their own, and the youngest son, William, stayed to take over his father's farm. Russell recalls hearing that while the Captain was away, William (his father) hired and supervised men for farm work at the age of 14. When the Captain came home, full of seagoing discipline and a sailor's notions of how a farm should be run, the men soon quit. Except for Tom Martin, who worked on the Moreland farm for more years than anyone can remember. After the Captain died, William asked Tom why he stayed on when the others quit. "Well, if the Captain told me to do something the wrong way," Tom replied, "I went ahead and did it the way he wanted." It says much about the men and the times that this solution occurred to only one man among many. Tom remained a bachelor and worked for William all his life. "He lived alone, and I mind when he died," Russell says. "Poor old Tom. The rats had him half eaten up before anyone found him."

William married Annie Arthur in the first year of the new century. Russell, their third child, was born in 1906, and Art, Russell's youngest brother, in 1916. The Moreland-Arthur ties were close: William's younger sister married Annie's older brother, and after Annie died in 1922, William married her sister Fannie. Like many young couples then, William and Annie lived with his parents, sharing the big brick house on Moreland Hill. The Captain had retired from the sea in the 1890s, and he and Jane both lived to be 89. Photographs taken toward the end of their lives show him as a stern-faced man with a white beard and the deep-set eyes of a sailor; her face is softer, with humour in her eyes and grandmotherliness in the set of her mouth.

The old man was not always stern, though. A proud Presbyterian all his life, he was no teetotaller, and Russell's brother Paul writes in his memoirs of the year there was a sawing bee at Moreland Hill, complete with steam engine and circular saw, to cut the winter fuel into stove lengths. The Captain kept a few barrels of hard cider in the basement for such occasions, and he made sure no one suffered from thirst. In the afternoon, someone got careless with the governors on the steam engine, and it roared dangerously out of control, scattering drunken woodcutters in all directions. When order was restored, Grandmother Moreland went down to the cellar, opened all the spigots and watched until the remaining cider seeped into the earthen floor. The Captain never made cider again.

Russell was only 5 years old when the Captain died. Nevertheless, his life bridges the gap between two cultures so different that they seem almost unconnected. Russell's youngest grandchild (Bill's 4-year-old son Mark) was born in the mid-1980s, into a world of space exploration, satellite communications, lasers, heart transplants and the threat of nuclear annihilation. Russell's oldest grandparent (Captain James) was born in Ireland in 1821, into a world of horse-and-buggy travel, superstition and folk medicine. Mark was born as close to the start of the Korean War as the Captain was to the French Revolution, as close to the beginning of the technological revolution as the Captain was to the industrial revolution. When the Captain was born, Napoleon was still alive, and Wellington and Thomas Jefferson and Simon Fraser. The Battle of Trafalgar was as recent for him as the Tet Offensive is for Mark, the death of George Washington as close as that of John Kennedy.

Russell spans this generation gap, overlapping its extremities. He remembers a world without television, radio, telephone, electricity, cars, planes, anaesthesia, antibiotics, plumbing or income tax – a typical pre-World War I rural Canadian childhood. He remembers the day they got their first car, a McLaughlin-Buick. His grandmother, Captain James' widow, refused to ride in it – at first. "Then, when we finally did talk her into going for a ride, she always wanted to go. Whenever you got the car out, there she'd be in her good dress, and you had to take her, y'know. You couldn't say no." When the old matriarch got out of the car after each trip, she would say, "Rosie, get your leg up." Russell never understood what she meant.

The farm on Moreland Hill was destined to go to Russell's youngest brother Art, so when Russell graduated from the one-room elementary school in Sunbury, he made an effort to continue his education. The nearest high school – with four teachers – was in Sydenham, a village 15 miles west of Sunbury. Russell pedalled his bicycle down the mud road to Sydenham each Monday morning, boarded with a family there for $5 a week and pedalled back home again on Friday night. He enjoyed studying and excelled in subjects like Latin and algebra that require clear thinking and a good memory, but in January, the 15-mile bicycle ride became too much. He never went back.

Russell worked on the farm for a few years, but he was a young man with no responsibilities, free to enjoy the restless spirit of the 1920s. He went out west to work in the prairie wheatfields. The Ontario boys who were the best horsemen drove the grain binders that cut and tied the sheaves of wheat, but Russell was never very good with horses. "You're supposed to know what the horses are going to do before they do it," he says. "I was always the last to know." Russell stooked the sheaves; that is, he walked behind the binder and propped the bundles of wheat against each other to dry. The stubble was stiff and sharp, and a day of stooking would leave the front of his pants below the knee in shreds. At night, Russell patched his pant legs, and when the patches wore out, he turned his pants around and wore them backwards.

But what he remembers most about those days are the fires. After the sheaves were threshed, the farmers would burn the huge piles of straw that remained. Russell would walk out at night under the prairie sky, and all around him, the horizon would glow orange, as if the sun were setting in all directions at once. "They should have known better," he says now. "Straw is a wonderful soil builder, and it was a terrible thing to waste it like that. They don't do it now, I'll tell you."

Russell was not surprised by the dust bowl of the Depression years, when the irreplaceable prairie topsoil, robbed of the organic matter it needed to resist wind and drought, blackened the sky as it blew away. Today, the danger of substantial wind erosion is returning, as farmers, even in eastern Canada, enlarge their fields by removing the tree-lined fencerows that shelter the soil. "I don't like to see these fellows cut down all the trees," says Russell. "They're going against nature. And I'll tell you, you don't want to go against nature."

Russell spent the summer of 1931 working on a Great Lakes freighter. He made 33 trips, hauling iron ore from Duluth, Minnesota, to the steel mills in Chicago, Illinois, and saved every penny he made – "The other fellows always went out and got drunk, but I was never interested." When his father called him home in the fall, he had a nice little nest egg. "Dad was worried about me. He never liked the water, and he didn't even know how to swim – and him the Captain's son – so he bought this farm for me." The 100-acre farm, with house and barn, cost $7,000. Russell's father put up $5,000 and threw in some cattle and a team of horses. They bought it from a Mrs. Gillespie, who had just lost her husband and daughter to tuberculosis. Neighbours warned Russell to stay out of the house, but he disinfected the place and moved in anyway.

Ruth Makin grew up a few miles from Sunbury, in Ida Hill, a crossroads village on the Rideau Canal. She was a bright girl who moved quickly through the grades in her one-room elementary school and graduated at the age of 10. She went to high school in Kingston and planned to be a teacher, but she developed a slight hearing problem that a doctor predicted would get worse. By the time she realized he was wrong, she had already decided not to put her parents through the expense of sending her to teachers college in Ottawa. Instead, she stayed home, where she kept a flock of chickens and earned 25¢ an hour giving piano lessons. One Sunday afternoon, after Ruth and her father sang a duet at the Sunbury Presbyterian Church, Russell asked her to go for a drive with him.

Ruth agreed, but she confesses now that it was Russell's older brother Les who really interested her. In fact, she says, *all* the girls were interested in Les. At that time, Les was good-looking, brash and charming. He was often seeing two or three girls at the same time, and Russell says that when one girl told him to stop dating another because she wasn't going to play second fiddle to anybody, he grinned and told her she was lucky to be in the band at all. That's the way Les was, but it was quiet and fun-loving Russell that Ruth ended up with. Ruth is now 76, slightly stooped and, since she broke her hip two years ago, very slow in her movements. This is new to her, and she still apologizes for it. "Oh, I'm so slow," she says, embarrassed when someone has to wait for her. "Isn't it awful?"

Aware of their mortality in the casual manner of the elderly, she and Russell enjoy the time they have left. One afternoon, Russell spots a notice in the paper proclaiming the 60th wedding anniversary of a couple they know. "How long have we been married?" he asks her. "Fifty-five years?"

Ruth shakes her head. "Darned if I know."

"Well, we likely won't make it."

"Not likely. We're on our last legs now."

They are quiet for a moment, then Russell looks over at her. "That's a long time to be married to one man."

"I'm satisfied."

"Well," harrumphs Russell, "you're easily satisfied."

"No," she says softly, holding his gaze, "I'm not."

When Russell began milking his own cows in The Dirty Thirties, dairy farming was a seasonal occupation. His cows had their calves in April, and after that, he milked them twice a day until fall. About the first of November, he cut back to milking once a day, and when the really cold weather arrived, he quit altogether. In between, he planted his grain and corn, brought in the hay and harvested the crops. In the winter, he fed the cows, fixed his machinery and cut firewood for the next year. Every morning for eight months of the year, Russell trucked his milk in 30-gallon drums to the cheese factory across the road, and before he came back, he filled the drums with whey to feed to his pigs and calves. "Pigs were a big thing then. We'd never have got the place paid for without them. 'Mortgage lifters,' they called them." The property taxes were paid from the proceeds of the 75 turkeys Ruth raised each year, and she also kept a flock of 100 chickens. In the early years, she bought 200 day-old chicks every spring, then plucked and dressed the fattened roosters for market in the fall and shipped eggs to Montreal year-round. Later, when she could buy sexed chicks (all females), Ruth had her own egg route in Kingston. Once a week, she delivered 30 dozen eggs, holding a wooden basket in the crook of her elbow as she counted out each customer's order.

In those days, Russell and Ruth lived close to the land, in touch with the seasons and far from the Depression-era poverty and turmoil in the cities. They were independent – not rich, but by dint of hard work and thrift, not poor either – and God-fearing, liked by their neighbours and respected in their community. It sounds like an idyllic life, but it is easy to let time filter out the long hours of brutally hard work, work that broke the health of less sturdy couples, and the isolation – roads were not ploughed in winter, when the only method of transportation was horse and open cutter. They had no electricity until after Tom was born in 1936, and they went without a milking machine for another year after that. They had 25 purebred Holsteins then, and it took an hour and a half, morning and night, to milk them by hand, even with the help of the widowed Mrs. Gillespie. "She stayed and helped us," Russell remembers. "And say, now, could she ever milk."

Ruth nods. "I was never any great shakes myself." Good enough, though, to squirt a pure stream into the open mouths of a troop of begging cats. Ruth has always been a lover of animals – so much so that if she finds a wasp in the house, she catches it in a jar and releases it outside – and although she grew up in a village, she has always enjoyed farm life. Russell, of course, was born to it, and he struggled with the horses and worked as hard and as well as he knew how. Mr. Gillespie, his predecessor, had been a precise man and good with horses. Each day in the spring, he had paced off a section of land, then fitted, sowed and harrowed it that same day. "He was a good farmer," the cheesemaker across the road told Russell one day, "but you know, you grow twice as much crop on that land as he did."

Russell's father died in 1942 of complications arising from a goitre. "I'm glad he died before the fire. He would have felt pretty bad." The fire – probably electrical, no one knows – started in the early-morning hours of that winter's coldest day, February 15, 1943, the day after Valentine's Day. "We were fortunate," Russell says. "The fire killed all the cattle." In that weather, with no shelter, no feed and no way for a truck to get to them (the roads were not ploughed), they were better off dead. They were lucky, too, that the smoke got them in their sleep. "The cattle never moved. They were all lying down, quite peaceful." The next day, Russell checked the pen where he had kept a sow and her batch of piglets. "They were lying down too. There was one big lump of ashes and all these little lumps beside it." Russell once witnessed another barn fire that started while he was playing hockey at an outside rink near Sunbury. Nobody could get the animals out, and as the fire spread, they listened to the terrible, shrill bawling of the cattle, followed by a sudden silence that was, in its own way, even more terrible.

"Until the fire, I could always go to sleep – just drop off like that," Russell says with a sharp gesture. "Since the fire, though, I can't. You know, you lie there, and oh, I don't know, stuff goes through your head."

In 1944, Russell's neighbour to the east, who owned the 50-acre parcel the Morelands now call Tom's place, was killed by a train as he drove a wagon and team of horses across the tracks. "He lived by the tracks all his life, but I guess you get used to it, and he just forgot to look." The noise of the steel-rimmed wagon wheels masked the sound of the approaching train, which struck the front of the wagon. The horses, unhurt, ran the quarter-mile to the house and stopped in the barnyard, where they stood shivering and waiting to be unhitched. The train also stopped, and curious passengers disembarked to survey the wreckage.

The widow asked Russell if he would buy the farm, but he insisted that she first offer it to her husband's family, who lived on the other side of her property. At the time, she was not on good terms with her in-laws. "She asked them for $7,000, and when they turned it down, she sold it to me for $3,500."

In between milking and cropping and buying more land, Russell and Ruth raised five children. ("That was *your* fault," he says. "Not entirely," she replies.) It was, Ruth says, like raising three families: Tom and Anne were born in 1936 and 1939, Bill and Jean in '45 and '47, Emmy in '52. "After Jean, we had the family picture taken. I thought that was it," she says. "I was 43 years old when Emmy was born. Mind you, my mother was 42 when I was born, and I was an only child."

"An only child – that's like a farmer I know who went golfing," Russell interjects. "He got a hole-in-one on his first round and never went back. He figured, what was the point? He was never going to do any better than that."

Their three girls all became teachers, fulfilling the goal their mother never realized. Anne and Emmy are still teaching, and even Jean, who earned an Honours B.A. in political studies, taught for three years. Tom followed his natural mechanical abilities, and Bill went to the Kemptville College of Agricultural Technology. He graduated in 1967 but was content to farm in partnership with Russell until he finally bought out his father in 1983. After 52 years of running the show, Russell was glad to give it up. Like Bill, he finds the responsibilities, the decision making, the *managing* of the farm to be more troublesome than rewarding. He loves the work, loves turning up the black dirt with the plough in the fall and dragging the teeth of the cultivator through the frost-softened soil – loves it with the transparent joy of a child moulding beach sand in his fingers. Now, in what passes for retirement, he can do that work without the worries of ownership.

And like Tom Martin, his father's hired hand, Russell does what he's told even when he thinks it's wrong. At least, that's the theory. And in all but a few instances, it is the practice too. But Bill still calls Russell "the boss," and when the boss makes a suggestion, Bill usually takes it to heart. Thus, when Russell offers the opinion that there are not enough hay wagons to bring in the hay efficiently, Bill says, "The boss says we need a new hay wagon," and he buys a new one the next day. Such instances are rare, though, and Russell can say with understated parental satisfaction, "Bill's a pretty good manager."

In all, it is a happy situation, based on pride, trust and a sense of tradition. Bill respects the work Russell has done to build the farm into a workable business and is happy to have his father's help. Russell takes a proprietary pride in the direction his son is taking the family business and is thrilled to remain useful and to continue the work he enjoys. "The farm is a good place for old people," he says. "There's always something for them to do."

After the fire, Russell replaced his lost herd of registered purebred Holsteins with what are called "grade" cows. They were Holsteins in every respect, not crossbreds or mongrels, but were not registered with the Holstein Association of Canada. If they were dogs, people would say they "didn't have papers." In 1973, Bill decided to build a new herd of registered purebreds. He bought 13 pregnant heifers for $650 each from a neighbour who was selling his farm. "That was a fair outlay of cash then," notes Jean. She remembers the trouble they had with that bunch. "The only people those heifers ever saw were the hired man who fed them and the inseminator. They were" – she rolls her eyes expressively – "slightly wild."

A heifer is a young cow, the bovine equivalent of a filly. There is no male counterpart – a young bull is just called a young bull. Strictly speaking, a cow is a calf until she is a year old, a heifer until she bears a calf, and then a cow, but in practice, heifer is a looser term. First-calf heifers or second-calf heifers are cows that have had one or two calves. That's the limit, though – third-calf heifer is a term only an auctioneer would use. Bill bought bred heifers, animals between 15 months, the age at which Holsteins are bred, and 24 months, the age of motherhood farmers aim for when they plan their heifers' pregnancies. Holsteins have a 278-day gestation period, a little over nine months, and they are expected to bear calves at 12-month intervals for the 8 or 10 years of their productive lives. By calving, the cows not only supply their own replacements but also freshen their milk flow, which starts to decline three or four months after parturition. Thus, a cow is said to "freshen" when she calves, as in, "Vicky will freshen on June 13."

Cows are "dried up" (not milked) for about two months before their due date, so an official milking period – known as a lactation – is 305 days. The milk production, measured in kilograms, for the most recent 305-day lactation of every registered Holstein in the country is on record, providing a handy comparison of a cow's worth. In the inevitable shorthand of barn-aisle conversation, "Vicky's three-oh-five is seventy-four-ninety" (almost 7,500 kilograms, more than 16,000 pounds, about 1,600 gallons). A 305 of 7,490 is nothing special for a 5-year-old cow these days, though it is half again the average of 30 years ago. Bill has several cows with 305s in excess of 10,000 kilograms, and his herd average, as of May 1, 1987, is 8,195.

Of course, there are too many variables to compare the value of two cows realistically based only on their 305s. Age, for example. Production peaks when cows are about 7 years old, and it is unfair to compare the 305 of a 7-year-old with that of a 2-year-old or a 10-year-old. Even the time of calving has an influence – cows calving in the winter produce more milk in a year than those calving in the summer. To overcome these differences, Canadian farmers use an indexing system called Breed Class Average (BCA), making it possible to compare any two cows in the country on equal footing. BCA works like the Consumer Price Index: the average production in 1955, when the system was begun, was set at 100, and all production records are expressed as their relation to 100. A production of half the average is 50; twice the average is 200. To achieve a BCA of 100, a 5-year-old cow calving in December would have to have a 305 of 5,357 kilograms; a 2-year-old calving in June would need a 305 of only 3,857 – 1,500 kilograms less. Vicky, with her 5-year-old 305 of 7,490, has a BCA for milk of 153.

But the ability to produce large quantities of milk is only one quality that farmers value. They also want the milk to be high in butterfat and protein; that is, not to be watery. So indexes have also been established for annual production of fat and protein (in kilograms), and a cow's BCA is always given as three numbers: milk, fat, protein, in that order. Vicky's BCA is 153-172-161, well below Bill's current herd average of 173-175-184. A triple-200 BCA is not rare – Bill has a half-dozen of them – but it still turns heads. Bill's top cow, Seven, named for the 7-shaped splash of white on her forehead, has a BCA of 239-254-255. Wow.

The 13 bred heifers Bill brought home in 1973 had calves and gave milk – and their heifer calves had calves – daughters and granddaughters, and so began a lineage of cow families made real by flesh and by paperwork. Not all of them stayed, of course. There was Gloria, who was sold the week after she kicked the milk tester in the chest. "We knew he had a heart condition," Jean remembers, "and when she kicked him, *we* all just about had a heart condition." And May, who had to have her hind legs restrained at every milking. "The way she'd kick, it was like an involuntary muscle spasm, as Charlie Brown says." They put up with her for two years, because she was the most productive cow of the bunch, but finally "beefed her," as Jean puts it – sold her for slaughter.

Now, of course, all those cows are gone, even the good ones like Rita and Ava and Sue and Komet, the one that went to the zoo. But their heritage remains. Jean uses a simple naming technique to make order of the complex genealogies: all the heifer calves born in one year have names beginning with the same letter; cows in the same family have similar-sounding names. Sue, one of the quiet ones from that first bunch, had Jujube that year, and Jujube's first calf – as a 2-year-old – was Lulu, Mark's favourite cow. Lulu begat Ooly (who begat Rooly and Toolip), Qulu ("That was tough, that Q-year") and Tutu. And so on. After the T-year, Jean went back to A – Alice and Arol and Alissa – rather than face finding names for the years U to Z.

Ava is the matriarch of another important Rustowil cow lineage. Her first calf, Juanita, was unremarkable, but her second calf was Krave – better known, because of the number on her forehead, as Krave Seven, the farm's best and oldest cow. "You can't count them as a major cow family until you get some daughters," Jean says. "Seven had heifers, and that's great, but none of them really panned out." Seven's first calf, in the M-year, was born dead, then she produced five heifers in a row: Oleven ("We beefed her after two years"); Pavlova ("A real pet – you'd swear she understood you – but she didn't milk, so we shipped her to the U.S."); Quasar ("Big and lazy – we beefed her in her second lactation"); Rave, mother of Ava and Brave ("That was a deal with the Agriculture Canada experimental station at St-Hyacinthe: they gave us the semen, and if she had a bull, they would take it – but she had a heifer"); and Savour, who was delivered of Averil by caesarian section ("Her uterus was attached to the wall of her stomach, and we couldn't rebreed her"). Of the five, only Rave remains. Seven then had a bull calf, and although her 305 as a 10-year-old was 12,966, it looked as though she was not going to get rebred. Three times she was unsuccessfully inseminated with a $75 vial of frozen semen before the neighbour's bull did the job the old-fashioned way. She is due to freshen on September 10 and will turn 12 years old in November. It will almost certainly be her last chance to produce a worthy successor. "She had lots of heifers," Jean protests in her defence. "We just never found the right bull for her."

Seven had two full sisters – Octavia, whose granddaughter, Atavia, Jean hopes will turn out like Seven, and Quava ("She had her only heifer calf on March 2, and her heart failed on March 3"). The sire of Seven and her sisters was Clinton Camp Majesty, a bull now noted for passing on to his daughters the traits of good milk production and strong feet and legs. When Bill bred him to Ava as an experiment, he was a young, unproven sire, but after that, he used him often. Majesty died in the fall of 1986 at the age of 13, but Bill owns 25 vials of his semen, valued at $50 or $60 apiece.

Another important cow in the history of Rustowil is Iva, whom Bill bought in 1970, even before he purchased the baker's dozen. "Iva was a nice-looking cow, and she milked so easily," says Jean. Unfortunately, her teats leaked, leaving her prone to udder infections from constantly lying in the wet, so she was sold to a buyer in the United States. Before she went, though, she had two daughters: Godiva and Hivite. Hivite produced Jive, Kiev and Liv (as in Ullman), whose first daughter was Nivea. Bill has a trophy that Nivea earned by recording the highest composite BCA in the county three years in a row. Jean describes Trivia, Nivea's daughter by Majesty, as "our best 2-year-old." Godiva produced Iva II (I-year), who begat Iva Lou and Iva Nou (L- and N-years). Iva Lou begat Iva P who, in the R-year, begat – ready for it? – Iva Rived. Godiva's K-year calf died of a broken neck when it stuck its head through the bars of the bull pen and the bull objected to the intrusion. Then she had Lively, who had twins (Quiver and Quaker) and was the first Rustowil cow to have a double-200 BCA (milk and fat). After that, Godiva had a couple of bull calves, followed by twin heifers, Olivier and Olivia (as in Sir Laurence and de Havilland). Olivia had bulls for three years, then three heifers in one year – Majesty twins (Alissa, Alicia) in January and Alice in December.

There were other purchases as well. Bill sent Jean to the dispersal of the Maeford herd near Ottawa, at which 55 cows sold for more than $200,000. Prices ranged from $1,250 for an 11-year-old to $13,000 for a 5-year-old classed as Excellent, putting her in the top 2 percent of Holsteins in Canada. Jean bought Glory ($3,100), Jewel ($2,100) and Treasure ($6,700), then realized that Bill had forgotten to sign the cheque he had given her. She filled it out for $11,900 and forged Bill's signature on the bottom. "Fortunately, his writing is so primitive, it wasn't hard."

At another sale, Bill liked the look of Crissy, a young cow with a well-attached udder. "All right, now," said the auctioneer. "Let's get this fine-looking heifer started at $1,500. Who's going to give me a bid of $1,500?" This is standard technique for auctioneers, who know exactly what the animal is worth. They call for an opening bid higher than the animal's value, bidders start at about half or two-thirds of that number, and when the animal sells for less than the first number mentioned, the buyer goes home with the feeling, at some level of consciousness, that he or she has gotten a bargain. Knowledgeable bidders do not agree to the auctioneer's opening price any more than Lee Iacocca agrees to Bob White's opening list of demands. But Bill wasn't paying attention, and he waved his hand in agreement. "Fifteen hundred dollars," sang out the auctioneer. "I have 1,500. Do I hear 16?" There were, of course, no further bids. "Sold to Bill Moreland for $1,500." It was one of those moments when you feel the eyes of everyone in the room are on you. "I really felt foolish," Bill said later.

Bill bought Tidy and Princess with $4,000 he received when he sold Kiev. Years later, a local auctioneer brought a buyer over to look at Seven. The man offered $10,000 for Seven, which Jean turned down; then he offered $3,500 for one of Tidy's granddaughters. Not really interested in selling, Jean countered with a request for $5,000, a figure she thought much too high. The buyer declined, but the next night, the auctioneer stopped by at 10 p.m. with another buyer. Jean, who was in the barn checking on a cow that was due to calve, showed him around, and when they got to Tidy's granddaughter, she said light-heartedly, "I guess I overestimated this one. I thought she was worth $5,000, and I was only offered $3,500."

The buyer didn't even blink. "I'll give you $5,000 for her."

"So there we were," Jean says, "at 10:30 at night in the barn, him counting out 50 hundred-dollar bills."

Not all of Bill's deals have worked out so well. He bought Tara for $3,000 from the best herd in the country, a herd with an *average* double-200 BCA. Near the end of her first lactation, Tara had what Jean calls "some guck" in the right hind quarter of her udder. It cleared up with treatment, but after she calved, the left hind quarter was shrivelled up. Tara will never exceed 75 percent of her potential; she is what farmers term a three-quartered cow. "Yeah," Bill grimaces, "a thousand dollars a quarter."

Late in May, Jean cooks up a major trade with Danny Hulton. It's a straight three-for-one swap – no cash involved – that sends Olivier, Tidy and Shiva to Danny's farm on Wolfe Island in return for one cow. "He gets three cows, and we get one," says Tom, with a heaven-help-us roll of his eyes. "And she thinks we're getting a good deal."

"It's good for both of us," says Jean, unperturbed. "All Bill cares about is milk production. If a cow can't produce, he doesn't want her. But Danny doesn't care about that at all. You take Tidy, for instance. Her BCA for milk is 50 points below our herd average, but it's 20 points above his." It seems reasonable to wonder why a dairy farmer would not be interested in milk production. Danny is more interested in the cows and their pedigrees than their products. His specialty is salvaging older cows that are past their peak of production but can still bear a calf or two and have the bloodlines to give him an exceptional – and therefore exceptionally valuable – heifer.

Olivier, daughter of Godiva and twin sister to Olivia, is now 8 years old and reaching the end of her productive life. Most of Bill's cows keep themselves presentable, but Olivier usually lets her tail fall in the manure gutter or lies down in some mud or manure. No matter how often she is cleaned up, her hind legs are always caked with the stuff. Speaking for everybody, Eileen says, "I can hardly wait to get rid of that pile of manure."

Tidy, whose granddaughter sold for $5,000 in the middle of the night, was a promising-looking heifer, but her first pregnancy went wrong, resulting in a mummified fetus. This is a rare and bizarre complication in which the fetus dies at about the sixth month of pregnancy but is neither aborted nor reabsorbed; rather, it and the normal uterine fluids dry up, becoming literally mummified. Bill and Jean first grew concerned when Tidy, though visibly pregnant, passed her due date without filling her udder or showing any other signs of imminent birth. The veterinarian – Bert Wilson at that time – induced labour with an injection of estrogen and removed the fetus, filling the barn with the putrid, lingering smell of rotted flesh. Tidy has had no further reproductive troubles, but she did not freshen until she was 3 years old and has not lived up to her potential.

Shiva, the last of the three, though one of Godiva's Majesty daughters, does not milk well, and Bill dismisses her as "a lazy old fart." He means she should eat more and produce more than she does, and he often speaks of such animals as if they were just not trying. It is not entirely an anthropomorphic notion. Shiva is not an aggressive animal, and she is content to let herself be pushed away from the feed wagon by other cows. It may be that shy is a better word than lazy, but the result is the same – she lacks the drive and initiative to get ahead in her world. "I'll be glad to see the last of those three," says Bill.

Danny, a tall, loose-jointed young man with a big smile and the kind of build described in western novels as "rawboned," is happy to take them off Bill's hands. "He's got his father's farm, so he doesn't have any big money worries," Jean says. "He likes to save these old cows from the slaughterhouse. They're all from good families, and they're all in calf. If Tidy has a heifer, he may get his money back on it in just one generation. So he's getting what he wants. He loves doing this."

Danny borrows a truck to pick up the cows, but its box is not large, and Bill and Jean are hesitant to put all three cows in it.

"Well, let's see if they'll fit," says Danny. They do, though not without being crowded. "This way, they won't get hurt," he concludes. "They haven't got room to fall down."

Bill doesn't say anything, but after the truck is gone, he shakes his head. "I wouldn't have even tried to get them in one trip."

Danny returns at 4:30 with his end of the bargain, a young, predominantly white cow that is an excellent milk producer but has no special pedigree or conformation. She settles into her new stall, and Danny says apologetically, "She won't give much tonight. You milk earlier than I do."

Jean nods. "What's her name?"

Danny does not answer. Instead, he gives Jean a long, sideways look that asks, "What, you think I know my cows by name?"

Later, her papers reveal her name is Connie. Bill is happy with her production and her attitude. He has what he wants, and so does Danny.

"It's just another way for the government to make a few extra bucks on the backs of farmers."

Bill is pulling a small trailer behind the smaller of his two green John Deere tractors. It is a pleasant day in early May, and he and Tom are heading for the wooded slope behind the Quarry to get some wood for next winter. Tom, delighted to have a chance to work outside instead of in the barn, can't stop smiling; but Bill, who should be enjoying the cool weather and the refreshing interlude between planting barley and corn, is exercised over a recently proposed change in the tax law.

"You used to have a choice between using cash accounting and accrual accounting. Now, [Finance Minister Michael] Wilson is going to make everybody use the accrual system." The cash system allows farmers to report income when they receive it and deduct expenses when they pay them. Capital expenditures aside, it is relatively simple: I made this much money, I spent this much, therefore I made (or lost) this much. With accrual accounting, income is reported when a sale is made (sometimes not in the same tax year the payment is received), and expenses are deducted not as they are paid out but as the materials bought are used, so a farmer can't purchase, say, a three-year supply of herbicide and deduct the total cost in one year.

Proponents argue that accrual accounting gives a more realistic picture of farm finances because it figures into the calculation of income all the stored grain and other assets in a farm's inventory. Bill disagrees. "It's not a true reflection of the financial situation. For example, my inventory changes with the price of cows. A few years ago, cattle were up to about $1,100 or $1,200. Then they were way down for a while, and now they're about $800. Well, I've got 80 or 90 cows, with the dry cows and heifers, and that $300 would make quite a difference. If the price goes up $300, that's income, and I have to pay tax on it. But it's all on paper – I haven't actually earned any more than the year before." If the potential value of Bill's cattle increased by $25,000, it would double his present income and quadruple his taxable income. Even though his actual income has not changed, he would have to pay several thousand dollars more in income tax.

"Of course, if the price goes down, then that's a loss," he says, spreading his hands in a gesture of literal evenhandedness. "But there's no forward averaging, and it makes it hard to do any financial planning." Given the choice, 9 out of 10 Canadian farmers have opted for cash accounting, and they are not happy to have their minds changed for them. The long-term effects of the proposal are not yet clear, but one thing is certain: farmers will be footing heavier bills from their accountants. "It's not fair," Bill insists.

Nevertheless, he shrugs off his frustration when they arrive at the woodlot. The unusually dry weather has made it possible for him to get the tractor through the low spot Russell indicated when he said, "You're kind of licked with your tractors," but Bill is stopped by the disorderly growth of saplings and mature trees ahead. At this point, many landowners would pick a more or less straight path, with few trees, to cut themselves a roadway, but Bill treads less heavily on his land than most. With the tractor shut off, he and Tom open a crooked path through the woods, taking advantage of natural spaces between the trees and cutting down only a few dead or dying saplings. Where Bill must decide between ease of access and the cutting down of a living tree, he never chooses convenience. As a result, the roadway zigs and zags so much, it can hardly be discerned from any one spot. These days, such an approach is labelled "environmentally sensitive," but although Bill is not environmentally unaware, his motivation is that of a sensible, practical man who has received this land from his father and intends to pass it on to his son.

They follow the course of switchbacks to a clearing near Bill's fence line, across from the scattered ironwoods that so offend his sense of resource economy. With Tom operating the chain saw and Bill stacking and giving directions, they clear up some standing and leaning deadwood. Tom is in his element, and he handles the saw with the deceptive ease of an experienced woodcutter. As is true with users of other dangerous equipment, those who operate chain saws do so at first with a care so exaggerated, it is hazardous; as they attain some proficiency, tense caution disintegrates into reckless overconfidence; those who pass through these stages unscarred develop a lasting and ingrained carefulness. Fear, then contempt, then respect. Tom has progressed well into the third category, and he expertly trims the limbs off more than enough poles to fill the trailer.

Finished, Tom silences the saw. With their jackets now off, he and Bill stand and look across the fence. Bill has his hands on his hips, thinking; Tom waits, hands stuck behind his red suspenders, fingers laced across the front of his plaid shirt. "It sure is a shame to see that wood go to waste," Bill says again. "It's been lying there for years already, and it won't be any good next year." He sighs. "If anybody's ever going to get any use out of it, Tom, we'd better take it home with us." They clamber over the fence, and as Tom trims the fallen trees, Bill throws them in a pile on his side of the wire. Bill Moreland, outstanding member of the community, pillar of his church, stealer of wood. He does not skulk or glance over his shoulder or apologize. "If anybody ought to be arrested, it's the guy who left this wood here to rot." Like the rest of us, Bill has a clear sense of right and wrong that does not necessarily coincide with a strict interpretation of the law: waste is wrong; making use of some discarded trees, even if they are on someone else's property, is right.

At noon, they open the lunchboxes Eileen packed for them and sit at the base of a large maple. As is their habit, Tom stretches his legs out and leans comfortably against the tree, while Bill sits on his bunched-up coveralls, without a backrest. And as usual, Tom eats in silence, finishing well before Bill, who – between bites – ponders current affairs out loud. The lead item on the morning news is the revelation that part-time actress Donna Rice spent a good part of the weekend at the home of U.S. presidential candidate Gary Hart while his wife was out of town. Hart will withdraw his candidacy later in the week; today, he is denying that anything happened, but his protestations go unheeded.

Bill is genuinely mystified by Hart's behaviour, which he sees as poor judgement and a lack of self-control. He falls to decrying modern morality and its effect on young people in a what's-the-world-coming-to manner usually observed in older men, and as he speaks, the season's first blackflies descend, encouraged by the dissipation of the chain saw's smoky exhaust. Like commandos crawling under barbed wire, they work their way one at a time under Bill's glasses, which he is finally forced to remove. "I was pretty green about girls when I was 16," he says, wiping his finger on the knee of his pants to remove the squashed blackflies. "Now, they get them going steady when they're 12 years old. That's too young to get started with that. Judas Priest, by the time they're 15, they want to do more than just hold hands. It's only natural." In a vain attempt to chase away the blackflies, he waves his arms like a television evangelist.

Tom, who is being ignored by the flies, is grinning hugely. "I sure like coming to the woods with someone the bugs like the taste of better than me."

"Yeah, go bother him for a while. I'm not *that* much better looking," Bill says, shooing blackflies toward Tom with his hat. "Anyway, I believe you have to keep control of kids. At that age, they just don't have the, I don't know, the experience, I guess, to hold back when they should. I didn't know girls existed when I was 12, and my father pretty well kept me under control when I was 16 and 18. It didn't hurt me, and I think it did me a lot of good." Bill has been adding to the wide strip of fly corpses on his pant leg and now looks as though his leg has been run over by a motorcycle.

Neither man smokes, and they have milk in their thermoses rather than coffee, so they do not linger after they have eaten. Tom works enthusiastically through the afternoon and, despite some pointed hints from Bill about the time, well past the start of milking. "He's just like a beaver," Bill says. "Once you get him started, you can't get him stopped." On the way back to the barn, Bill looks at his watch in the gathering dusk and wonders if Jean has been left alone to milk. "I hope Eileen is back from Kingston, or we're in big trouble." Eileen, well aware that the men would probably be late, made sure she was home in time to help Jean milk. Bill drops Tom at the barn and unloads the trailer full of wood with "help" from Mark. Afterwards, Mark sits on his lap, and Bill lets him steer the tractor back to the barn. When Mark forgets to straighten the wheels after making a turn, Bill, though tired and hurried, is patient, helpful and encouraging. It is a nice father-son moment — "quality time," in social jargon — as Bill helps his son keep the powerful machine under control. A metaphor for things to come.

Last year, Bill grew his corn beside the barn, where the barley is now up as green and rank as a lawn that needs mowing. This year, as part of his system of crop rotation, he will plant the corn "at Pearl's," a 100-acre farm next to Ed Johnston's place that Bill bought in 1981. It lies on the concession north of the home farm and is divided in half by a paved north-south road. The side next to Ed's has the house, barn and 45 acres of alfalfa hay; across the road are 50 acres of rolling cropland divided by a drainage ditch into two fields that, except for a portion of the upper field planted in barley, are bare, waiting for corn.

The farm used to belong to Pearl Garrett, a bright, lively schoolteacher whose only child, a boy about Bill's age, died young. "He was a lovely boy," Ruth Moreland remembers, "but there was something wrong with his spine. It was terribly sad." When Pearl's husband died, she sold the farm to Bill, with the condition that she could live in the house for the rest of her life. With no desire to become a landlord, Bill readily agreed, but now, for two reasons, he regrets it. Pearl is ageing rapidly, and her ability to continue to care for herself is in doubt. Eileen, especially, feels responsible for her well-being, a worry neither of them wants. Also, Tom MacFarlane, who is currently living in a row-housing project in Gananoque, wants to move, and Bill would like to offer him Pearl's house as part of an employee benefit package. This would be ideal, in Bill's view, because he would not have to worry about renting the house, and there would be someone living there to look after the calves. Bill has divided the barn into three pens with access to separate exercise yards – one each for heifer calves 3 to 6 months, 6 to 9 months and 9 to 12 months, when they are brought back to the main barn. If Tom were living in the house, he could keep a closer eye on the calves than anybody does at present.

It is an awkward situation for Bill and Eileen. They are genuinely concerned about Pearl, but what they want for her – to live somewhere where she is not alone – is also very much to their own advantage. They do not want to be seen to be pushing the old lady out of her home, yet they feel leaving it is the best thing for her.

In her marvellous book *Much Depends on Dinner*, Margaret Visser contends that corn and its by-products – corn oil, corn syrup, cornstarch – are as important to our society as buffalo was to the Plains Indians. Together, North Americans grow 250 million tonnes of corn each year; individually, we consume three pounds of it every day. She continues:

"You cannot buy anything at all in a North American supermarket that has been untouched by corn, with the occasional and single exception of fresh fish – and even that has almost certainly been delivered to the store in cartons or wrappings that are partially created out of corn. Meat *is* largely corn. So is milk: American livestock and poultry are fed and fattened on corn and cornstalks. Frozen meat and fish have a light cornstarch coating on them to prevent excessive drying. The brown and golden colouring that constitutes the visual appeal of many soft drinks and puddings comes from corn. All canned foods are bathed in liquid containing corn. Every carton, every wrapping, every plastic container depends on corn products – indeed, all modern paper and cardboard, with the exception of newsprint and tissue, is coated in corn."

Corn oil, she goes on to explain, is a popular cooking fat and is found in margarine, mayonnaise, salad dressing and soap. Corn syrup is widely used as a sweetener in candy, ice cream, some liquors, soft drinks, condensed milk and ketchup. Cornstarch – "white, odourless, tasteless and easily moulded" – serves as a neutral carrier in everything from baking powder, icing sugar and instant potato flakes to toothpaste, detergents and painkilling pills.

"Modern corn production grew up with industrial and technological revolutions," says Visser, "and the makers of those revolutions made whatever they wanted to make – antibiotics or deep-drilling oil-well mud or ceramic spark-plug insulators or embalming fluids – out of the material at hand. And that material was the hardy and obliging fruit of the grass which the Indians called *maïs*." Currently, corn has become the basic ingredient in biodegradable plastic, and it is even being touted as a replacement for road salt.

Individually and collectively, we are dependent on corn. Equally, though, corn depends on us. Like other grains, corn is a grass; unlike them, it does not grow in the wild. If agricultural production of corn were to cease – an unlikely event, given that corn is grown on every continent except Antarctica and is harvested somewhere in the world every month of the year – it would become extinct immediately. Of all the cultivated crops in the world, corn is the only one for which this is true. Wheat, rice, tomatoes, pumpkins – everything else – would continue to grow wild in some uncultivated corner of the world; corn would not because it cannot reproduce itself. It is not infertile: each plant sets a cobful of seeds without difficulty, lining them up in neat rows. But the cobs are so carefully wrapped in a protective condom of heavy husk, they are unable to discharge the seed into the soil. The kernels rot in the husk. Without humans to perform the mechanics of reproduction for it, corn would disappear.

So where, if it relies on humans to survive, did it come from? In a word, Mexico. At least, that is where the genetic changes to make it human-dependent took place. The only wild relative of corn currently in existence is *teosinte* (literally, God's ear of corn), a tall wild grass that looks more like sugarcane than corn. Native Central Americans began selecting teosinte-like plants for increased production 5,000 years ago, eventually turning a quarter-inch-long spike with unprotected, self-seeding grains into the husked eight-inch-long cobs reverently presented to Columbus and other explorers and settlers. By that time, *maïs* constituted 90 percent of the diet of some American people and was as integral to their culture and society as it is to ours today.

In modern Canadian dairy farming, many varieties of corn are grown, but for only two purposes: silage and grain. To make corn silage, the plant is cut off at ground level and sliced like a cucumber at one-quarter-to-three-eighths-inch intervals – leaves, cobs, stem and all – then packed in a silo. As a feed, corn silage is low in protein but high in fibre and carbohydrates, and per acre, it provides more digestible energy and plain old calories than does any other crop. Grain corn is just the kernels, like so many cans of niblets, rock-hard because they are harvested after drying on the cob. Pound for pound, all grains – corn, wheat, oats, barley – are about equal in feed value (to a cow), but corn is the most palatable (to a cow), and if cultivated carefully, it yields the most bushels of grain per acre (to a farmer).

Bill grows only grain corn, which he harvests as high-moisture corn. High-moisture is a relative term – compared with fresh corn off the cob, it is still pretty hard and dry. But it contains enough moisture (about 22 to 25 percent) that it would rot if left in a pile or stored in an ordinary grain bin. Bill avoids this by storing it in an airtight silo; without oxygen, the corn cannot decay, so it is held there in a kind of anaerobic limbo. He never removes more corn from the silo than he will use in 24 hours. Bill feeds about 200 tonnes of high-moisture corn a year, half of which he grows himself. What he buys costs him more than $100 a tonne, $11,000 to $12,000 in all. He is hoping that his crop yield will exceed three tonnes per acre (100 tonnes from 30 acres) and will have a similar value. But first, he must get it in the ground.

Bill does not plant his own corn. He hires the job out to another dairy farmer, Jim Greenlees, who makes a circuit of the area every spring. Jim's father used to plant corn for Bill's father. Now, the sons are in their early 40s, but they went to public school and high school together, and out of the other's hearing, each refers to the other as Billy or Jimmy. Face to face, they try to maintain their middle-aged dignity and usually remember to say Bill and Jim. By the middle of May, Jim has worked his way around to the Moreland farm. It is good timing – Russell takes the last pass over the field in the morning, and Jim arrives to plant in the afternoon. But Russell is not happy with the condition of the field, and he tells Bill it is too rough and contains too many rocks. This time, however, Bill does not heed his advice. "It'll have to do, Father. Tom can pick some more rocks when he's cultipacking." Russell grumbles a bit, but he doesn't argue.

Jim is a big, strong-looking man with a belly-over-his-belt build that keeps his pants riding low and makes it hard for him to keep his shirt tucked in. By the time he arrives at Pearl's, he has worked all morning and is covered with a fine dust that gives his face a funeral-parlour pall, but he is in high spirits. "It looked pretty bad at 5 o'clock, when I first went out," he says, lighting a cigarette. "It was just pouring rain, but it dried right up, and I was planting corn by a quarter after 9. It's a hell of a nice day now." Indeed it is – sunny and, with the wind dropping, warmer by the minute; however, the rain that fell on Jim's farm this morning did not fall on Bill's.

Jim is driving a red and white International Harvester tractor, model 844 (two steps up to the cab), with a four-row Allis-Chalmers Air Planter mounted on the back. "This is supposed to be the most accurate corn planter on the market," Jim says, with an I-don't-know-but-that's-what-they-tell-me shrug. Each of the planting mechanisms is independently mounted on the planter frame so that all four corn rows are planted at the correct depth. "The old ones had them all together, so if you came to a furrow or a hump, it'd put the corn on top of the ground on one side and about six inches deep on the other." Every time Jim lowers the planter to begin a row, a long arm with a disc on the end drops down from one side or the other of the planter and scratches a line in the dirt beside him. Coming back up the field, he uses that mark as a guide, lining up the outside of his front wheel with it to keep the

CORN PLANTER

rows evenly spaced. When he lifts the planter at the end of each row, a flip-flop mechanism automatically selects the other disc marker – first left, then right, as he goes back and forth across the field. As well as looking nice, straight, even rows provide better growing conditions for the corn and make it possible to harvest the crop with less waste.

Each of the four planting wheels has its own corn bin and is monitored by what Jim identifies as "a seeing-eye sort of thing." When the planter is working correctly, four lights in the cab flash as the seeds pass the seeing eye: if one of the lights stays on, that bin is empty; if it stays off and a buzzer sounds, that planter is plugged. "You have to be careful, though. It's sensitive enough that a shadow will set it off." He steps ahead and shades the planter, then steps back, causing the buzzer to go on and off. "You don't bother to stop if it goes off when you're under a tree." From the bin, the seeds fall beside the planting wheel, a 16-inch disc marked by a row of dimples an inch from its outer edge. Most of the aboveground part of the wheel is enclosed in a sponge-lined hood that is pressurized by a small air blower of the kind used in car heating systems – hence the name Air Planter. The air pressure holds each seed in a dimple on the wheel until it passes the sponge, when it falls into a furrow cut by a knife on the front of the planter. It is commonly accepted to be, as Jim says, the most trouble-free planting system on the market, 99.9 percent accurate.

As well as opening a furrow and depositing the seed, the planter leaves a double strip of fertilizer a couple of inches on either side of the seed – "The old kind used to dump the fertilizer and the corn out together," says Jim, "but if you got a rain right away, sometimes the fertilizer would burn the seed because it's too strong" – then it closes up the furrow and packs the soil around it. All in all, it is a wonderful machine, and Jim paid $8,000 for it in 1980. "I don't know if you can buy one like it for $15,000 now," he says, adding that the new models have more features, such as a monitor for the fertilizer level and digital readouts showing the number of acres planted and the number of seeds planted in the last acre. "It sure takes the guesswork out of it, and that's nice, but every time they put on something else, it jacks the price up a little bit." A five-figure price tag for a machine that is used only one day a year explains why Bill would rather have Jim do his planting for him. Jim, who grows only 20 acres of corn himself – "I hope to get it planted later this week" – justifies the expense by doing enough "custom" planting for relatives and neighbours to make the machine pay for itself.

Bill meets him in the lower part of the field with a gravity box full of fertilizer and 10 bags of corn seed. Some farmers take great pride in the brand of corn they grow and go so far as to put little signs in each field that identify the brand and its hybrid by name and number. Bill affects no such ostentation; indeed, he has purchased two different brands – four bags of PAG and six of Northrup/King – and, of the latter brand, two different hybrids, PX9060 and PX9161. His only concern is that the different types be planted consecutively and not mixed. Each bag costs $82 or $84, depending on the brand, and contains 80,000 kernels of corn, 10 for a penny. Bill is aiming for a plant density of 60,000 plants per hectare, which he calculates as one bag of seed for every three acres.

Jim pours the four bags of PAG into the four bins on his planter. The seed is already coated with a fungicide to protect it from decay organisms while in storage, but Bill hands Jim four instant-soup-mix-sized foil packages of DL Plus, a purple powder labelled as an insecticide/fungicide for the control of wireworms and seed-corn maggots in the soil. It contains diazinon, lindane and captan, and the label, in part, reads:

> Exposure to captan may produce long-term health effects. To minimize exposure, follow directions outlined on this label. **PRECAUTIONS: Never handle material with bare hands.**
>
> Do not breathe dust. Avoid spilling on skin or clothing. When treating or handling treated seed, work in a well-ventilated area, and wear a respirator, goggles and rubber gloves. Do not use leather or cloth gloves. Wear clothing that completely covers arms and legs to minimize exposure. Change contaminated clothing daily, and wash thoroughly before use. Wash hands, face and arms thoroughly after handling Agrox DL Plus and before drinking, eating or smoking. Shower after use or at the end of the workday. Do not contaminate food, feed or any body of water. Lindane is toxic to fish, birds and other wildlife. Label unplanted, treated seed as follows: "Poisonous to man and animals. Do not use for food or feed purposes. Do not sell to oil mills. This seed has been treated with captan, diazinon and lindane."

Jim tears open the packages with his bare hands and dumps one into each seed bin. The powder has a unique smell, as distinctive and pleasantly off-putting as a dentist's office. Despite the warning label, Jim is not wearing a respirator or goggles or rubber gloves. His shirt is only halfheartedly tucked in, and his sleeves are rolled up. As he pulls a gnarled stick from a pipe that is part of the planter frame and stirs the bins to mix the powder with the seed, Bill nods in approval. "Glad to see you don't like to get that stuff on your hands. Some of the old guys used to put their hands right in there."

"No, you read the directions on this stuff, and it scares you. You're not supposed to touch it or breathe it. You can't eat or smoke or anything." He stirs up a purple fog, which settles on his hands and enters his lungs. "I get enough of this stuff on me anyway. Does this field look square to you?"

"No, I think it's a little narrower at the north end."

"Well, where do you want the short rows?" At some point, the north-south rows will not reach from end to end – the choice is to work from one side to the other and leave the short rows against the far fence or to come in from each side and leave a kind of herringbone pattern in the middle. Jim favours putting the short rows against the far fence, where they will not be seen from the road. Bill would like them left in the middle so that the combine will have more room to manoeuvre at harvesttime. In the give-and-take of rural diplomacy, this is a delicate situation: Bill, who owns the land and is paying for the work, clearly has some right to say how it should be done; on the other hand, Jim is using his own equipment and has his reputation to consider, for, in the way of small communities everywhere, those who know who owns the land will also know who planted it. Both men are independent – and independently minded – businessmen. They restate their positions, but although neither wants to risk bad feelings by insisting on doing it his way, neither offers to give in. They let the matter drop for the moment, and the discussion turns to fertilizer.

Bill has already harrowed in 100 pounds per acre of urea, a nitrogen fertilizer, and now he consults his soil analysis, which recommends 225 pounds per acre of 20-40-15. The numbers represent the fertilizer's nitrogen-phosphate-potash (NPK) rating and mean that 100 pounds of the fertilizer contains 20 pounds of nitrogen (N), 40 pounds of phosphate (P_2O_5), 15 pounds of potash (K_2O) and, by implication, 25 pounds of filler. The N is made by processing atmospheric nitrogen under pressure and heat with hydrogen and carbon dioxide from natural gas; the P is calcium-phosphate rock from a mine in Florida treated with sulphuric acid from a sour-gas well in Alberta; the K is potash from Saskatchewan, purified and crystallized into granules. Clearly, the costs of transportation and natural gas are a large part of the price of farm fertilizer, which jumped dramatically during the energy crisis of the mid-1970s. Currently, though, this is offset by a worldwide fertilizer surplus, and fertilizer prices are lower now than they were five years ago. Bill's 20-40-15 cost him $575 a tonne, $58.50 for the 225 pounds he needs per acre.

While Bill is consulting his soil analysis, Jim flips through the owner's manual for the planter. He can vary the amount of fertilizer it deposits by changing sprockets on a drive gear. "It's set at 218 pounds to the acre now, and the next setting is, uh, 232." He grins at Bill. "You're right in the middle."

For Bill, the choice is 7 pounds per acre too little fertilizer or 7 pounds too much. He wants to use all the fertilizer he's got, but he doesn't want to run out either, and he is aware that the planter is unlikely to be exact. "I wonder if it's putting it on a little heavy," he says. This is a conversational gambit they both use, introducing an idea by saying "I wonder if . . ." as though it were a philosophical question they might want to stop and have a learned discussion about.

"Yeah, I think it is a little heavy. I wonder what would happen if we left it like it is."

Having tested the water and found it to their liking, they both dive in and agree to leave the setting at 218 pounds per acre. "Now," Bill says, with a nod to the planter, "How much does it hold?" There are two fertilizer bins on the planter, and Jim says that each side holds seven 55-pound bags, right full. "Okay," says Bill, and does the math in his head, saying it out loud so Jim can catch him if he makes a mistake. "Let's see, 7 times 55, that's 350 and 35 is 385 pounds to a side — that's 760, 770 to a load. I've got 3 tonnes, that's 6,600 pounds, and 30 acres at 225 is, uh, 6,750, but that's all right because I've actually got an extra 600 pounds. This piece of ground is 15 acres, so at 225, that's 2,250 plus half of that is 1,125 makes 3,375 — is that right? 3,375? — and 770 a load is, uh, a little over four loads." His eyes focus again. "If it takes five loads for this piece, then it's too thick."

Jim begins to plant, and since nothing more was said about the short rows, he will leave them up against the far fence, where they do not show. But before he gets through the first load of fertilizer, Bill returns to say he has been talking to Jack Curtis, whose fields Jim finished planting that morning, and Jack felt that the fertilizer application was a little light. Jim changes sprockets, and the field ends up taking almost five loads, just within Bill's limit.

When Jim stops to refill the fertilizer bins, he lights a forbidden cigarette and leans against his tractor wheel. "These people are pretty good farmers," he says, in an understated way that means he thinks they are very good farmers. "You look at this field. It's in good shape — nice and moist, well worked up, good and smooth. I've been some places where the field is so rough, you couldn't see the marker." He is talking about the same field Russell was complaining to Bill about. "And there's no rocks in it. You don't mind doing something like this. You go some places, and there's rocks as big as bowling balls just lying in the field. Rocks are hard on a machine like this," he adds, waving his cigarette at the planter. "Rocks and groundhogs," he says, as if repeating a slogan. "The two things a farmer can do without."

He watches the hydraulic auger fill his fertilizer bins. "I never saw one of those work before. Never dreamed they'd work so good. Sure beats handling all them bags." He grins. "Why, there's nothing to this corn planting if you got all this machinery." Later, Russell and Ruth, out for a drive, stop by the field and watch. Jim drives stolidly up and down the field, squinting at the marker through the smoke from an ever present cigarette. It is dull, wearisome work, all the more so because of the care needed. "I never saw anyone so particular," says Bill, a classic instance of the pot calling the kettle black, and indeed, there is as much admiration in his voice as disparagement. "He's almost as bad as his father. You'd see Earl planting, and he'd be right up like this." He grabs an imaginary tractor steering wheel with one hand and fender with the other, then leans out past the fender and twists his head sideways to squint through one eye at an imaginary front wheel. "You'd get your rows straight, all right, but you'd get an awful crick in your neck."

Ruth watches 40 or 50 gulls wheeling in loose formation, then landing to investigate the freshly turned dirt. "I always wanted to find a sea gull's nest with some babies in it," she says. "But I never did."

Jim finishes the first 15-acre field that afternoon and returns in the morning to plant the field north of the ditch, but it soon becomes clear that he will run out of fertilizer and seed before he is done. The field is 30 acres, and Bill, who wanted only 15 acres of it in corn, paced off what he thought was half the field and planted it in barley. In fact, it turns out that he left 19 acres to be planted in corn. He hurriedly supplies Jim with two more bags of seed and another tonne of fertilizer.

Ironically, he would have had enough fertilizer if he had not asked Jim to recalibrate the planter.

—————

Meanwhile, back at the barn—on a dairy farm, there is always a meanwhile, always a barn full of cows that must be milked twice a day and bred and calved and fed and doctored and watched with the vigilance of a guardian angel—Paul O'Neill, the youngest of the vets who have taken over Bert Wilson's practice, arrives to perform three services: a minor surgery, heat checks and pregnancy checks.

First, the surgery. The patient is Peggoty, a 6-year-old mostly black cow with a BCA of 202-219-199. Since her last calf, she has been bred three times without success, and although the usual rule at Rustowil is three strikes and you're beefed, Peggoty is milking well enough to deserve an extra chance. The diagnosis of her problem is an advanced anus. In a normal cow, the anus is under the tail, and directly below that is the vulva and vaginal opening, a four-to-six-inch-long vertical slit. When a cow defecates, she does not, as a dog does, look embarrassed and hump herself up in the middle so that her anus is more or less pointing to the ground. Rather, she just raises her tail and lets fly—sometimes, if she is walking, in midstride. Cows are not fussy about their toilet: as an elderly farmer once told me, "Cows are just like people—when they get up in the morning, the first thing they do is have a shit. The only difference is we get out of bed first."

At any rate, Peggoty is not normal. Her anus is not directly above her vagina but is set well into her body, leaving a kind of shelf between it and the back of her legs. Her vaginal opening, rather than being vertical, is draped over the edge of the shelf so that the top of it is horizontal. When she defecates, a residue of manure is usually left on the shelf, and when she has soft stool, which, being on a high-energy diet, she often does, the residue is a puddle that dribbles into her vagina. "Not," says Paul, raising his eyebrows, "the recommended way to get pregnant." His solution is to close most of the vaginal opening, leaving only enough room at the bottom to pass urine and accept semen.

He washes the manure off her backside, then gives her an epidural, which will mask most of the pain but still allow her to stand. "Let's see if this is the right spot," he says, slipping a needle between her vertebrae. Peggoty jerks forward and kicks at him; Paul nods. "She thought it was the right spot." When the anaesthetic has taken effect, he gets Tom to hold her tail out of the way and begins. Starting a couple of inches from the bottom of the vaginal opening, he uses a pair of surgical scissors to cut a clothesline-thick strip of skin from the lip of the vulva – up one side and down the other. It takes very little time, and there is not much blood. He then stitches across the opening so that the two raw edges are forced against each other, then sticks his finger in the opening below them. "There, that should be enough room."

He explains to Jean that when she takes the stitches out in a couple of weeks, the two strips of cut flesh will have grown together, effectively sealing the top part of the opening and hopefully allowing her to become pregnant. When she calves, the force of her contractions will tear apart the narrow strip of newly joined flesh, and she will bear her calf normally. Afterwards, Paul will repeat the operation, so she can be rebred. Not a particularly bright future, but better – for both Bill and Peggoty – than the alternative: a short walk in a long abattoir.

"Kind of loose, aren't they?" Jean asks, meaning the stitches, which are about an inch apart.

"They only have to keep out the wind and a little manure, Jean," Paul grins. He has the Dale Carnegie habit of always using the name of the person to whom he is speaking. They chat for a while. Jean asks about his new house, which he will be moving into soon. He has to go to Ottawa to retrieve his furniture, stored there when he and his wife went to Africa for four months last year. There, they spent three weeks a month doctoring children and the rest of the time doing agricultural consultant work. "We didn't do any actual veterinarian work, Jean. We just made suggestions on how they could improve their production. Basic things, like letting the cattle get a drink of water."

Paul puts away his instruments, and they move to the bottom of the barn, where the heifers are tied. He tests three heifers for the onset of heat by palpating their walnut-sized ovaries. "Breed her tomorrow, Jean," he says of one, and "In four or five days, Jean," of another. Then he does pregnancy checks on five cows that were bred a month or more ago. At 35 to 40 days after conception, a calf embryo attaches itself to the uterine wall, where it can be felt as a jelly-bean-sized lump.

All of this palpating and feeling – a wonderfully convenient and inexpensive diagnostic tool – is possible because of a peculiarity of bovine anatomy: the spine (which, of course, is horizontal), the rectum (a continuation of the large intestine) and the reproductive tract (vulva, vagina, cervix, uterus, oviducts and ovaries) are lined up one on top of another like the lines of type on this page. By donning a shoulder-length clear plastic glove, Paul can insert his hand – in fact, his whole arm – into a cow's rectum and, through its muscular wall, feel his

REPRODUCTIVE SYSTEM

CERVIX
UTERUS
OVARY
OVIDUCT

RECTUM
VAGINA
VULVA
BLADDER

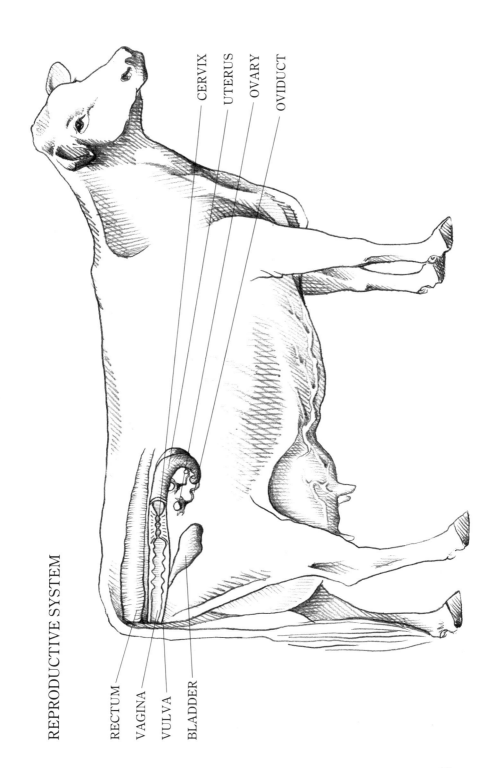

93

way from vagina to ovaries, hidden under the hipbones. Fortunately, a cow's rectum, designed to pass more than 100 pounds of manure a day, can accommodate such manhandling with little or no discomfort to the cow. After registering an initial expression of wide-eyed surprise, most cows go back to chewing their cud while Paul massages their internal organs.

And, of course, the ability to feel around the reproductive system makes artificial insemination that much easier. The technician reaches into the rectum, grabs the cervix and, working by feel, inserts a straw containing thawed semen into the vagina and partially through the cervix. All in all, it is rather like pulling on a pair of mittens and trying to put a pencil in a pencil sharpener with the lights out. In the early days of artificial insemination, technicians blew through the straw to deposit the semen; now they depress a plunger.

Paul uses the take-'em-by-surprise entry technique when inserting his gloved hand for an examination. He pulls the tail to one side and, without warning, plunges in his hand with one smooth motion, not stopping until he is in up to the wrist. Later in the month, when Paul's partner, Brian Willows, comes out to do some more "preg checks," he uses the "rocket" entry, a two-stage booster technique in which he inserts his fingers – tips together as if trying to slip on a bracelet – up to the second knuckle, pauses momentarily while the cow relaxes her sphincter, then thrusts in up to the wrist. Before the examination can begin, both men usually find it necessary to reach in the full length of their arms and scoop out a couple of handfuls of manure. When Brian is introduced to a visitor who enters the barn while he is groping a cow's innards with his left arm, he lets go of the cow's tail and proffers a handshake as casually as if he is holding a martini in his other hand instead of a cow's uterus.

The results of these spring preg checks are important to Rustowil because they have had a rash of missed breedings. At Paul's suggestion, Bill has tried to correct the problem by adding more dietary phosphorus to the mineral supplement, but this solution takes time to prove itself. Paul's check showed five out of five pregnant, but Brian's check has the hard cases, like Rave, bred for the first time since she aborted in March, and Solivier, bred for the third time this spring – her last chance before being shipped. Brian finds a jelly bean in Rave's uterus and waits, with his brown, dripping left arm held away from his body, while Jean writes down the good news in a spiral notebook that advertises the Howie Meeker Hockey School on the cover.

"That's a gift," she says with a grin, but her smile fades as they move to Solivier. Two years ago on Thanksgiving, when Solivier was a 2-year-old heifer still on pasture, she delivered her first calf, or rather calves – twin bulls, both dead. In the excitement – Bill and Eileen had a houseful of company – it was noted only that she gave birth on the day Stidler was due, so she was mistaken for Stidler, who later delivered a heifer, Alive, and was assumed to be Solivier. It was a mistake that would occur only with the relatively unfamiliar first-calf heifers. "That's what happens when you're too busy," says Jean. "We only looked at the calendar, you see. They were both kind of black and white, and when you don't see them all summer, it's easy to get them mixed up. Normally, we would have been suspicious if some cow had twins on the wrong date, but there are twins in both cow families." The mistake was discovered months later by the milk tester, who makes a positive identification of each cow by the numbered tag in its ear, rather than its markings or due dates, and the cows were renamed.

"Solivier's bull calves had been dead for a while," Jean remembers. "The vet had to remove some of the pieces – it was a real mess – and then she got an infection. But it cleared up, and now she's milking well." But she was hard to rebreed after the infection; now she is experiencing the problem again and may be on her way out. Brian searches out her uterus, his face vacant as if he were groping for a dime in a pocketful of change, then glances over at Jean. She is leaning against a stanchion, pen poised above her notebook with exaggerated nonchalance that ill conceals her tension. "I don't know how to tell you this, Jean, but . . ."

"Oh, no." Her arms fall to her sides without writing in the book.

". . . she's pregnant."

"What did you say? Oh, don't do that to me." Her grin returns, and she scribbles in the notebook. "I guess that new mineral of Paul's is working."

"Yes, he's really up on all that nutritional stuff. He keeps me on my toes. You know, he always carries some balloons in his pockets to give to the kids. I went to this one place where Paul had been the last few times, and their little girl came out to watch. When I was done, she was looking at me, and the farmer said, "She's waiting for you." I didn't know what he meant, so I asked her if she wanted me to lift her down – she was sitting up on a rail – but she shook her head, no. So I washed my boots and asked her if she wanted me to wash hers too, but she just shook her head. I didn't know what was going on, but finally, the farmer told me that Paul always gives her something.

"Well, I ran out to the car in a terrible sweat and looked through the glove compartment and finally found a package of gum. I gave her a piece, and she ran off to the house as happy as can be. You know, I've been going to that farm for eight years, but her mother said that when I drove up the driveway, she said, 'Is it Doctor Paul? Is it Doctor Paul?' He just started in January." He shakes his head and peels off his glove, neatly turning it inside out and dropping it by his medical case.

"How's Bert getting along?" Jean asks as he gathers his equipment. "Do you see him at all anymore?"

"Yes. In fact, I saw him just yesterday, and he's fine. He and Marion are going out west in a couple of weeks."

"Is he getting all that stuff done for Marion? I hear she's got a list of all the things he didn't do over the last 37 years."

"Oh, yeah, she's got him on the go. Except she had him out weeding the garden, and he weeded out most of the flowers too. I was talking to her, and she came out of the house, and there was the garden, all this bare dirt and a couple of wilted flowers that looked like they'd had their roots trimmed back pretty good. She just kind of closed her eyes and said, 'Ohh, that man.' I think his retirement is harder on her than it is on him."

———————

Bill is a traditional farmer, raised and educated in the mainstream of conventional agricultural practices. That is not to say he is incapable of innovation or independent thought – certainly his ideas on what constitutes a seedbed are radically different from what he was taught in agricultural college. But when he strikes out on his own, he does so out of his sense of practicality rather than from a commitment to some theoretical position. In what he calls, with a roll of his eyes, "my spare time," he attacks a backlog of farm papers and agricultural magazines, scouring them for ideas that will make some chore easier or cheaper. He constantly reevaluates his methods in the light of what he learns from the experience of others.

Bill uses commercial fertilizers because he has found them to be the easiest and cheapest way to get a good crop. He produces and ships half a million litres of milk a year and (almost incidentally) 15 or 20 tons of beef on the hoof. Most of that food is extracted from a six-inch layer of dirt that covers his farm – topsoil to plant roots to alfalfa and barley and corn to cow to market, where it sustains human life ("building strong bones and healthy teeth") and eventually disappears into sewers and cemeteries. Those soil minerals, transformed by plants and cows into human nutrition, are irretrievably gone from Bill's farm. He slows the loss by returning his cows' manure to the land and planting green-manure crops, but he needs to import some fertility from off the farm to make up for the daily migration of nutrients to the city. The granules of rock and natural gas he orders from the Co-op are the most efficient way for him to do that.

Weeds are a different matter. Only his annual crops (barley and corn) need protection. Once established, alfalfa and other grasses form a thick, weedproof sod. In the grain crops, some weeds mature early, spreading their seeds before harvesttime, then coming back the next year in a force 100 times stronger than last year, perhaps strong enough to overpower the crop. Others mature late, and their moist green seeds, harvested with the dry grain, cause overheating in the grain bin and spoil the crop. With its underseeding of alfalfa, Bill could not cultivate the weeds in his barley crop even if a tool to do so existed. As for the corn, herbicides are easier and more effective than cultivation and, until recent years, not all that expensive. Currently, the price of farm chemicals has risen along with everything else, except, perhaps, the price of corn, which sells for no more than it did 20 years ago.

Added to this economic pressure is an environmental awareness that is increasing on two fronts. Farmers are responding to public concerns about pesticide residues in food, and they are gaining an appreciation of their own role in the ecological scheme of things. Farmers are, after all, consumers and as much a part of social trends as everybody else – in the 1980s, they are as concerned about fitness, day care and wilderness preservation as any other group. But, also like other people, they resent being told how to run their affairs by inexperienced outsiders. Farmers believe a good deal of the bad publicity about pesticides is unwarranted, and they feel that, like chain saws, agricultural chemicals are safe farm tools when handled and applied properly – tools they must be allowed to use to stay in business. Few of those who object to the use of herbicides, they say, have to watch a crop costing thousands of dollars in a field the size of several city blocks be slowly strangled by weeds that could have been controlled with one application of a liquid that the government of Canada – based on the results of half a million dollars' worth of tests – has declared safe.

Still, Bill applies relatively small amounts of chemicals to his crops. "We've gone back to cultivating corn, so we don't do too much spraying," he says. "But we do some, and I'd like to get away from it. It would save a lot of money, for one thing. I know it can be done, because there are fellows who are doing it. What I should do is take the time to join one of these organic-farming organizations and talk to some of the people with a little experience at it. It seems like a lot of them are European, and they've got generations of experience to draw on. I'd like to know more about it."

Until then, he will continue to protect his investment chemically. Bill uses a preemergent spray on his corn – that is, a herbicide that kills weed seeds before they come out of the ground – so a couple of days after Jim Greenlees finishes planting the corn, Bill hauls out his spray equipment: an old flatbed truck fitted with a 700-gallon water tank and a tractor-mounted sprayer. The truck, a 1953 Mercury that once belonged to Bell Telephone and then to a stock-car-driving friend of Tom Moreland's, cost Bill $500. The sprayer, a 1985 model made in Sweden, cost him $4,500. It consists of a 180-gallon pressurized tank with pump and agitator and two 17½-foot booms fitted with spray nozzles directed at the ground. The booms fold up for travel, overlapping like crossbones under the pale skull of the tank.

It should be remembered that "weed" is a word invented and used by economists, not botanists. A weed is simply an alien, and what is a weed on one farm may be a valuable crop on the next. A plant species may be both a weed and a crop in different fields on the same farm or in the same field during different growing seasons. One of the "weeds" that Bill hopes to eliminate from his cornfields is the alfalfa that grew there as a hay crop the year before. Clearly, since there are fields of alfalfa on either side of his corn, he has to make sure his spray stays where he wants it.

There are several forces at work that may interfere with this goal. The first is dry weather. As the humidity falls, water-based pesticides are more apt to evaporate or be caught in convection currents and, like miniature gliders, ride a thermal out of the field. Bill uses an oil-based herbicide that is less affected by evaporation, and he makes an effort to spray just before a rain, when the air is humid. The next factor, and probably the best known, is wind, and Bill is scrupulously careful not to spray unless the wind is below the recommended 11 kilometres an hour. "It's just crazy to spray when the wind is blowing," he says. "Not only are you spraying half the countryside, you're not getting a good spray pattern on your crop. It's just a waste of money."

But it is not quite that simple. Bill has only about a week to spray the preemergent, and he often cannot wait for perfect conditions. He began spraying the top part of the cornfield on Thursday evening but stopped after half an hour when a breeze sprang up. A brief shower that night ensured the success of what he had sprayed – moisture acts as a catalyst for the herbicide – but Bill is chafing about not having finished the whole field before the rain. There is no foreman to supervise Bill's herbicide application, no bylaw enforcement officer to oversee the wind speed in his field, nothing to stop him from spraying his crops in a tornado if he wants to, except his own sense of responsibility and his belief that it is a waste of time and money.

Now, on a calm but dry Saturday in mid-May, this belief is coming up for reevaluation. With no rain in the forecast, his decision on Thursday to stop spraying has become a trade-off – an improved spray pattern for, perhaps, a reduced kill rate. Philosophically, Bill knows he was right to stop spraying, but he is all too aware that many other farmers are not as conscientious as he. Now, he is caught in a compromise, and it has made him irritable, a state of mind not helped by the fact that he wanted to start spraying in the morning but was delayed by having to run a couple of errands. It is after lunch before he drives the old Mercury to Pearl's – the exhaust, unfettered by a muffler, assaulting the still air – and backs the tractor and sprayer out of a shed into the barnyard.

The tank is still half full, so he starts the agitator and examines the nozzles, which are clogged with sludge and must be disassembled and cleaned. "Ahh," he says in disgust. "Everything takes so frigging long to do." His frustration is not eased by the knowledge that this delay is of his own making – he should have rinsed the nozzles before putting the sprayer in the shed. Physical activity is Bill's remedy for mental indigestion, and farm work never fails to assuage his worries and frustrations. As he begins to clean the nozzles, the haste and tension visibly fall from his shoulders. This is Bill at his happiest, lost in the pleasure of making a machine perform better, and he is soon whistling tunelessly to himself. "I really like to get something done," he says later. "I guess that's an old-fashioned idea, but I think that people who sit in offices and play with numbers all day must be really frustrated." Planning and record-keeping are necessary parts of Bill's role as reluctant manager, but they do not qualify as "getting something done."

As he cleans the nozzles, Bill inevitably spills herbicide on his hands. It looks like watery, off-white paint and has the same this-is-going-to-give-me-a-headache-if-I-have-to-smell-it-all-day fumes. "This stuff isn't too bad," he says, carefully washing his hands from the tank on the back of the truck when he is done. "I'm glad I don't work with a lot of insecticides." Although the herbicide label advises users not to swallow the liquid or inhale the spray mist, it only cautions, "Avoid prolonged contact with skin," a much milder warning than the "Wear long sleeves and rubber gloves" found on most insecticides.

Driving up and down his field at about 4 miles per hour, Bill sprays a 180-gallon tankful on nine acres every hour. At 35-foot intervals, a device on each end of the spray boom deposits a splotch of an environmentally innocuous foam – sort of a cross between shaving foam and bubble bath – that marks the edge of the spray pattern. The foam evaporates in half an hour but remains visible long enough to help Bill avoid overlaps or missed spots. Even with hourly stops to refill the tank, Bill finishes spraying the corn that afternoon. It is May 16, and all that remains of his planting chores for this year is to spray the barley. That has to wait a couple of weeks, until the alfalfa has three leaves and is sturdy enough to survive the treatment.

Including the herbicide for the barley, Bill's expense sheet for planting looks like this:

SEED

144 bags (25 kg or 1.1 bu each) certified barley seed @ $6.95/bag	$1,000.80
7 bags (25 kg or 55 lbs each) alfalfa seed @ $7.85/kg	1,373.75
5 bags (25 kg each) red-clover seed @ $3.08/kg	385.00
11 bags (25 kg each) grass seed @ $3.81/kg	1,047.75
4 bags PAG corn seed @ $84/bag	336.00
8 bags Northrup/King corn seed @ $86/bag, less $4.30 for prepayment	653.60
12 pouches corn seed fungicide treatment @ $1.50/pouch	18.00

FERTILIZER

3,582 kg of 30-50-40	$ 895.12
4,160 kg of 45-30-20	1,081.60
1,100 kg of 19.5-19.5-19.5	258.09
3,814 kg of 20-40-15	1,106.45
500 kg of 8-32-16	149.50
1,364 kg of 46-0-0 (urea)	327.36

HERBICIDE

24 litres MCPA	$ 95.50
60 litres Cobutox	450.00
30 litres Dual	574.50
14 kg Atrazine	78.00

CUSTOM WORK

Jim Greenlees	$ 350.00
TOTAL	$10,181.02

Add to the cash outlay of 10 grand a couple of hundred gallons of diesel fuel, thousands of dollars in machinery depreciation and maintenance – including a new clutch in the big Ford tractor – and a month of unstinting labour by three men, all of it abandoned in the ground like buried treasure, waiting for rain and warm weather to pry open the pirate's chest of emerald growth and golden grain. Bill is surprised how much moisture is in the ground after such a dry spring, but he would like a good rain, both to activate his herbicides and to germinate the seeds. But wishes are not rain clouds, and the rain gauge Bill keeps outside the barn remains empty for the rest of May.

BOOK IV

MILKING COWS

Udders. Fifty of them on the fifty black-and-white Holstein cows lined up in Bill's barn. Udders the size of soccer balls, udders the size of beach balls, udders of infinite variety: white ones, black ones, white ones with black spots and, there on the end, one that is black halfway down, as if it had been dipped in white paint; long ones, wide ones, oval ones, oblong ones; soft ones, hard ones, smooth ones, lumpy ones. All the udders are covered with baby-soft hair. All have four hairless pink or pink-and-black teats – farmers say "teets," never "tits" – that are themselves a commonwealth of individuality. Long, short, thin, thick, cylindrical, carrot-shaped, smooth, wrinkled, pointed, round. Two hundred of them, most pointing to the ground like fingers, some pointing forward, a few pointing outward and one pair pointing inward so much that they cross.

A cow's udder is a magnificent structure, an engineering marvel, a great pyramid of genetic architecture. Pound for pound of body weight, a woman nursing triplets produces proportionately less than half the milk of a high-yielding Holstein cow. To match the cow's output, the woman would need a 60-inch chest. And to meet the standards for structure and shape that farmers demand of their cows' udders, she would have to carry her oversized breasts high and firm, with not enough sag to hold a pencil – an anatomic wonder. And in their own way, that's what the 50 udders in this barn are.

To begin with, an udder is not just a hollow bag that fills with liquid. It is flesh, and aside from such obvious differences of form as size and the number of nipples, the function of the bovine mammary system is similar to that of any other mammal. Actually, the cow's udder consists of four distinct mammaries farmers call quarters – one for each teat. A ligament that suspends the udder from the body's centreline divides the udder into left and right halves, and membranes separate the front and hind quarters. Each quarter drains into its own teat and cannot be milked from any other; the hind quarters are usually larger, holding about 60 percent of the milk. The teats are hollow, and at the very bottom, a tiny sphincter muscle holds back the flow of milk. If this opening is small or the muscle tight, the cow is said to be a hard milker; if it is too loose, the teat will leak and, worse, let bacteria into the udder – a prime cause of mastitis.

The milk-producing parts of the udder are microscopic spheres called alveoli. The inside of each alveolus is lined with a single layer of cells that transforms blood into milk, which collects in the hollow centre, then drains into a ductule. The lining of the alveolus draws

MAMMARY

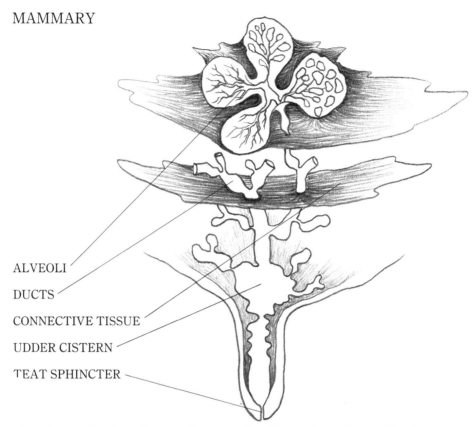

ALVEOLI

DUCTS

CONNECTIVE TISSUE

UDDER CISTERN

TEAT SPHINCTER

vitamins and minerals directly from the blood, transforms blood sugar (glucose) into milk sugar (lactose), strings together its own amino acids to make casein and other milk proteins and squeezes out some droplets of fat of its own manufacture. It takes 500 gallons of blood passing through a cow's udder to make 1 gallon of milk. Then, as a thousand rivulets join to become a river, the alveolar ductules become ducts, then larger ducts leading to a pint-sized cistern above each teat. Imagine the Montreal Forum full of ping-pong balls, each one tied to a fibre, the fibres braided into strings, then cords and finally massive ropes that focus on the face-off circle at centre ice, waiting for a whistle.

That whistle is the milk let-down reflex, for as milk is made, it is held in the ducts and the hollow centres of alveoli. Milk production is an ongoing process, working on a back-pressure system that slows the pace only when the udder is full. Usually, this means production proceeds unimpeded for 10 or 11 hours, then falls sharply – thus a twice-a-day milking schedule is suited to all but the most spectacularly productive cows, which are milked three times a day. If the back pressure is not relieved for 35 hours, milk production stops entirely, and the contents of the udder are slowly turned back into blood.

Teats are sensitive to touch, warmth and wetness and, when exposed to these stimuli — as by the sucking of a calf — they alert the cow's pituitary gland to release the hormone oxytocin. This causes muscles wrapped around the alveoli to contract. Milk is literally squeezed out of the upper part of the udder, and it collects above each teat, waiting to be drawn out. This effect, referred to as the cow letting down her milk, occurs about a minute after the stimulation and lasts for five or six minutes. Cows that are nervous or uncomfortable also release adrenaline, which counters the oxytocin, and they are said to hold back their milk — although, in truth, the response is involuntary. Farmers who fail to make milking a pleasant, relaxing experience for their cows do not stay in business for long.

When a calf braces its feet and reaches out its head for a drink of mother's milk, it wraps its tongue around a teat and sucks with surprising force. The manipulation and moist warmth initiate the letdown reflex, and the suction draws a stream of milk from the teat. When the calf swallows, the suction is momentarily released, an on-off cycle repeated 50 or 60 times a minute.

Hand milking works by pushing milk out of the teat rather than pulling it out. The uninitiated often try to milk a cow by squeezing the teats like elongated tennis balls, but this simply pushes the milk along the path of least resistance — back up into the udder. To force milk into the pail, you have to close off the escape route by first squeezing thumb and forefinger together at the top of the teat. The other fingers are then tightened in descending order, resulting in a forceful stream of frothy white liquid — about an ounce per squeeze, depending on the size of the teat. A good hand milker, working both hands in a practised 2/4 rhythm, can fill a pail almost half as fast as can a milking machine.

Most of the early mechanical milkers, dating back to the 1870s when they were called lactators, imitated hand milking. The most successful used a hand crank to turn four pairs of rollers, each pair repeatedly caressing a teat from top to bottom. The first vacuum-powered milkers were cruel and ineffective devices using a constant suction that drew blood as well as milk to the bottom of the udder, but in 1895, a pulsator was introduced that more closely imitated the on-off action of a sucking calf. This design has been refined over the years but not substantially changed.

Bill's milking system consists of a vacuum pump, which generates about two-thirds as much suction as does a calf, two loops of pipe that circle the barn (a metal one for the vacuum, a glass one for the milk) and five portable milking units.

MILKING UNIT

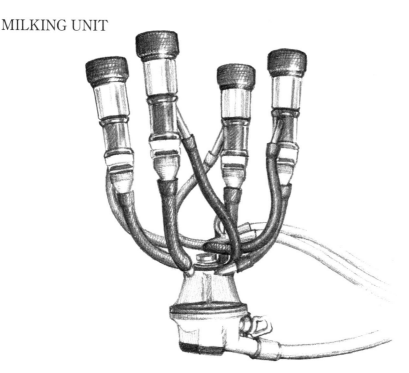

This equipment has replaced the old system in which the milking units were attached to an airtight stainless steel pail that hung from the cow's hips on a leather strap. After each cow was milked, the pail was carried to the milk house, where it was emptied into the cooling tank. With the pipeline, this time-consuming and knee-wearing work is avoided entirely – Bill, Tom, Jean and Eileen can work their way up the line of cows without lifting anything heavier than the plastic-and-rubber milking unit.

At each cow, the procedure is the same: Wash the teats and the lower part of the udder with warm water (to initiate the let-down reflex), dry it (to prevent chapping), draw a stream or two of milk from each teat into a strip cup (to make sure each teat is operational, to check that the milk is not clotted, bloody or otherwise showing signs of infection and to give the oxytocin time to squeeze milk out of the alveoli), plug the vacuum line and the milk line into the twin pipelines above the cow's head, and slip the four teat cups into place. These are held on the teats with a suction ring at the top, and the milking unit is suspended below the udder by the power of its own vacuum.

VACUUM MILKER

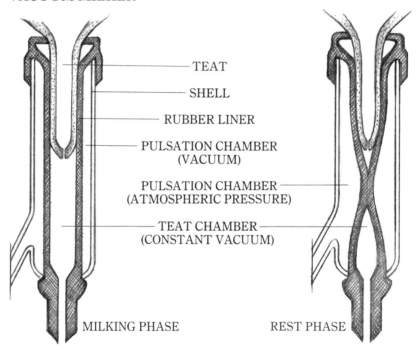

TEAT

SHELL

RUBBER LINER

PULSATION CHAMBER (VACUUM)

PULSATION CHAMBER (ATMOSPHERIC PRESSURE)

TEAT CHAMBER (CONSTANT VACUUM)

MILKING PHASE

REST PHASE

Each teat is now held in a two-part cylinder: an inner flexible rubber one with constant vacuum pressure, and a hard plastic outer one in which the pulsator alternates between a vacuum and a nonvacuum. When pressure in the outer ring is negative, milk is drawn from the teat through the inner cylinder and thus to the pipeline; when the outer chamber fills with air, the rubber tube collapses, stopping the flow of milk and massaging the teat. Like a calf, the machine draws milk 60 times a minute, and to match the construction of the udder, 60 percent of the vacuum pressure is directed at the hind teats. In this way, all the quarters are milked out at roughly the same time.

At least that's the theory. In practice, every cow is an individual, and the Morelands know what to expect from each quarter of every cow. Scotty's left hind quarter milks out slowly, for instance, so Bill sits down beside her as the machine works, massaging that quarter to speed up the flow of milk. As the other quarters empty, he kinks each vacuum line and slips it off, until finally, only the one remains. Leaving a machine on an empty udder is painful for the cow and damaging to the udder, so Bill tries to slip the milker off just as the last stream is drawn out of each quarter. Finally, each teat is dipped into an iodine-based concoction (called, appropriately, teat dip) that coats the teat and helps to seal the hole in the bottom against bacteria.

As practised by the Morelands, milking is a smooth flow of unhurried activity. Strip cups are passed back and forth, udders are washed at just the right time, and the teat dip is presented when needed. Except for the occasional "Is Lily ready?" or "Where's the teat dip?" little talk about the process is necessary, and what there is centres on changes in the routine.

"Squida's right hind quarter is milking out a bit slow."

"Stattice is still not finishing her grain."

"Is Scotty on our cull list? I'm getting tired of doing this."

———

The relationship between humans and cattle goes back far beyond the unrecorded day that a village boy first reached between a cow's hind legs to squeeze out a stream of milk – and was no doubt soundly kicked for his impudence. There are 30,000-year-old cave drawings portraying hunted animals that are unmistakably bovine. Not that they would be confused with a modern Holstein, Hereford, Charolais or Brahma. The proud beast in the cave drawings is an aurochs (one aurochs, two aurochs), the now extinct progenitor of all that we call cattle. It was a splendid creature, standing more than six feet tall at the shoulder and fitted with gracefully curving horns that swept forward to deadly points three feet apart. The aurochs once dominated the Eurasian landmass but did not prosper when civilization invaded its habitat of woodland spotted by meadows. The last known aurochs, a lonely old cow kept walled in a forest preserve in what is now Poland, died in 1627 of old age – and, for all we know, a broken heart.

The history of the aurochs' domestication and integration into agriculture is uncertain, but it is probably not part of the story of agriculture that many of us learned in public school. In this version, a nomadic band of hunter-gatherers tires of running down aurochs or chasing them over a cliff and builds a fence around them or, perhaps, kidnaps a few calves and raises them in captivity. It seems unlikely, though, that a wandering tribe of hunters would be culturally suited to such a stable life, and they certainly wouldn't have the technology (fences, bridles) or knowledge (pasture management, feed gathering) to become stock farmers. It would appear far more likely that animal domestication began with a society of peasant landowners – people used to living in a community, to gathering quantities of plant food, to storing up produce for periods of dry or cold weather.

It even seems unlikely that the aurochs was the first animal to be domesticated. This honour probably belongs to the dog or the pig, whose ancestors were scavengers that might reasonably have been expected to hang around the outskirts of such communities. With overlapping boundaries and a commonality of diet, animal husbandry was more inevitable than insightful. Even in modern primitive societies, there are records of village women suckling baby pigs.

But it is a huge jump from feeding a piglet human milk to feeding a child aurochs' milk. Why choose this huge, dangerous beast to tame? Why risk life and limb to domesticate any animal that isn't already hanging around the village anyway? One theory currently popular is that when the coexistence of people, pigs and dogs became a fact, the next group of animals was kept around for religious reasons, and the aurochs was chosen because its swooping horns were thought to symbolize the curve of the new moon. In other words, aurochs became cows to provide priests with a convenient source of throats to slit. As religious thinking became more advanced, the sacrificial beasts were hitched to their own altars and paraded through the streets; thus were draft animals created. Castration, too, was probably religious in its inception, and the accompanying behavioural changes an unexpected benefit. Meat and milk were the last discovered uses of domestic cattle, according to this theory, and it is given credence by contemporary art, the oldest of which shows only priests yoking oxen and milking cows.

Once tamed and turned to food production, the aurochs was trimmed down to size – about two-thirds of its size in the wild – and its horn span greatly reduced, and that was about the extent of cattle breeding for the next 7,000 or 8,000 years. Cows bred indiscriminately, and although pronounced regional variations developed, they were unplanned and unsought. It was not until the pioneering work of British cattle breeder Robert Bakewell in the late 1700s that the notion of selecting cattle to breed for a desired trait gained any credence. Disciples of Bakewell selected a few generations of Durhams for meat and milk production and renamed the breed the Shorthorn, for which they established the world's first cattle registration book in 1822.

In Canada at that time, there were two breeds of cattle. The Canadien, descended from French cows brought over by colonizers dating back to Champlain, was popular in Lower Canada. Most of these animals had been unceremoniously pushed off ships and left to swim to their new homes in rough-hewn barns on the shore of the lower St. Lawrence River. The other breed, ubiquitous in Upper Canada and New England, was an undistinguished and unnamed mongrel ranging in colour from yellow to brown, black or red. Both breeds, if they can be called such, were stocky, unproductive and notable only for their ability to survive long winters on poor rations. It was said that when they staggered out of their drafty barns in the spring, they were in such poor condition that, unless the sun was shining very brightly, it took two of them to cast a shadow.

Nevertheless, old-world advances in cattle breeding were soon felt in the colonies. The Americans were quicker to see the advantages of the new breeds, and as much Canadian breeding stock came from the United States as was shipped directly from Europe. By 1850, Devons and Shorthorns were established in Upper Canada, while Ayrshires, loaded on ships in Scotland to provide milk for transatlantic passengers and then abandoned in Montreal, had gained a foothold in Lower Canada, especially in the Eastern Townships.

Until the middle of the 19th century, there was no dairy industry in the Canadas; rather, cows were kept for the milk, butter and cheese they supplied to the farm kitchen, and the excess, though used to pay off a credit at the general store, was still considered more an aspect of self-sufficiency than a source of income. Wheat was what farmers in the Canadas concentrated on, and for many years, it was an easier and more profitable crop than beef or milk. The 1851 census of Canada West reported cheese production of 2 million pounds and butter production of 16 million pounds – figures that say as much about the preference for buttermilk over whey for feeding hogs as the relative consumption of butter and cheese.

Later, though, markets opened up in Canada West, in the United States – particularly just before and during the Civil War – and in England. Besides, wheat yields were faltering as the natural fertility of the soil began to wane. The result was a growing interest in dairying as an enterprise that would stand on its own rather than as a sideline. When a group of farmers in Herkimer County, New York, established the first cheese factory, the last piece fell into place. Previously, cheese production had been a back-of-the-stove kitchen operation, and the results were predictably inconsistent. The idea of leaving the cheesemaking to a full-time professional – either an independent proprietor who bought the milk and sold the cheese or an employee hired by a consortium of farmers who paid his wages from their profits – made for the consistency that gave rise to a new agricultural industry.

In 1864, the first two cheese factories in British North America were established near Norwich, Canada West. There is some dispute concerning which of two men deserves to be called the father of Canadian cheesemaking, a Canadian named Smith or an expatriate Herkimer County native called Farrington. It seems that Farrington began construction of the first brand-new cheese factory in Canada, but Smith, although he started later, produced Canada's first commercial cheese in a converted barn. With his greater knowledge of the process, though, Farrington went on to become Canada's leading cheesemaker and is now generally recognized as the pioneer of cheese factories in Canada. At the time of Confederation in 1867, there were 235 cheese factories in Ontario; by 1880, there were 550, and the industry had spread to other provinces as well. Most of them made a hard cheese, an imitation of that from the village of Cheddar in southern England.

By that time, too, the dairy breeds from the English Channel islands of Jersey and Guernsey were established in Canada, as were the Hereford and Angus beef breeds. All were good British stock, but in 1881, the inevitable happened: the Holstein-Friesian arrived. This tall, skinny, gangly, spotted beast – most other cows in Canada at that time were solid-coloured – was a native of Holland and arrived here from the United States, where it had been bred for almost 30 years. Traditionally, Holstein-Friesians are said to be a cross between white cattle from Friesland, a province of the Netherlands, and black cattle from Schleswig-Holstein, then a province of Prussia. It is ironic that the cows are almost universally known by the first, Germanic half of their original name when it was Dutch farmers who nurtured, developed and exported what has become the world's most popular breed of cattle.

The odd-looking black-and-white cow was praised by some Canadian farmers for its prodigious milk production and scorned by others for the milk's low butterfat content. Holstein milk was said to be "thin," "blue" and "watery." It was claimed by detractors that they could read the date on a coin dropped into a pail of Holstein milk and that the milk would rust their pails. Hyperbole aside, Holstein milk was not as rich as that from other breeds, but some of the complaints may have been voiced by those who realized they could no longer bulk up their product by adding water, a not uncommon practice in the days before the invention of milk-testing equipment.

In typical Canadian fashion, two provinces are squabbling for the honour of having imported the first Dutch cow, albeit from a line that had been bred in the United States for a quarter of a century. Manitoba and Ontario both claim to have imported Holsteins in 1881; however, it was Michael Cook of Aultsville, Ontario, who went on to become founding president of the Dominion Holstein Breeders' Association, and he was, if not the first, certainly the first important Canadian breeder. In the intervening century, the Holstein has risen to an unassailable position of eminence in Canada, representing 95 percent of all dairy cows. With a worldwide reputation for longevity and lifetime milk production, Canadian Holsteins are exported to 75 countries, and in many developing countries, an increase in milk production brought about by crossing local animals with Holsteins is the most common evidence of Canadian aid.

———

Around the middle of May, as he does every month, Bill receives a cheque for the milk he has produced, and as he also does every month, he takes it out to the milk house. With Tom and Jean looking over his shoulder, he unfolds it on the stainless steel of the bulk tank and gives everyone a chance to examine it.

The figures down the right side of the statement are the quantities of milk the truck picked up every second day, 15 shipments in all. They represent 30 days of milk production: a total of 41,228 litres. The area at the top of the statement marked QUOTA sets the limits of Bill's milk production under the Ontario Milk Marketing Board (OMMB) and is divided into GROUP 1 and MSQ (market share quota). These used to be called fluid milk and industrial milk: the former went to dairies, where it was separated, homogenized, pasteurized and sold as milk; the latter was processed into butter and cheese. Farmers who lived close to a dairy were able to sell fluid milk, and they were paid more for it than were farmers who lived close to a cheese factory and sold industrial milk. In Russell's day, fluid and

MILK CHEQUE

D194931

Licence No.
546321

Date	Amount

Pay to the order of

WILLIAM R J MORELAND
RUSTOWIL FARM
R R 1 JOYCEVILLE ONT
KOH 1Y0

DIRECT DEPOSIT - VOID/VOID
000426962 0359-0280676
Pay ********Dollars—and   ** Cents
The Ontario Milk Marketing Board

Canadian Imperial Bank of Commerce
6711 Mississauga Road (Markborough Place)
Mississauga, Ontario L5N 2W3

Per

⑊03922⑊010⑊ 01⑊008⑊⑊

STATEMENT FOR	APRIL	1987	POOL	PLANT	TRANSPORTER	LICENCE	DAILY MILK SHIPMENTS IN LITRES
			01	064702	33677	546321	

GROUP I 30 DAYS @ 815 DAILY IS 24,450

MSQ THIS DAIRY YEAR 205,798   MSQ NEXT DAIRY YEAR 205,798

TEST FROM	TO	BUTTERFAT	PROTEIN	KG/HL LACTOSE	SOLIDS NOT FAT		BUTTERFAT	PROTEIN	LACTOSE	SOLIDS NOT FAT
01	07	3.77	3.41	5.36	9.44	LAST MONTH'S AVERAGE	3.81	3.35	5.28	9.42
08	14	3.79	3.39	5.50	9.59	THIS MONTH'S AVERAGE	3.82	3.39	5.41	9.45
15	23	3.84	3.36	5.31	9.35					
24	30	3.89	3.38	5.46	9.43	BACTERIAL GRADE	1	OTHER TESTS S.C.C. 91	INHIBITORS NO	

USAGE	BASE PRICE AT 3.6 TEST	PERCENTAGE	LITRES	PRICE AT YOUR TEST	AMOUNT
PRODUCTION			41,228		
CLASSES 1 & 2	52.510	71.98	17,599	53.920	9,489.38
EXCLUSION	41.702	7.8	1,373	43.112	591.93
MSQ SHIPMENTS	41.702		22,256	43.112	9,595.01
				TOTAL VALUE OF MILK	19,676.32

KILOGRAMS OF BUTTERFAT FROM MSQ SHIPMENTS   850

	PERCENTAGE	LITRES			
MSQ SHIPMENTS: THIS MONTH	10.8	22,256			
TO PREVIOUS MONTH	54.8	112,755			
TO END THIS MONTH	65.6	135,011			
AVAILABLE MSQ % TO APR 30	85.0	174,928	CANADIAN DAIRY COMMISSION EXPORT LEVIES AND/OR REFUNDS		
OVER MSQ: TO END THIS MONTH			RATE	AMOUNT	
TO PREVIOUS MONTH					
THIS MONTH					
WITHIN MSQ THIS MONTH		22,256	4.65	1,034.90-	

TRANSPORTATION				ODHIC LEVY			
BASIC WITHIN POOL		EXTRA OUT OF POOL		DHI RATE	AMOUNT	TOTAL	
RATE	AMOUNT	RATE	AMOUNT				
2.0500	845.17			.03	12.37	857.54-	

OMMB LICENCE FEE				ASSIGNMENT SERVICE FEE	TOTAL	
ADMINISTRATION		PROMOTION				
RATE	AMOUNT	RATE	AMOUNT			
.2200	90.70	.6700	276.23	.15	367.08-	

OMMB REF.	DATE MO. DAY YR.	DESCRIPTION		AMOUNT
10006		FARM CREDIT CORPORATION	1	327.00-

41,228

PLEASE REPORT ANY ERRORS OR OMISSIONS PROMPTLY

Line	Litres
1	
2	2,848
3	
4	2,848
5	
6	2,783
7	
8	2,786
9	
10	2,717
11	
12	2,731
13	
14	2,786
15	
16	2,758
17	
18	2,745
19	
20	2,758
21	
22	2,731
23	
24	2,693
25	
26	2,606
27	
28	2,707
29	
30	2,731
31	

RETAIN FOR INCOME TAX PURPOSES   AMOUNT DUE PRODUCER   17,089.80

114

industrial milk had different standards of cleanliness; now all milk is treated the same, and what farmers receive for it depends not on its actual end use but on the kind of quota they own.

Bill owns 815 litres of Group 1 quota; that is, he is both allowed and required to ship 815 litres of milk every day, 24,450 litres in a 30-day month. If he fails to meet his quota at the end of the year, his next year's quota is set at what he actually shipped this year, and the unused portion of his quota is sold to someone who will fill it. Any milk he ships in excess of his Group 1 quota is applied to his MSQ. Bill's MSQ amounts to 205,798 litres a year, and he is required to produce 80 percent of that amount or else his quota is reduced proportionately. If, for example, he produces only 76 percent of his MSQ, his next year's MSQ is reduced by 4 percent. If he exceeds his MSQ, he is charged the full cost of exporting the butter and skim milk powder his milk would produce – a stiff penalty amounting to about 37¢ a litre.

Bill acquired most of his quota from Russell, who had received most of it at no cost because he was already dairying when the OMMB was established in 1965. In the intervening years, they both bought additional quota to meet their increases in production. For a long time, quota traded at a few cents a litre, but recently, its value has skyrocketed. Group 1 quota currently sells for a whopping $270 a litre, MSQ for about 70¢. Bill's quota – which represents nothing more than the right to sell a certain quantity of milk – is currently worth about $365,000. A handy retirement package should he decide to get out of farming but a terrible, crushing financial burden for a new farmer wanting to take over his operation.

The fact that the quota system would add a quarter to a half a million dollars to the value of a dairy farm was not anticipated by the people who designed it 22 years ago, and many farmers think that allowing quota to have a value is a mistake. Bill is, reluctantly, among them. "Yeah," he sighs. "I mean, it just makes it too hard for young people to get into farming. The average age of dairy farmers in Ontario is up around 50, and it shouldn't be that high. We've got to think about the future."

The price of quota is one of the few objections voiced about the system by farmers, who are almost universally in favour of supply management as a marketing tool. At its best, the system, which controls domestic and imported supplies, allows enough production to keep the price at a level that will give a medium-small farmer enough profit to live on. Critics, mostly consumers, complain that they could buy milk more cheaply if its supply were not controlled, and they are probably right – in the short term. Before the quota system was established, farmers went through a series of boom-bust cycles as production and prices fought like gladiators in the arena of market forces. They were never able to achieve a mutually acceptable standoff.

"What supply management allows me to do," says Bill, "is some financial planning." It is difficult to contemplate the addition of more cows and machinery or the purchase and improvement of land without any control over the future price of one's finished product. Of course, it might be argued that that is the situation faced by any widget manufacturer, but there are some substantial differences. By increasing (or decreasing) the supply of raw materials and hiring (or firing) workers, the widget manufacturer can raise (or lower) production to meet the changing market realities on a monthly or sometimes weekly or even daily basis. In dairy farming, the raw materials are crops, which take up to 18 months to bring on line, and the workers are cows, which take two years or more to start producing. Without some assurance of a stable price, the decision to expand production might just as well be made by a coin toss.

Other consumers point to the world price of milk, which is much lower than the price Canadians pay, as proof of the overpricing brought about by marketing boards. With her steamroller logic, Brigid Pyke responds, "Sure the world price of milk is lower. And the world price of labour is about a dollar an hour, but nobody expects Canadian factory workers to accept that. It remains one of the enduring mysteries of our time why Canadians will flock to their windows to light a candle in support of Poland's Solidarity and then expect the Canadian farmer to lie flat on his back and take whatever is offered for his produce." The argument ought to be settled by the fact that price increases for supply-managed foods have consistently stayed below the Consumer Price Index.

But of course, the Morelands and their helpers know the figures in the QUOTA section and the arguments they provoke only too well. Their eyes immediately drop to the next section, TESTS. There, on a week-by-week basis, is the percentage of butterfat in their milk, plus the protein, lactose, and solids not fat (SNF, representing the total of the protein and lactose plus a few minerals – everything that is not fat or water). Milk that is high in butterfat has always been rewarded, and the Morelands receive a premium when their milk's fat content exceeds 3.6 percent. "That's more like it," says Jean, who notices that despite a dip at the first of the month, they have gained a tenth of a percentage point. Bill's herd average over 12 months is 3.6, but he and Jean have set 4 percent as their long-term goal.

At a time when butterfat testing was the only readily performed test for milk solids and when butter consumption was high, a premium for butterfat made a lot of sense. Now, however, it does not reflect the reality of the marketplace. Two-thirds of all milk sold in Canada is 2 percent; the excess butterfat must be made into butter. Currently, Canada's butter production – 100,000 tonnes a year – is pretty well balanced to annual consumption – a little less than 10 pounds per capita. Although we sold 4,000 tonnes of butter on the world market in 1983 and 3,300 tonnes in 1987, the mountains of butter thought by many consumers to reside in some oversized freezer somewhere simply do not exist. True, there are stocks of skim milk powder, and the Canadian Dairy Commission must unload 60,000 tonnes a year, but sales are brisk, especially in the post-Chernobyl era, when purchasers – mostly Third World countries and the agencies that serve them – are leery of European food products.

These days, at any rate, fat is definitely out nutritionally, and SNF – protein, natural sugars and minerals – is in, so the push is on to convert dairy pricing to reward farmers who produce the marketable items. Still, a lot of farmers would take a financial dunking if forced to change horses in midstream, and resistance to the new system is high. The appearance of a figure for SNF on the milk cheque is part of a long-term effort by the OMMB to make farmers start thinking about something besides fat and prepare themselves for the change that will inevitably come. Average SNF content is about 9.1 percent. Bill is well above that, and he is one of the farmers who would earn more money on a bonus for solids than he does for fat.

The next section, MILK, is probably the most important of all, since it calculates Bill's earnings, but he and the others pay it little attention because they have no control over it. Bill produced 41,228 litres of milk, and he has paid for the right to sell 24,450 of those litres at the rate for Group 1 milk – what will appear in stores in bags and cartons of homogenized and 2 percent. But milk sales have been down lately – down to 71.98 percent of the quota allotted for Group 1 production – and Bill is going to receive top dollar only for the amount of milk that will actually sell, not for the amount he has paid for the right to produce. Thus, he can sell 17,599 litres of Group 1 milk, for which he receives not the base price (52.510¢) but the price at his test (53.920¢), which includes his bonus for butterfat content. Total: $9,489.38.

The bottom line of this section says that most of the rest of Bill's production (22,256 litres) is applied to his MSQ. He is paid an adjusted price of 43.112¢ for a total of $9,595.01. The middle line, another $591.93, represents the amount of milk (1,373 litres) that the dairies need in addition to what they use for milk. These are the so-called fresh products: cottage cheese, buttermilk, chocolate milk, restaurant coffee creamers. This amount of milk, set at 7.8 percent of fluid milk use, is purchased at the MSQ price but is not subject to the export levies and refunds applied to MSQ milk. Total for the month: $19,676.32.

MSQ UTILIZATION: Bill's 22,256 litres of MSQ milk represents 10.8 percent of his annual quota, and his accumulated shipments for the dairy year (starting August 1) total 65.6 percent of his quota. Thus, at the end of the dairy year's third quarter, Bill has shipped two-thirds of his allowed production – a bit low. Still, there is no penalty for being a bit low in MSQ, and there are stiff penalties for being a bit high. Bill can now work to raise his production in the last three months of the year, while a good many other farmers scramble to sell cows or buy more quota to keep from going over the limit.

The rest of the statement lists the expenses Bill and his milk have incurred: $1,034.90 to cover the cost of exporting skim milk powder, $845.17 to have his milk trucked to the dairy, $12.37 to the Ontario Dairy Herd Improvement Commission for BCA calculations and other record-keeping services, $90.70 for OMMB expenses (this is truly astonishing: how many other nonprofit groups run a province-wide organization on an administration fee that amounts to ¼ of 1 percent of the money they handle?), $276.23 for ads and commercials promoting milk and milk products and $327.00 against an old debt incurred when building the addition on the barn.

Bill's gross income for April, then, is $17,089.80 – about average. That money, plus an occasional cheque for selling a culled cow or some extra grain, pays for everything: land, wages, machinery, purchased feed, hydro, taxes, vet bills, debt (the farm owes about $68,000) and interest. In 1986, the farm grossed $186,023. After all the bills were paid (including $12,000 to Eileen for the work she did), Bill had $20,458 left over. This represents his salary, and based on an 84-hour work week, it works out to about $4.75 an hour – 50¢ more than minimum wage.

A family income of $32,000 is well above the poverty level, but it is hardly upper-middle class. Still, there are circumstances that make Bill and Eileen's earnings seem more than they are. They pay no mortgage, have no personal debt, survive as a one-car family because the farm truck is always available, and have no commuting or child-care expenses. In addition, they do not smoke or drink, they spend little money on clothes and hardly any on what most people classify as recreation – an occasional dance, lunch after church on Sunday, a rare movie. "Bill was never one to throw money away," says Russell.

In practice, Eileen's wages are spent on groceries and everyday incidentals; Bill's pay the bills – telephone, hydro, heating oil. There is usually enough left over for Bill to buy his limit in retirement savings plans, and last year, he claimed $3,600 in charitable donations, mostly to their local church and the organizations it supports. There were more too – hundred-dollar bills stuck in envelopes and mailed anonymously to people in the community in need of hope and a bit of a boost. Bill and Eileen believe that prayer can accomplish miracles, but they have not forgotten that it takes cash to buy groceries.

All in all, there is seldom more than $500 in the bank account and often a good deal less. "Sometimes we have to phone up the bank and say we need a $2,000 loan till such and such a time," says Eileen. "That's cheaper than using an overdraft. Gracious, they cost an arm and a leg." How does it feel to be capital-rich and cash-poor? "Oh, it sort of annoys me sometimes to think that we work this hard and have no money. It doesn't seem to bother Bill, but I think if we were in debt, it would." At the same time, Eileen realizes that they think and act like people with more money than their bank statements would indicate.

"Well, if we want a holiday, we don't stop to think what it costs. We know the money is there." Last February, they went to Florida for two weeks, travelling on a bus tour. While there, in an odd combination of parsimony and impulse spending, they invested $10,000 in a time-share condominium. "It's nice to know there's a milk cheque coming every month. Two years ago, when we bought some extra milk quota, they took it right out of our milk cheque, and I remember that month we got a $72 milk cheque. That was the only time we ever really felt a squeeze." They are lucky to have no substantial debts. Many farmers have their milk cheques cut in half every month to pay off a heavy debt burden.

"We just let the farm carry us," says Eileen. "I think that's unusual, because most farmers owe too much money to do that. Lots of times, there's nothing left over at the end of the month for Bill to take as a salary, but we're building his estate all the time. We bought Pearl's place in 1981 for $82,500, and now it's paid for. We put every cent into paying that off." Home, job, investment, life savings – the farm is everything to them. And it could turn into a millstone. "Sometimes I think about free trade – what if it came through and the value of our quota went down to nothing? Or if something happened to Bill? I used to not worry about things like that, but now I wonder – who wants to spend three-quarters of a million dollars on a farm these days?"

––––––––––

Every two days, the truck – "Cold Beautiful Milk," say the white and blue letters on its stainless steel tank – backs up to Bill's milk house and drains the bulk tank. As he does at all the farms on his route, the driver takes a sample of the milk that will be tested for fat, SNF, water and, if necessary, bacteria and drug residues. A meter measures the amount of milk, and before he leaves, the driver hangs a receipt on a clip nailed to the milk house wall. For Bill to meet his quota, each receipt should read "2,700 litres." Sometimes it does.

The milk from Bill's farm is delivered to Beatrice Dairy in Kingston, where it is processed and packaged, then shipped to stores and school cafeterias. The dairy business is competitive and cutthroat, so although Beatrice's management gives occasional tours of the plant, cameras are not allowed on the premises. The person who gives the tours is Rick Light, a pleasant young man of medium height and even features who is not amused by the suggestion that he should call himself Rich and thereby sound like an ad for one of his company's products. Rick is friendly and polite, but when he wants to make a point in a conversation, he has a habit of leaning forward in a posture that reveals a hardness of character one might otherwise miss.

As the plant's quality-control manager, he needs that spirit when he tells other employees they are not doing their jobs well enough. "I'm known as 'that aggravating bastard,'" he says, "but it's part of the job – I have to tell the truth. We have excellent quality in this plant. It's consistently in the top few out of hundreds across the province. But it takes a lot out of you to maintain that standard. I'm definitely not the most popular employee here."

Still, he says, he likes the job. "Yeah, there's always something happening. I do some of the work on the machines myself, because I don't like the maintenance guys getting their greasy hands on the sanitary equipment." Rick has never met Bill Moreland or visited his barn, and to him, Bill is just one of the many – he won't say how many – anonymous farmers whose milk comes into the unloading bay in the back of a truck. Each tankful of milk is sampled before it is unloaded, and inspectors look at it, smell it, taste it and check it for bacteria and for antibiotic residues. If there are any irregularities, they turn to the individual samples so that they can identify the source of the problem. After the milk is metered into a storage tank, the trucks are washed and rinsed before they are allowed to leave. "Wash trucks at 140 degrees for no less than 15 minutes," reads a sign at the back of the truck bay. Rick won't say how much milk is processed at the plant, but there is enough storage for 240,000 litres of raw milk.

The working part of the plant is no bigger than a couple of suburban living rooms and resembles a modern sculpture done in stainless steel. "The raw milk comes from the storage silos to the balance bowl through this pipe," Rick says, pointing at a stainless steel line overhead. The balance bowl is nothing more than a stainless steel holding tank the size of a double laundry tub that feeds the other equipment. Milk is pumped from it to the regenerator, a heat exchanger that takes heat from pasteurized milk it is cooling and uses it to warm the raw milk to 157 degrees F before sending it on to the separator, which looks like a small rocket nose cone set on a table.

The separator, bought from a Swedish company for about $130,000, is little different from the first prototype patented by Swedish engineer Gustaf de Laval in 1878, which forced the relatively light fat globules out of the milk by centrifugal force. Little different, that is, except for capacity – this model spins at 8,000 rpm and can process 20,000 litres an hour. Whole raw milk enters through a pipe in the top and exits as skim milk and cream through two pipes in the bottom. The skim line heads directly to two homogenizing machines – "the homos," Rick calls them – but the cream line divides into two. One feeds back into the skim line, adding either 2 percent or 3.25 percent cream, depending on the milk product desired, and the other directs excess cream – Bill's milk, for example, is currently 3.8 percent – into another storage silo. This plant, which makes no cream products, ships 80,000 pounds of excess cream every week to another plant that produces table cream, whipping cream and the rest.

Between the separator and the homogenizers, the line is interrupted by a petcock, from which a test sample is drawn every 10 minutes to verify the butterfat content, and by the vitamin feeder, which drizzles additives into the milk: vitamins A and D in 2 percent, vitamin D in homo. "A is a fat-soluble vitamin," Rick explains, "so we need to replace what we take out in the cream. Vitamin D is the only thing we ever add to whole milk. Some people think that because we have a long shelf life, we must add something, but it's not true." The addition of vitamin D to milk has practically eliminated rickets, a disease once endemic among inner-city children.

The homos, with capacities of 12,000 and 6,000 litres per hour, are the bottleneck of the whole process: their combined output equals the plant's 18,000-litres-an-hour capacity. The largest of the homos is a stainless steel box the size of a Volkswagen beetle, but its working parts – three shiny pistons, each about a foot long – would fit in most bathroom sinks. A huge crankshaft – "about this big," says Rick, spreading his arms wide – drives the pistons, generating 2,000 pounds per square inch of pressure and a lot of noise. "The pistons draw in milk on the back stroke, then force it through a very small space on the forward stroke – hammer it through, really," says Rick. "That shears the fat globules into very small pieces that stay in suspension in the milk. They don't collect at the top of the container." Butterfat globules, squeezed out of the cells that line the udder's alveoli, are normally six to eight microns in diameter; the homogenizer reduces them to about one or two microns. "Basically," Rick says, lowering his voice, "the milk just has the shit knocked out of it."

From homo to pasteurizer: "Government regulations only require us to hold the milk at 161 degrees for 16 seconds, but we get it up to 175 for 30 seconds. We find the higher temperature gives us a little better shelf life because we have a better kill on the bacteria. The minimum might not ensure a total kill. Well, you never get a total kill, but 99.999 percent." After being pasteurized, the milk, now ready for sale, is cooled to 45 degrees in the regenerator, then "dialled" into one of seven finished-product tanks: a 50,000-litre silo for 2 percent, a 55,000-litre one for homo, and smaller tanks used at various times for skim, chocolate, ice cream and milk shake mixes, buttermilk and egg nog (in season).

All that remains before putting the milk (cooled to 34 degrees in the silos) on store shelves is to package it in bags or cartons. The carton machines, in another part of the plant, are as fast and as fascinating to watch as bottlers and other such machines, but the bagger is a triumph of mechanical engineering, transforming a roll of plastic into bags of milk at the rate of 90 a minute. The forerunner of this machine used to form bags from the roll of plastic film, then fill them one at a time as they passed under a tap. The new machine never shuts off the flow of milk. The plastic is pulled off a roll on the back of the machine – imagine a 50-pound roll of Saran Wrap – and sterilized with ultraviolet light as it comes over the top. It is then formed and sealed into a tube that a spout fills with milk. Below the spout, the tube is cut and sealed at 1⅓-litre intervals – the seal at the top of one bag forms the bottom of the next bag.

There are four such machines at this plant, each forming, filling and sealing a bag of milk every two-thirds of a second, then dropping the bags onto a conveyor belt leading to one of two machines that automatically drop three of them into a larger bag. This is closed with a plastic tab and dropped into a plastic milk case of the kind used by university students to hold their record collections. Two machines put four 4-litre bags in each case and stack the cases six high for storage in the cold room – five stacks a minute, and all done in a space no larger than many living rooms.

From the cows' udders to Bill's bulk tank to the milk truck to the storage silo and through the separator, homogenizer and pasteurizer to the bagger and the store shelf, the milk has never seen daylight or been in an open container. The first time it is exposed to air is when the bag is cut open in someone's kitchen. "The biggest problem we have is that milk is such a great medium to support growth," Rick says. "Anything will grow in it, and that's why it's so critical to keep everything clean." To monitor the success of this rigorous fastidiousness, he keeps a cooler full of samples in his laboratory, a cramped room overlooking the separator, the homos and the pasteurizer. Compared with the aggressive gleam of the stainless steel outside the room, the ordinary cleanliness of the lab looks almost dingy.

Milk in cartons is given a "best before" date 15 days after the day it was packaged; milk in bags, 18 days. The cooler holds samples from each day's production for the last two weeks, one shelf per day. As Rick explains the dating system, he reaches into the cooler and pulls out a 250-millilitre carton of homo. "See, the best-before date on this is" – he realizes the carton is open – "oops, we use that one for our coffee. Well, anyway, we hold it for a couple of weeks at 45 degrees. Milk should be held at less than 40 degrees," he says. "That's the industry standard. We try to abuse it at 45 degrees, and then we plate it" – run a standard platelet count – "to see if it meets the code. Most of the time it does. We're very good here."

"Hey," says an assistant, "we're the best."

"Yeah, we are. At least, we were the best in Ontario last year and the year before."

———

Milk processing has not always been a world of soap and stainless steel. When Russell bought the farm in 1930, milk was commonly squeezed by hand into an open pail, then strained to remove the cow hairs, dead flies and whatever else may have dropped into it. Held overnight in 30-gallon cans set in cold water, the milk was delivered to a cheese factory the next morning. In those days, dairies were rare, but it was said there was a cheese factory on every corner – 30 in Russell's township. Russell and Ruth were especially lucky to have one directly across the road from them. In the mid-1950s, when the factory was the only one of those 30 still operating, it was run by Lawrence Walker, but when Russell began farming, Lawrence's father was the cheesemaker. "I was born right in this house in 1918," says Lawrence of the red Insulbrick-covered house beside the factory site. "That was a rough year for Dad – I was born in September, and my mother died of the flu in October. There he was, left with six little kids."

In 1925, the factory burned to the ground – "right in the middle of the summer, when the milk was at its highest." In those days, farmers milked only during the warm weather, and milk flow peaked in mid-summer. "They had it rebuilt in six weeks, a 50-foot-square building with a steel roof. The contractor made the blocks right here by hand." This was the building Russell remembers, with horse-drawn wagons backed up 100 yards down the road, each farmer waiting his turn to pull up the circular drive and unload his cans of milk on the factory's receiving dock. The morning wait was as much a social ritual as a business necessity, and Jean remembers that she learned to identify Ed Johnston's booming laugh from their house before she recognized his face.

"Yessir," Ed says, "there was a lot more milk produced in the country then than there is now." Actually, Ed is wrong – milk production in Canada has remained virtually the same for 50 years. What he means is that there were a lot more dairy farmers then; currently in Canada, one-third of the farmers (on 20,000 dairy farms) produce the same amount of milk (about seven billion litres a year).

In its heyday, the Woodburn Road Cheese Factory handled milk from 60 farmers – as much as 30,000 pounds of it every day. After the milk was weighed and tested for butterfat content, the cheese-maker placed it in a vat to which he added rennet and a lactic-acid culture. He then held the mixture at 86 degrees until it turned into a solid mass, called the curd. "You cut the curd into tiny cubes, heated it to about 103 degrees and drained off the whey," says Lawrence. "Then you spent the rest of the day trying to get the curds back into a solid again." With the bulk of the whey gone, the cheesemaker spent about three hours turning and piling up the cheese, using wooden paddles in the early years, then mechanical agitators. Finally, he cut the curd into strips, salted it and pressed it in hoops overnight before packing the cheeses in boxes for ageing. When things went well, the cheesemaker's day was over at 5 o'clock, but sometimes, if the curd was reluctant to solidify, the job dragged on until 8.

It took 10 pounds of milk to make 1 pound of Cheddar, so at one point, the factory produced 3,000 pounds of cheese a day, packaged as thirty 100-pound cheeses. Before being set in the storeroom to age, the cheeses were cured for eight days and turned top for bottom every day. The process has not changed in several hundred years, except that "now they take the milk in these tank trucks and hold it in stainless steel tanks. And the milk is pasteurized. That's why you don't get the natural Cheddar taste you used to get." Sometimes, though, the taste was a little too natural. "The farmers would bring their milk in in the morning and fill the cans with whey to take home and feed to their calves and pigs. Then the cans would sit out in the sun all day – all covered with flies – until the wife came out in the afternoon with her dishwater to wash them. But the whey was stuck right on by then, and they couldn't get it off. It affected the quality of the milk, all right, made it kind of yeasty."

Lawrence Walker took over the factory from his father in 1943, the same winter that fire destroyed the Morelands' barn. It was the year after Lawrence was married – "I've been married for 45 years now," he says with a twinkle. "That's an awful sentence, y'know, and no time off for good behaviour" – and his wedding pictures show a dark-haired, good-looking young man with a strong jaw. After a lifetime of cheesemaking, the evidence of former strength remains, but his hair is now white, and he moves slowly, joints and hands swollen with arthritis.

The factory was an odd combination of independent business and community project. Lawrence owned the building and equipment, but he worked for the farmers, who owned both the milk and the cheese. "It's like taking your car to a garage," he explains. "The mechanic owns the garage and the tools, but you own the car and he works for you." At a meeting held every spring, the cheesemaker and the patrons met, as Lawrence says, "to set the price of the making. There was me trying to get the price up and them trying to get it down. Some years, the meeting would go on for hours, all this haggling over a couple of fractions of a cent a pound."

The first year Lawrence took over from his father, he got 3¢ a pound; 15 years later, when the factory closed, he was up to 4¢ a pound. For that, he worked seven days a week making the cheese and arranging for its sale through the Cheese Board. Friends on a trip to Great Britain once brought him back a gift of his own cheese that they had bought in a store not far from the village of Cheddar. Proceeds of the sales went to the secretary/treasurer of the farm group, usually the wife of one of the farmers, who paid her husband and the other farmers based on the number of pounds of butterfat they delivered to the factory. She also paid Lawrence for the making, and "I hoped I had enough to pay off my creditors."

During the war, with the price of cheese as low as 10¢ a pound, farmers got less than $1 per hundredweight for their milk; in more prosperous times, the price of cheese was closer to 40¢ a pound, and the farmers received more than $3 per hundredweight. In the early days, the cheeses were shipped out in boxcars kept cool with ice packed in both ends. The railroad cars also brought in coal to power the steam boiler that heated the vats and powered the pumps. The farmers spent a couple of days together each year, unloading the coal from the cars and hauling it up to the factory in their wagons. In winter, when the factory was closed, they hauled blocks of ice to the icehouse.

They were less cooperative about the whey. "Oh, there was always a big row about the whey," Lawrence recalls. "In the spring, when the big flow was on, the calves and pigs were still small and nobody wanted it. We had a big ditch out there"—he gestures behind the house—"we used to dump it in. It's a good thing the environmental people weren't around then. It got pretty ripe in the hot weather, I can tell you. I remember once, we had some visitors—people who came out from the city for the day —and their kids got into it. Oh my, what a mess." He chuckles and scratches the back of his head. "Anyway, in the fall when the calves and pigs were big, everybody wanted the whey, but there wasn't as much. A farmer might bring in four cans of milk in the spring, and when the milk flow slowed down, he would have only two or three cans of milk. But he still brought four cans so he could take home the same amount of whey. Sometimes we pumped water into the whey tank all day so everybody could get some."

As a marketing system and a way of life, the cheese factories served both the public and the farmers well, but they depended on a rural society in which most people owned a cow or bought their milk from a farmer-owned dairy. By the 1950s, those days had pretty well passed, and the independently owned cheese factories were on their way out. "Things really tightened up after the war. I remember Kraft opened a cheese factory on Wolfe Island – they had all stainless steel equipment and lots of help. The government said this is the way it ought to be, and they made it so everybody had to follow them."

Dairies were also growing in size and popularity. "They offered more money for the milk, so they took all the bigger farmers, the ones who could afford the electric can coolers and that other stuff. Because the dairies, you see, had higher standards." In the summer of 1958, Walker was processing only 12,000 pounds of milk a day and trying to run things alone because he couldn't afford to hire a helper. In the fall, he closed the factory for the winter and never reopened it. Three years later, the building, then rented to a welder, burned to the ground. All that remains as a memorial to the past is the paved circular drive, now wrinkled by frost and lined with seams of grass.

Russell was one of the few farmers who stayed with the factory until the end. "Oh, I should have quit sooner – there was lots who coaxed me to do it – but I was the biggest supplier for the last few years. If I had quit, the place would have closed down, and I kind of felt responsible for keeping it going. But boys, shipping whole milk to the city – that was the price!" Russell had already switched to 80-pound milk cans, built the milk house and installed an electric can cooler, so in the spring of 1959, he was ready to ship to Kingston. His first contract was with Kingston General Hospital – the one built on his great-grandfather's grave site. "They would order the milk one day – about 10 cans on average – and I'd take it in the next. They bottled it right there." After four years, the hospital stopped doing its own bottling, and Russell signed on at what was then Cloverdale Dairy. Twenty-five years later, the dairy is owned by Beatrice, and Russell's son is still shipping milk there.

―――――

Toward the end of May, Bill puts his cows out on pasture, divided into the three natural groupings: milking cows, dry cows and bred heifers. The latter two groups are transported three or four at a time in a homemade trailer hitched to the back of a tractor – the heifers to the Quarry and the dry cows to a rented pasture down the road. After each trip, Bill or Tom shovels the manure out of the trailer and sprinkles some coarse sand on the wet floorboards to improve the footing for the cows. Now and then, Jean stands on the trailer tongue and talks to the nervous animals as they are ferried to pasture, telling them to be proud of themselves because they come from good stock or reminding them of the pleasures of a summer vacation. "Sometimes," she confides, "I think they understand every word I say. Other times, it's like talking to a brick wall."

With the heifers on pasture, the lower half of the barn is empty – Jean puts newspapers over the water bowls so that they stay clean – and the feeding and manure-shovelling chores are dramatically reduced. "It makes it a little easier around the barn," Tom says. "On the other hand, you have to keep an eye on the cows on pasture. That's why we feed them every day – to bring them up to the gate where we can have a look at them." He shrugs. "It evens out as far as chores are concerned."

Bill knows that some farmers put their young cattle out on pasture in the spring and hardly see them until fall, but he does not approve. "It's pretty easy to lose one if you don't see them for three or four days. They can get pinkeye or hoof rot so bad, they're never right again. We've even lost the odd one here. A lot can happen in 24 hours." Quality care takes an effort, though. Yesterday, only 13 of the 21 dry cows on pasture came to the gate when they were called, and Tom, whose job it was to find them, spent a couple of hours on the four-wheeler scouring 100 acres of bush and rough pasture until he found them and chased them up to the gate.

Strictly speaking, the 48 or so cows Bill is milking twice a day are not put out on pasture, although they are let out in a green field. The 10-acre patch of grass is more properly termed a paddock – not large enough to provide a summer's worth of pasture, it serves to give the cows a place in which they can get some exercise and a taste of green grass. They reach it by walking down a narrow, fenced corridor from the paved exercise yard beside the barn. The first day, Tom feeds them a big load of haylage in the yard before opening the gate to the paddock so that they do not gorge themselves on the succulent grass.

Bill, on the smaller of his two John Deere tractors, hauls a round bale.

Bill in the barn. "Milking cows is what it's all about."

Eileen milking. "This is my favourite part of farming."

Eileen in the milk house getting ready for milking.

Russell Moreland, Bill's father, still helps with the chores.

Jean Scott, Bill's sister, is the herdsperson.

Bill's day starts at 4:45 a.m.

Bill and Eileen assist at a birth.

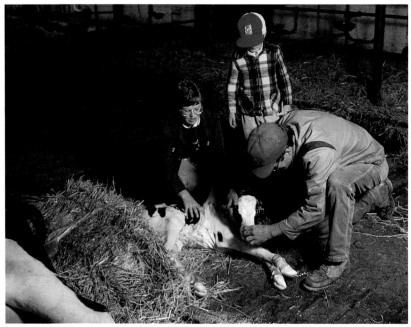

Mark joins them to examine the new calf.

134

At milking time, Eileen feeds the calf milk from its mother.

An aerial view of the home farm after harvest.

Like tourists in the tropics, their digestive systems are sensitive to sudden changes in diet. In fact, they will be allowed in the paddock for only an hour today, and it will be another 10 days before they settle into their summer schedule: out from 8:30 till noon and back out again from 6:30 p.m. (after evening milking) till 5 a.m.

For the cows, this is a special day. They have not set foot on anything but concrete or the straw on their rubber mats for six months. They diffuse into the paddock like cream into coffee, running in all directions and kicking up their heels like lambs. "They're remembering their childhood," Jean says with a fond smile. Soon they slow to a trot, slack udders flapping from side to side, and then to a walk, blowing through their noses from the unaccustomed exertion. Some of the young ones explore the fence line, others strike out across the field, then stop and change direction as if they had just remembered an appointment. A few haven't gone past the patch of bare dirt in front of the gate. In a normal year, this area would still be a mud puddle, but now, the cows are pawing dry dirt over their backs, enjoying a pleasant dust bath. Sako kicks up a little cloud of dirt and, in the same motion, makes a convulsive little jump-kick – like a fat woman with a shaker of talcum, she is dusting the insides of her thighs.

The older cows, more sedate than their daughters and granddaughters, begin to eat. Now a cow eating grass is a wonderful thing, as perfect in its own way as a cheetah running down an antelope or a grizzly pawing a salmon out of the froth of a mountain stream. The modern Holstein cow is a beautiful machine, a creature moulded by humans to turn more grass into more milk with less waste than any other creature on the face of the earth. As with deer and other ruminants that expose themselves to predators every time they leave the shelter of the forest to graze in a meadow, a cow's digestive system allows her to ingest huge quantities of food quickly and to chew it later, safe from hungry eyes. Today's cow, weighing as much as a good-sized moose, hardly able to run because of the beach ball between her hind legs and so domesticated that she is puffing before she gets across the field, is still defined by this neolithic vision of the world.

A cow has eight bottom teeth across the front of her mouth and a full set of 24 molars but no canine teeth and no top front teeth. Where her top teeth should be is a thick dental pad, which means that a cow cannot bite off a stalk of grass – demonstrate this on your front lawn by trying to cut a blade of grass between a butter knife and the palm of your hand. Instead, a cow holds the grass between teeth and pad and pulls her head sideways, tearing off the grass like someone tearing a piece of paper on the edge of a table. Feed a cow a handful of hay or full-length grass, and she will not – cannot – bite it off a mouthful at a time; instead, she will swallow it whole, pausing only to moisten the stalks with saliva and soften them with her molars. Given the structure of a cow's muzzle, she cannot get her teeth closer to the ground than about two inches – a cow would starve to death on a golf-course fairway.

More important to a cow than her teeth in the act of eating is her tongue, which cow anatomy texts call "the main organ of prehension." She uses it to grab her food, wrapping it like the end of an elephant's trunk around a mouthful of grass or, in the barn, scooping away some of her neighbour's grain. A cow's tongue is rough, like a cat's, pale rather than pink and about a foot long. A cow habitually reaches her tongue out of each side of her mouth and sticks it into her nostrils, which are perfectly placed and shaped to accept its tapered end. She repeats this grooming with the satisfaction and fastidious regularity of a dandy wiping his moustache as he eats a bowl of soup.

And thus, with gluttonous determination – cows have been seen grazing for 40 minutes without raising their heads – accompanied by much nose licking and the sound of tearing grass, begins the 180-foot-long trip through the astonishing world of the bovine alimentary canal. The first 3½ feet, the length of the esophagus, are easy – the cow simply swallows – but then it gets complicated. As any schoolchild knows, cows have four stomachs. Well, yes and no. Certainly, there are four distinct organs, and one of them has four compartments, so in a sense, they have four stomachs twice; on the other hand, only one of those organs – not the one with four compartments – is actually a stomach.

First is the rumen (from the Latin word for gullet; hence, ruminant, an animal that chews its food a second time, and ruminate, to chew on a problem). The rumen is a vast cathedral of an organ, divided into four chambers by architectural muscles called pillars. It can hold about 300 pounds of material – in liquid terms, just under 200 litres, about 42 gallons. *42 gallons.* Imagine an oil barrel almost full of grass tucked away under a cow's ribs, or its equivalent in a 165-pound human: a stomach the size of a 5-gallon gas can. The rumen is always half full of liquid, and the grass turns its contents into a hearty green broth. The walls and pillars of the rumen push the soup around in a circle like a slow-motion washing machine, and fingerlike papillae on its sides absorb nutrients from the soup, principally carbohydrates that are used for instant energy. Of course, much of the grass in the rumen is too coarse to be easily digested, so when the cow has eaten her fill, she finds a quiet spot to chew her cud, and this involves the reticulum.

RUMEN AND RETICULUM

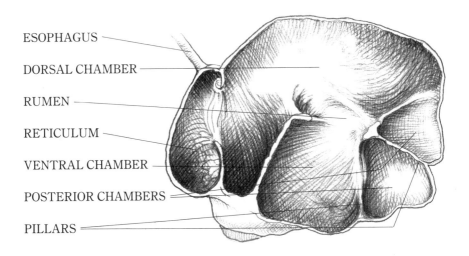

ESOPHAGUS

DORSAL CHAMBER

RUMEN

RETICULUM

VENTRAL CHAMBER

POSTERIOR CHAMBERS

PILLARS

If the rumen is a cathedral, the reticulum is the rector's office; if it is a washing machine, the reticulum is the pump. With a capacity of about 10 quarts, the reticulum is separated from the rumen by a low wall over which the rumen soup sloshes. The reticulum differs from the rumen in function, not content. Its walls, which are honeycombed rather than fingered, do not absorb nutrients, and it serves more as a traffic circle than as part of the alimentary freeway. Both the esophagus and the passage to the next organ open into the reticulum, and its muscular wall is responsible for passing along the thoroughly digested bits and screening out the wads of cud to be rechewed.

Since cows do little chewing of their food before swallowing, they can ingest all manner of sharp objects, such as nails and short lengths of wire. These and other indigestibles accumulate in the reticulum.

If, while the reticulum is squeezing up a wad of cud, some piece of metal punctures it, the cow will die. Such deaths are relatively common, and farmers even have a name for the condition: hardware disease. Many, including Bill, combat it by slipping a magnet about the size of a roll of nickels down the throat of every cow in the herd. It lodges in the reticulum, where it attracts and holds metallic intruders – one such magnet retrieved at an abattoir had 25 nails clinging to it like shipwrecked survivors to a life raft.

So the reticulum gathers a wad of unchewed grass, known as a bolus, and the cow burps it up and masticates it. There is something irresistible about watching a cow chew her cud. She gets a look on her face as though she is thinking about something, and the tennis-ball-sized bolus can be seen travelling up her neck, then suddenly appearing in her cheek, where it sticks out like a baseball pitcher's chaw of tobacco. Then the methodical side-to-side grinding of the cud between the molars (some cows grind from left to right and others from right to left. Are they right- or left-brain dominant?) for about 45 seconds before the bolus is swallowed, and the whole process starts over again. Cows will not ruminate unless they are healthy, safe and relaxed – another throwback to the neolithic past – so a cud-chewing cow is a happy cow. Her placid contentment, visible from across the field, is contagious, and her unrelenting rhythm of burp-grind-swallow is as mesmerizing as any hypnotist's chant.

But while rumination may soothe frayed human nerves, it is hardly relaxing for the cow. In fact, it is common for people to think of a cow's life as an easy one, like a dog's – you know, sleep a little, eat when they're hungry, chew their cud for a while, make milk without trying, stand around a lot. Not so. Cows are classic type A personalities, driven by genetics to suck gallons of milk out of their bodies every day – an underfed Holstein will have an udder full of milk on the day she dies from starvation – and it's all their digestive systems can do to keep up. Even with good rations, some cows can't offset the daily nutrient loss and lose weight during their lactation – "They live off their backs," say farmers, who compensate by getting them overweight ("putting a back on them") when they are dry.

All cows struggle to stay ahead of the game, but rumination takes time. A cow grinds her teeth together about 24,000 times a day just chewing on her cud, a chore that takes a full eight-hour shift. She must sleep for eight hours, and for a dry cow on pasture, the rest of the day is spent eating grass – another 16,000 jaw movements and no time to put up her feet. High-producing milk cows are fed silage and grain and protein supplements that are easy to eat and require little rumination, but it is still difficult to get enough feed into them to keep them from living off their backs too much. In the winter, Bill feeds his cows 11 times a day. "But," he says, "you can't feed them all the time, because they have to have time to chew their cud."

As well as grinding the food into smaller, more easily digested bits, rumination also serves to add saliva to the bolus, and as with any other part of a cow's diet, the quantities involved are not dainty. A cow on pasture produces 100 pounds of saliva a day; in the barn, the same cow produces 50 pounds of saliva for every 10 pounds of hay she eats, and she may eat 40 pounds of hay a day. That's a lot of spit, and one of its purposes, in addition to lubrication, is chemical. Cow saliva is alkaline, with a pH of 8.2, and it counteracts acids produced in the rumen or ingested in feeds like corn silage, keeping the pH in the rumen about neutral – 6.5 to 7.5. Cows fed a lot of grain or other feeds that require little mastication can suffer from acid indigestion because they do not make enough saliva. Some farmers solve this problem by adding sodium bicarbonate to the diet; others, like Bill, prevent it by making sure their cows get enough roughage to promote proper salivation.

And so, back into the rumen soup. The wonderful thing about the rumen, aside from the fact that there is room for it inside the cow, is that it is more like a septic tank than a stomach. Instead of secreting juices that break down its contents, the rumen is a more or less inert tank that provides an environment for microorganisms that do the work. Zillions of living plants (bacteria, yeasts) and animals (protozoa) live in the rumen soup, munching and fermenting it into digestible components. Some of the microorganisms turn cellulose (plant fibre) into fatty acids that are absorbed by the rumen wall; others process the soup through their own digestive systems and produce vitamin K and all the B-complex vitamins; still others break down plant proteins into amino acids and build them up again into proteins of their own. The proteins and vitamins are tied up in the bodies of the microorganisms, which die and are washed into the stomach and intestines, where they are broken down by digestive juices and absorbed into the bloodstream. In a sense, then, a cow is part carnivore – it ingests only plants, but it lives on the meat of dead protozoa.

There are two side effects cows must endure because of this teeming, fermenting rumen soup. The first is swamp gas: a potent

DIGESTIVE SYSTEM

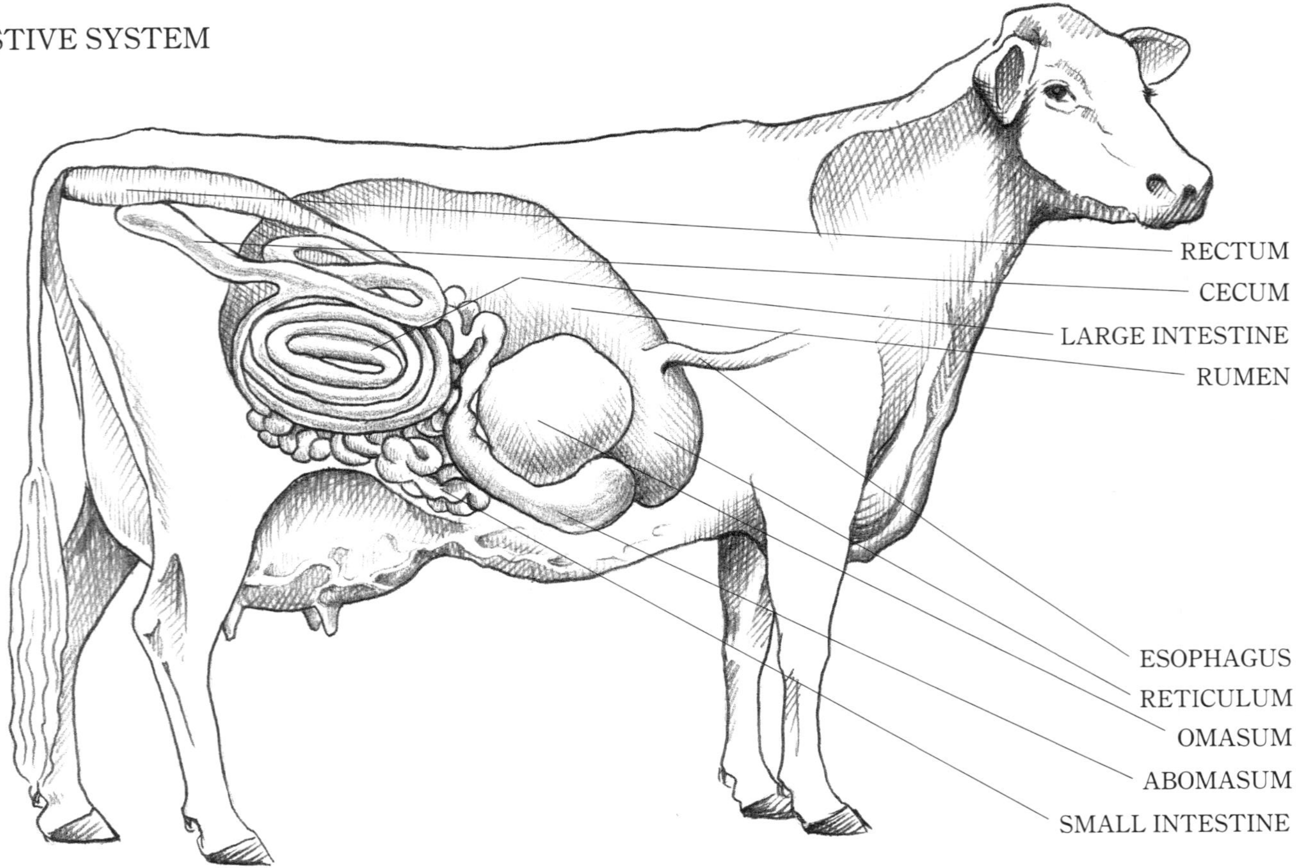

RECTUM
CECUM
LARGE INTESTINE
RUMEN

ESOPHAGUS
RETICULUM
OMASUM
ABOMASUM
SMALL INTESTINE

142

combination of methane, ammonia, hydrogen, hydrogen sulphide, carbon dioxide and carbon monoxide. A cow normally belches – discreetly, of course – about 200 gallons of these gases every day. An excess of some feeds, such as fresh alfalfa, can cause foaming in the rumen that interferes with eructation, or belching. The result is bloat, a self-descriptive condition that can kill in hours if not treated. In its later stages, the only cure is to stab the cow just below the short ribs on the left side, where the rumen is close to the skin, thus allowing the gas to escape, like air from a punctured balloon.

The other side effect is incidental to all fermentation: heat. Largely because of the rumen soup, a cow will never freeze to death; in fact, she has a constant excess heat production of about 3,000 BTUs, as much as most portable electric heaters. This is a bonus for farmers who, like Bill, keep their barns well ventilated in winter. Bill maintains the air temperature in the barn between 50 and 60 degrees F, believing that fresh air is good for the cows and cool temperatures keep bacteria at bay. The downside of the trade-off is that cows suffer in the summer heat. Feed consumption and milk production both drop at temperatures above 80 degrees, and as Bill points out, "It's a lot easier to keep them warm in cold weather than to keep them cool when it's hot."

The other half of a cow's four "stomachs" includes the omasum and the abomasum, each with a capacity of about four gallons. The first consists of many layers, or plies, that squeeze the juice from the soup and pass on the solids; the second is the only true stomach, and it does not differ much – except in size – from a human stomach. It secretes acids and enzymes, including rennin, the substance that curdles milk for cheesemaking, and it prepares the food pulp – shredded, fermented and compressed but still green – for digestion in the intestines. The small intestine (135 feet long and 2 inches in diameter) and the large intestine (only 35 feet long but up to 5 inches in diameter) draw out most of the remaining nutrients, although many proteins are passed in the feces. Anaerobic bacterial action in the large intestine causes putrefaction, giving cow manure its distinctive aroma and familiar colour. The entire process, from grass to manure, takes about four days, three of which are spent in the rumen.

As wonderful as the modern Holstein is at transforming huge amounts of grass into huge amounts of milk, things occasionally go awry. Perhaps the most common – and most dreaded – of these glitches is mastitis, an inflammatory condition of the udder caused by injury or infection. At any given time, one-third of the dairy cows in Canada have subclinical levels of mastitis in one or more quarters. They are walking disasters waiting to happen, because such low-level infections can flare up into acute attacks with the least provocation, such as attaching the milker too early or leaving it on too long, both of which damage the udder by causing suction without milk flow. The infection can also be passed from one cow to another by the milking machines, so Bill is careful to milk his healthiest animals first. Other causes include damp bedding and access to swampy ground, which expose the udder to excessive amounts of bacteria; narrow stalls, which increase the chances that a teat will be stepped on; high door-sills or other projections that may hit the udder; and stress, which reduces the cow's natural resistance to infection.

Even at the best of times, though, high-producing cows are under stress from their high-energy diets, which have to be "hot" enough to maintain milk flow and body weight. And then there is the processing of all that milk — like any machine kept close to the red line for months on end, udders are prone to overheating. Already on the edge, it takes only a little bump to push them over. Farmers notice the first symptoms of mastitis at milking time: one quarter of an udder is warmer than the others, or the milk contains clots. Hence the use of a strip cup, which gives farmers a twice-a-day opportunity to examine the milk from every quarter of every cow.

Antibiotics are the only effective treatment for mastitis. This means a four-day course of treatment and a further 5 to 10 days (depending on the drug used) waiting for the antibiotic to work its way through the cow's system until there are no residues in the milk. During this time, the cow's milk is pumped into a pail instead of the pipeline, and the pail is emptied down a drain. Even after the infection has cleared up, though, the infected quarter will not return to its former level of production. The cow suffers the fever and discomfort associated with any bacterial infection; the farmer suffers short-term and long-term losses of income as well as the cost of the treatment and the bother of individual milking. A 10-day loss of milk from a high-producing cow can amount to more than $200.

One of Bill's high-producing cows, though she is well past her prime now, is Lulu, Mark's favourite. Bill has not been able to breed Lulu after her last calf in November, and by all that makes sense in the business of dairying, he should have sold her to bring a younger cow on line. It is not her placid nature or the endearing chin whiskers she has sprouted in old age that have saved her from the bologna factory; rather, it is her special relationship with Mark, who would be heartbroken if she were shipped.

In early June, Lulu picks up some mastitis in her left hind quarter. Bill and Jean both examine her, and although they do not speak, the look they exchange says it all. The next night, the infection has spread to the front quarter, and her temperature soars to 106 degrees from a normal of 101. Bill calls the vet, whose advice is as simple as it is predictable: sell her. But first they have to control the fever. Penicillin is the obvious treatment, but then Bill would have to keep Lulu for an extra 10 days – the "withdrawal period" required by law to ensure that there is no antibiotic residue in her flesh. He is not confident he can keep the poor old girl healthy for that long, so he opts for the only other choice available, a whopping dose of aspirin to try to bring down the fever. Bill forces four tablets, each the size of two knuckles of his little finger, down her throat and waits. At 2 a.m., when he gets up to check her temperature, it is down to 104. In the morning, though, it has climbed to 105 again. Bill gives her three more aspirins, but he says, "I think we're losing the battle."

Amazingly, Lulu's temperature drops to 103 at noon and is normal by afternoon milking. Nevertheless, the writing is on the wall – not only is it bad financial judgement to keep her, it would probably cause her needless suffering. Her reproductive system has already conked out, and it seems her lactation system is seriously impaired. Her time has come, and even Mark realizes at some level of understanding that she has to go. He remains dry-eyed as he poses with her for a final picture. "It was kind of awful," Eileen says afterwards. "Like some sort of last rite or something."

The morning Lulu is due to leave, Mark and Eileen are at the library. Lulu walks onto the truck without making any fuss, a lady right to the end. "I guess if you're going to go," says Jean, "you might as well go with a little dignity." Later in the week, a cheque arrives in the mail. Lulu weighed 1,915 pounds and brought 61¢ a pound from a man who shipped her to the Ontario Stock Yards. "Over $1,100," says Jean. "You know, that's more than we'd get for her as a milker."

"I didn't plan to have Mark at the library when she left," says Eileen. "It just worked out that way, and that's fine. I even thought about not taking him out to the barn before we went, but then I thought no, he ought to have a chance to say good-bye. So I asked him if he wanted to say good-bye to Lulu or just go to the library. He thought about it and said, 'Well, Mommy, she is my favourite cow.' " At this, Eileen starts to cry, not sobbing but quietly leaking big teardrops down her cheeks. "Oh, this is silly," she says, taking off her glasses and mopping up. "I'm not really that sad about it, but I just think of Mark and how awful it is for him."

Later that afternoon, when Mark bursts into the barn, he is confronted by an empty stall where Lulu has stood for as long as he can remember. He stops and stares. While the cows on either side methodically swallow their hay, Lulu's neck chain hangs forlornly empty. Jean watches Mark, and when his chin begins to quiver, she steps over to give him a hug.

"Mark," she says, kneeling beside him, "I think Princess is lonely. I saw her out in her doghouse after you went to the library, and she looked really sad. Maybe you could go out and cheer her up. I think she'd like that."

Mark pauses to digest this information, then seems to reach a decision. He leaves the barn as he entered it—on the run.

BOOK V

CUTTING HAY

Bill begins cutting hay the day after the Oilers win the Stanley Cup – Monday, June 1 – and despite the old saw advising farmers to make hay while the sun shines, he chooses a muggy, grey day with rain in the forecast. The knack to getting good hay in the barn is to outguess the weather. Living grass is more than 80 percent water, and freshly cut hay would rot if it were simply collected, compressed and packed away in the mow of a barn. It takes two to four days, depending on the humidity in the air, for individual blades of grass to dry out to 15 to 20 percent moisture, when they can be safely baled. If all goes well at haying time, the weather stays dry and the hay is harvested while it retains most of its nutrients and its appetizing green colour. If it is rained on, especially when it is nearly dry, the hay turns brown and brittle and the goodness is washed out of it. The more it is rained on, the worse the damage.

So why is Bill cutting hay just hours before what will likely be the first rain in weeks? "Well, it doesn't hurt the hay too much if it gets rained on right away," he says. "At this time of year, it's better to cut just before a rain than to wait and hope you're going to get a break of three or four days of good weather. If you wait until it's sunny to start cutting, you're liable to get rain when you should be baling. Or you may *never* get a break. Then it gets too mature, and all you've got is a bunch of junk." Hay is most nutritious while it is still growing, before the plants turn fibrous and woody at maturity. To achieve a balance between quality and quantity, the ideal time to cut hay is when the alfalfa buds are just starting to open into purple flowers. By the time the whole field is in bloom, nutrient levels have dropped and the plant stems have become coarse and unappetizing.

Bill cuts hay with a mower-conditioner, a tractor-driven machine that, as its name implies, does two jobs at once. An 11-foot-wide sickle bar, which cuts on the same back-and-forth principle as an electric hedge trimmer, mows the grass a couple of inches above the ground, and a revolving reel sweeps the cut hay into the conditioners, also called crimpers. They consist of two rubber rollers remarkably like the wringers in an old-fashioned washing machine. Each roller is about eight inches in diameter, and they both have raised ribs that mesh in a herringbone pattern. The rollers do not actually wring water out of the plants, but as the hay passes between them, the plants are kinked by the herringboned ribs – the leaves, soft and pliable, are unaffected, but the stems are bent at regular intervals. Without such crimping, the stems, which retain the most moisture, would not dry

out sufficiently until the leaves, which are the most nutritious part of the plant, were so dry and brittle that they would shatter into powder when disturbed. When the field is baled, they would blow away in a dark green fog.

Tom is going to do the cutting today, and when the tractor is fuelled and the mower-conditioner is greased, Bill explains the field to him. About eight acres, it is bounded by the cow paddock, the west fence line, the county road and the driveway up to Bill's house, which jogs into one corner of the field. A border of battered-looking peonies on the field side of the driveway has been a minor source of contention between Bill and Eileen for years. "Oh, they're a real pain," says Eileen. "You have to cover them with a sheet when the men are spraying, and they are always backing equipment over them." This year, she has decided to give up the fight. "I'll just let the men have it."

Bill reminds Tom of the field's danger spots, the places where a careless operator can break a tooth on the sickle bar. "You can see the concrete around the woodpile" – Tom nods – "and there's an old well over there by the fence, but it's filled in with rocks and covered with railroad ties, so you should be able to see it. But watch for the culvert under the drive just on the other side of that knoll, and that big tile along the road. And for heaven's sakes, don't run over Eileen's peonies."

Tom starts the tractor and slips the cutter into gear; then, with the sickle bar chattering and the rollers humming, he pulls into the field. He looks a bit awkward at first, as if trying to look in three directions at once, and so he is: ahead to see where he is going, behind to see if the machine is running properly and to the side to run the end of the nine-foot bar as close to the peonies as he can without mowing them down. Imagine riding a bicycle down the sidewalk with a nine-foot-long fishing pole tied under the seat so that it sticks out to your right. The trick is to keep the end of the pole as close as possible to the picket fence without touching it. It has been a year since Tom has cut hay, but he is making it look easy by the time he swings around the woodpile. Bill watches. "Tom doesn't have a whole lot of machinery experience," he says, "but he's got good judgement. The only thing I can do is tell him everything I know and then turn my back. That's what Dad did with me. I guess it's the least I can do for him."

He walks across the soft stubble where Tom has cut and measures a growing alfalfa stalk. It comes almost to his belt. "I wish it was all like this," he says. "Still, it's not as bad as I thought at first. It's grown a lot just in the last few days." Near-greenhouse conditions of high humidity and record-nudging temperatures over the weekend have given the crop a last-minute boost. But all is far from well, as Bill discovers when he examines a stalk of cut hay. The crop is so thin that the stalks are passing through the conditioner without being crimped. When Tom has made his first round, Bill pulls him over, and they adjust the gap between the rollers. The setting, about a quarter-inch apart, was fine for last year's crop, but this year, it needs to be halved. Bill shows Tom how the adjustment is made, then tries to get him to decide what the setting should be. "Is that enough, Tom?"

Tom grins. "I don't know. It's your machine – you decide."

"Darn. I thought maybe if you decided, I could blame you if it's wrong."

At lunch, most of the talk is about haying. Bill recalls a trip to southern Alberta where, in the parched Palliser Triangle, he saw fields of alfalfa supported by huge water-driven wheels that irrigated what Bill calls "a round mile" at a time. "You could see the whole operation at once," he says. "Cutting in one place, baling in another, picking up bales in another. They had no rain to worry about, and everything was done to a schedule, so there was always something to do – cut or bale or whatever." The neatness of the system appealed to him. "But it would be pretty boring," he concludes. "Like putting on bumpers at a General Motors plant."

Tom, who has already put in a seven-hour shift today performing such varied duties as shovelling manure, milking cows, feeding them, fixing machinery and cutting half a field of hay, grimaces. "Wouldn't that be awful? After you put on a thousand of them, there wouldn't be anything left to learn. I can't imagine it."

In the contemplative silence that follows, Mark asks if he can ride on the tractor with Tom. The answer, without hesitation, is no. Every tractor company and farm safety organization preaches that a tractor is no place for riders, but few farmers heed the advice. They know it is stupid, but they do it anyway. A 10-year study by the Ontario Farm Safety Association shows that 8 of the 40 people killed each year in farm accidents are children, and of those 8, 6 are killed in tractor- or machinery-related mishaps. Last year, a neighbour of Bill's let his young son stand on the tractor platform while he was mowing a field of hay. Lulled by the motion of the tractor and the rhythmic chatter of the sickle bar, the youngster went to sleep and fell off the tractor. Had he fallen to the right, he would have been gobbled up by the voracious maw of the mower-conditioner. Luckily, he fell to the left and was unharmed, but his father was so shaken, he could not bring himself to get back on the tractor for the rest of the day.

"Mark is always falling asleep on the tractor," says Bill. "I like to have him on my lap or between my knees, so I know where he is. Otherwise, I'm all tensed up, ready to jump on the clutch and the brake." Mark often rides with his "Bop" — Russell — in the big blue tractor with the cab, which he cannot fall out of, but Bill occasionally takes him on one of the open John Deeres too. This is an unusual lapse for Bill, who is careful to wear his hearing protectors, to put the tractor in low gear when working in a tight spot, to shut off the machinery before he works on it and to constantly remind others to be careful. "There was a story in *Hoard's Dairyman* once," Eileen recalls, naming the oldest and most respected of the many magazines aimed at dairy farmers. "It was written by a farmer whose wife was killed by a cow. She was in a pen with it, and when she turned her back, the cow knocked her down and attacked her. By the time they chased it away with pitchforks, the woman was dead. You know, we work around cows so much, we forget how big they are and how much damage they can do. Anyway, Bill left the magazine out and made sure we all read that story."

After lunch, Tom goes back to cutting hay, and Bill heads over to his brother's workshop, where he is working on an old corn cultivator he wants to put on the little tractor. Bill has four tractors: the big blue Ford, two green-and-yellow John Deeres and a grey 1955 Ford 860. The old Ford is gas-powered and looks like a garden tractor beside the big diesels, but it is a marvel of simplicity and durability. Bill uses it mostly for odd jobs like shuttling wagons, but this year, because his corn is planted in rows 30 inches apart instead of the usual 36, he needs it to pull the cultivator – the bigger tractors are too wide for the narrower spacing of the corn rows.

The cultivator, a series of splayed teeth that is dragged through the soil like a hoe, is an elderly six-row model. Bill is using it as a four-row, though, because the rows of corn were planted four at a time, and although Jim Greenlees was careful to keep his rows straight, they are not perfect. Small variations in the width of every fourth space distinguish the four-row sets in the field, and a six-row cultivator would make a mess of two rows on every pass. Bill has to change the spacings to accommodate the new row width, and as he loosens the cultivator teeth and shifts and measures and shifts them again, Ed Johnston drops by to get some welding done on a part from one of his ancient tractors. Bill has moved all the teeth but one when Ed leans over his shoulder and bellows, "That row's going to take a beating. Haw, Haw, Haw."

Bill grins back and stops to explain what he is doing.

"Well," Ed says, resting one hand on the cultivator for support, "that's where the horses had the tractor-drawn stuff beat. They'd just go ribbon straight. Yessir, that old team of mine was really something. Mind you, they were well trained – I raised them from colts myself. But that field there by the house, where the barley is this year, you could just tie a red rag on the fence at the other end, and as long as they could see that rag, they'd go right for it. You couldn't pull them off line" – he reins in a handful of air as if trying to make his team gee. "If there was any crookedness, it was the guy behind, it wasn't the horses. The boss" – Ed used to hire out himself and his team to the county – "just hated them, because on a heavy pull, they'd only go a little ways. About 20 rods was as far as they'd go, then they'd both stop, back up and loosen their neck collars, then away they'd go again for another 20 rods. Oh, you could practically go to sleep, and they'd do it all themselves. And when they were mowing hay, they'd mow about twice around the field, then head for a shade tree. You couldn't stop them, no matter what."

Ed is grinning broadly, and Bill, who has heard it all before, shifts the last tine into place. Ed pats the cultivator and, contradictorily, says, "That's a lot better than using the old horse."

"Yeah," Bill grunts as he tightens the last bolt, "I guess it would be."

"We used to have to get up and cultivate corn early in the morning before it got too hot."

Bill straightens up. "And whose benefit would that be for – yours or the horses'?"

Ed guffaws again, shaking his shoulders and showing the tobacco on his teeth. "It was good for both of us, I guess, good for both of us."

———————

Tom barely finishes cutting hay that afternoon before it begins to rain. It pours on Tuesday, rains again on Wednesday and drizzles sporadically on Thursday. Bill grows increasingly irritable. "This time of year is hard on him," Eileen says. "There are a lot of decisions to be made – to cut or not to cut. Bill hates making decisions. Sometimes I think he'd like to crawl into a cave and just ignore the world."

To prove her point, she calls to Bill, who is washing up for lunch, "Do you want ham or roast beef on your sandwich, Bill?"

"I don't care."

Eileen winks. "Mayonnaise or mustard?"

"Whatever you think."

"See what I mean? He just hates making decisions."

Normally, Bill takes two crops of hay per year – in early June and early July – and much of the first crop goes into the silo as haylage. Harvested at 45 percent moisture, haylage requires less drying time than hay, so Bill's schedule suits the weather, which is more likely to be hot and dry for extended periods in July than in June. Also, putting up haylage is faster and less laborious than hay making – all the work is done by machines – which is a bonus in years with a late spring, when planting chores overlap the first cut. This year, although the corn needs to be cultivated and the barley sprayed, planting is done early. Because of the poor alfalfa crop, Bill decides to make haylage with the second cut, which has a higher percentage of protein-rich alfalfa, instead of the first. Tom is delighted with the idea: "I'd much rather throw bales around now, while it's still cool, and spend the hot weather sitting on a tractor seat."

Although Bill has already rented some extra land, he is still worried about not having enough hay, so he goes to see Bob Norris, who owns 52 acres of clay loam a mile west of Bill's farm. Bob is a road-crew foreman for the provincial ministry of transportation and looks it – short, sturdy and middle-aged, with a beer-swollen belly and an aggressive, chest-out, bum-out stride that borders on a swagger. His career at the ministry overlapped that of Ed Johnston, and Bob remembers the days when Ed would grab a noon-hour nap under a tree after a morning of scything weeds, and the other men on the crew would tie his shoelaces together. "Bob's got a pretty good job," says Bill. "Those boys don't really kill themselves. In fact, I think they do more driving than working."

Bill has cut and baled Bob's hay for him – "custom-hayed" it – for many years. Bob has a barn and a few beef cows, and he and his two sons work pretty hard at looking after them, but he is a long way from making a living at it. Their sole piece of farm equipment is a rusty antique tractor that will rarely start without someone turning the hand crank on the front. For many years, Bob's land could not grow alfalfa because it was not drained and it was full of rocks and fence lines. When Bill was done with his own hay in the middle of July, he would go down to Bob's and take off a single cut of grass hay. At first, it was a good way to pick up a little extra cash, but as Bill got older, he found that after six weeks of worrying and sweating over his own hay, he was not interested in doing someone else's. "Besides, you'd go down there and get stuck in a mud hole somewhere or break something on a rock. I just got sick of it, so a couple of years ago, I told Bob that it was too hard on my machinery, and unless he got the rocks taken out and drainage tile installed, I wasn't going to come back.

"Well, I thought he'd get somebody else to hay the place for him, and that would be the end of it. The next thing I know, he's got some outfit to come in, and he spent $50,000 to get the place drained and cleaned up. When he asked me to take the hay off for him again, I couldn't very well say no after he'd done all that. So everything's the same, except now, he's got the whole place in alfalfa, and we have to take two cuts."

In fact, although it, too, suffered some winter damage, Bob's alfalfa is in better shape than Bill's this year, so Bill makes him a proposal. Instead of charging him 50¢ a bale to custom-hay the place, Bill will take Bob's crop of alfalfa and stick it in his own barn. Later, and for no charge, Bill will bring down an equal number of bales of poorer-quality hay. In Bill's eyes, it is a reasonable offer. He needs the high-protein feed for his high-producing cows, and Bob's haphazard collection of 20 crossbred beef animals could never make full use of it. From Bob's point of view, his cows will get all the nutrition they need out of the grass hay Bill will provide, and he will save a couple of thousand dollars.

Bob agrees to the deal. Russell is ecstatic. "We're lucky to have Bob for a neighbour," he says. "Damn lucky. There's a lot of people who wouldn't have gone along with that, but that Bob, now – he's a great fellow." When Bill tells Eileen about Bob's response, he says, "Of course, every second word was a gee dee."

Eileen's eyes light up with mock astonishment. "Just every second word?" she asks and adds that Bob is a wonderful fellow but "profane." Indeed he is. He swears with the regularity of a hockey player and the imagination of a regimental sergeant major. He operates on a three-tier system, each tier having its own theme. The first is a more or less constant background profanity with a religious motif. It is part of Bob's flair that he has transformed the old-fashioned exclamation "Bejesus!" into an everyday adjective, as in the sentence, "If this bejesus tractor doesn't start this christly time, we'll have to crank the bejesus thing."

The second tier involves the names and descriptions of various bodily parts, usually those concealed by a bathing suit. The third tier, used in times of severe stress, such as only happen about a dozen times a day, takes highlights from the first two and adds detailed portrayals of an astonishing array of bodily functions, several of which are ana-tomically improbable at best. Eileen is appalled by Bob's language, but she is quite fond of Bob. His performances, in fact, seem designed mostly to entertain his friends and to demonstrate to acquaintances, unsuccessfully, that he is not as nice a fellow as he appears to be. Bob has a heart as large as his vocabulary, and he would likely have ac-cepted Bill's offer solely on the grounds that it would help Bill, even if it did not save him some money.

The rain continues all that week and into the next – some days a steady downpour, others just a shower or two. Bill grows ever more restless and frustrated. "I don't know," he says heavily, when a sunny morning has turned into a cloudy afternoon with showers followed by black clouds and a hard rain. "You work like crazy all week to get the machinery ready, then you can't use it. Sometimes I wonder why I do this. This morning when the sun was shining, I was up and all hot to do something, and now I don't feel like doing a damn thing. I just feel like lying on the couch, putting a pillow over my head and ignoring everything." At lunch one rainy day when Bill is in town, Eileen quotes a Psalm during grace, "And help us remember this is the day the Lord hath made, and to rejoice in it. Amen."

She looks up and smiles slyly. "You notice I didn't say that when Bill was around."

The rains have not stopped Bill from cutting more hay. Indeed, he has to keep cutting – the rain is bad for it but not as bad as letting the crop get too mature. After spending another wet day working in the barn and the workshop, Bill is tired and discouraged. His face is pinched, and in its new lines and folds, it shows what Bill will look like as an old man. When the sky clears at suppertime, he thinks he should cut for a couple of hours until dark. He obviously doesn't feel like it, though, and Eileen tries to discourage him.

"Oh, I don't know what to do," he says, taking his glasses off and rubbing his face.

"I think you ought to stay home." Eileen does not operate the equipment, but she knows that accidents – lost fingers and hands, tractor tipovers – are more likely to happen when the operator is tired.

"Well, I know what you think," Bill says sharply, "but if we thought that all the time, we'd never get anything done. We'd be broke." He makes a face, then adds in a softer voice, "Mind you, we'd be happy."

In the end, he convinces himself that the ground is too wet and goes to bed at 9 o'clock, getting almost eight hours' sleep for the first time in weeks.

———

Bill has farmed enough years to have faith in the process of growth. He does not have to go out in his fields and look at the plants to see that they are larger than they were the last time he checked. He is well acquainted with the science of growth – air, water, minerals, sunlight, photosynthesis, respiration – and he even takes part in it, adding nutrients and killing weeds that interfere with sunlight or take up too much water. He knows about plant growth just as he knows rainbows are caused by the prismatic effect of water droplets in the air, as he knows the sky is blue because the atmosphere filters out the other wavelengths. But he is as pleased as the rest of us by the appearance of a rainbow or the piercing clarity of a cloudless sky. And he still goes out into his fields to oversee the crops as they burst from the ground.

By the end of the first week of June, the corn is about eight inches high and has four leaves. The plants are spaced at four-to-eight-inch intervals up and down the field, and the rows, 30 inches apart, are straight. When a breeze flutters the leaves, it looks as if the plants are hung on a series of clotheslines. Bill is pleased. The preemergent spray gave the corn a head start on the weeds, but now a green haze is slowly filling in the low spots and tractor tracks where the moisture is greatest. This is the time to cultivate, to uproot the young weeds while they are too young to recover from the trauma, but after a week of rain, the ground is too wet. Corn cultivation becomes another item on a growing list of things that should be done this week but aren't.

The barley is also in good shape – as green as Astro-Turf and as thick as a shag carpet. In the field by the barn, the tallest of it is knee-high, and Bill can no longer see his toes when he walks through it. It is tempting to think of plants as growing from the bottom up, as if the fully formed plant were being gradually pushed up from under the ground. Actually, plants, whether they be blades of grass or giant redwood trees, grow from the top – fresh material is added to the top, while the bottom, which never gets any higher, is broadened to support the new top growth. Stick an axe in an oak sapling at waist height, come back in a century, and the axe will still be at waist height, although the mature tree will be four times taller.

Barley, like bamboo and other grasses, grows by nodes. At the base of the newest (topmost) leaf is a round hole in the top of the plant. Inside the hole, like rifling in a gun barrel, is a tight green whorl that is the next leaf. As that leaf grows, it sticks out of the hole and unfurls itself, revealing the next whorl of growth in its centre.

So fast has the barley unfurled that it is already almost too tall to drive on – young plants spring back up after being driven on; older ones tend to stay down. It has grown up quickly enough to choke out all but the fastest and toughest weeds, but there are the odd stalks of pigweed and lamb's quarters showing, and a scattering of yellow rocket, known locally as wild mustard, has flourished near the laneway. Bill pulls the mustard by hand and shakes his head about the rest. "If I was to drive over this field now, my heart, it'd rimrack the whole thing. It's just too wet. Maybe it won't get sprayed this year, and I can save some money on spray." He doesn't look thrilled by the prospect, and spraying the barley is added to the list of chores that should have been done last week.

The genetic imperative of plants is to reproduce, with no consideration for personal survival. In contrast to animals, which usually do not get or stay pregnant when they are sick or injured, nothing makes a plant reproduce faster than impending death. Thus, houseplants can be made to flower by ruthlessly trimming their foliage. Prize garden vegetables are obtained by plucking off all of a plant's blossoms except one so that it will invest all its reproductive energy in a single fruit. In both cases, the plant is fooled into believing it is going to die, and so its vigour and reproductive urges are kicked into high gear. Bill's hay, after a week of rainy weather, decides this is its one chance to reproduce. It has become no taller or thicker, but it has begun to mature and blossom. Bill has to abandon his plan to make hay from his first cut. "If it ever stops raining, I'll have to get it all in in a hurry, and that means putting it in the silo."

Bill takes his forage harvester – like most of Bill's equipment, it bears the green-and-yellow markings of a John Deere product – over to Tom's shop for its spring overhaul. This machine picks up the cut and partially dried hay, chops it into pieces and blows it into an attached wagon. Bill paid $18,000 for the harvester in 1981. He uses it for 20 or 30 hours a year, and the rest of the time, it sits in the machine shed. "When I first got the big silo for haylage, I used to try to do everything perfect," he says. "I'd cut about 20 acres and wait a couple of days until it was at the perfect stage, 45 percent moisture or whatever, and bring it in. But then, when I was bringing that in, I should have been out cutting the next 20-acre batch. It was too much trouble. Now I just cut it all, 75 acres or so, and go until it's all in – work for maybe 20 hours straight and get it done all at once. It's not all perfect, but it's good enough. I've learned you can't do everything perfect." He says this with more resignation than satisfaction: he knows he can't do everything just so, but he doesn't like it.

The inside of the harvester is a mess, much of it covered with a quarter-inch-thick layer of last year's alfalfa juice that has turned to a gummy black rubber. It scrapes off easily, though, and the broken pieces smell like new-mown alfalfa. Bill shakes his head. "I should have cleaned this in the fall. I always put it away and intend to clean it later, but I never do. Dad was always one for that – put it away and get on with the next thing. I'd like to clean it, but part of the problem is that there's no room to do anything in the machine shed." The three-bay shed, 16 by 36 feet, was built in the days of horse-drawn machinery and is too small for Bill's needs. The harvester can be fitted in only by partially disassembling it, and even then, it is stuck behind other equipment. It is too much work to pull it out for a cleaning.

As Bill cleans and greases the harvester, Tom MacFarlane readies the forage wagons. These are enclosed on three sides, with a roof and a partial front. The floor of each wagon, about the size of a parking space, has a moving table; that is, a pair of chains along each side connected by lengths of angle iron, like the skeleton of a conveyor belt.

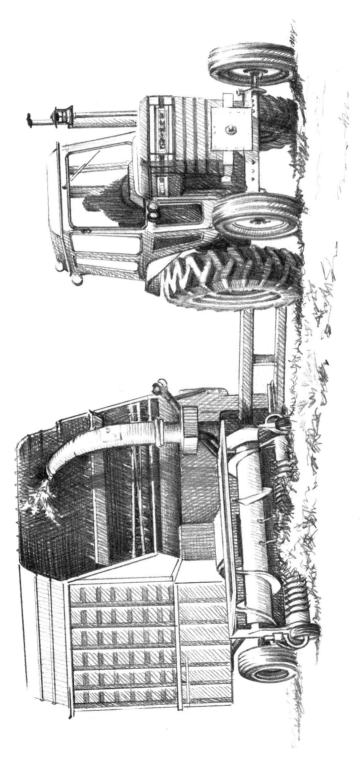

FORD TRACTOR PULLING FORAGE HARVESTER AND FORAGE WAGON

When the wagon is hooked to the power takeoff (PTO) – a drive shaft on the back of a tractor that powers external equipment – the chains move and the angle irons scrape along the floor, nudging the load of chopped forage up to the front, where slow-motion beaters chew away at it and drop the loosened bits onto a conveyor belt fitted across the front of the wagon. Thus, the wagon, after being filled by the forage harvester, can automatically empty its whole load from a two-foot-square hole in the front left corner. At any one time during the harvest, one wagon is being filled in the field, another is being unloaded at the silo, and the third is being transported to or from the field. It is an efficient, seamless process, or at least it is when nothing breaks down.

The heart of the forage harvester, the one mechanism all the others serve, is the cutter, an 18-inch-wide, 16-inch-diameter drum fitted with 12 full-width knife blades. The harvester picks the crop off the ground with sprung-steel tines, augers it to the centre and feeds it into the cutter with a pair of toothed steel rollers. The cutter, which spins at a terrifying speed and howls like a werewolf, chops whatever it is fed at ⅛-to-¼-inch intervals and flings the pieces up and out a curved pipe and into the wagon behind. It is a scary, dangerous machine, and there are a number of gruesome stories circulating in the farm community that feature a forage harvester as the instrument of dismemberment.

One of the most common stories, perhaps apocryphal, involves a harvester fitted with a two-row corn head; that is, instead of the hay pickup reel, it had a pair of mechanisms that grip stalks of standing corn at ground level, cut them off and feed them into the cutter. According to the story, a man was harvesting corn silage at his brother's farm, and the farmer's preschool son toddled into the field to see his uncle. Unseen in the tall corn, he was caught in the farthest of the two corn cutters. The uncle only became aware of what had happened when the machine plugged – he opened an inspection port behind the cutter and recognized the bloody pulp by the quarter-inch-wide slices of clothing. In one version of the story, the uncle staggered back to his brother's house in shock, was discovered loading a shotgun and had to be forcibly prevented from sticking it in his mouth and pulling the trigger.

Bill has not heard that story, but he does know a farmer he describes as "a big man, about 225 and a real bull – the kind of guy who wants to go and you just get out of his way." The man stopped to make some adjustments to his harvester, and before he got off the tractor, he took the machine out of gear, which is standard safety practice for farm equipment. But the inertia of the flywheel was still turning the machine, and he got his hand caught in the toothy grip of the rollers. "Once it's got you, you can't get out. By the time the cutter stopped, it had taken off all his fingers."

Paul O'Neill, the veterinarian, has advised Bill to give his cows more fibre by cutting his haylage in longer pieces, so Bill adjusts the speed of the cutter by changing a drive sprocket. Short pieces pack more tightly in the silo, excluding more air and giving a better-preserved product, but the longer pieces will improve rumination, allowing the cow to chew more cud and produce more saliva. He is just finishing the adjustment when Russell stops by to bemoan the weather.

"Well, it's our own fault," he says. "Yessir, our own fault. We shouldn't be taking hay off at this time of year anyway. My dad used to say, 'Dry May, wet June, makes the farmer sing a tune.' Dry May to plant the crops, d'ye see, wet June to make them grow, then harvest in July. We never used to start hay until after July 12 – Orangemen's Day. Not that we were good Orangemen or anything, but that's the way it was done." Orangemen's Day, commemorating the defeat of James II on Irish soil at the Battle of the Boyne on July 12, 1690, was an important social event in this area until after World War II.

"Yeah, they wanted me to become an Orangeman when I was a young man," interjects the usually taciturn Tom Moreland. "They're not supposed to have nothing to do with Catholics, these fellows, but the guy who asked me always bought his car from a Catholic car dealer, so I figured there wasn't too much to it. 'Course, that whole thing is all nonsense, anyway – it goes back hundreds of years."

"Yes," says Russell, "but things have changed now, and changed for the better. When I was young and living at home, Dad always told me to stay away from Catholic girls – that's the way people felt then. But nowadays, well, you take what's-his-name there on the other side of Gananoque – he married a Catholic girl. She goes to mass on Saturday night, then comes to our Presbyterian church on Sunday and teaches Sunday school. And that's the way it should be too."

———

Cows are not respecters of weekends, and on a dairy farm, there is no 37½-hour week. Tom and Jean get every second weekend off, plus alternate Wednesdays – three days off in a two-week cycle. They start work at 5 a.m. and quit at 6 p.m. With an hour for lunch, that's 12 hours a day, 60 hours one week, 72 the next. Tom and Jean take the same weekends off, leaving Bill and Eileen alone; but, of course, they work the same weekends too, giving Bill and Eileen every second weekend off. On their weekends, Bill and Eileen try to leave the farm, or else they find themselves getting sucked into one chore or another. Often, they visit Eileen's parents, who live an hour's drive away in Sharbot Lake, or stay with friends in Ottawa or on Wolfe Island. On the first weekend in June, black and rainy, they go to Bill's school reunion in Kemptville and miss a little excitement.

Tom and Jean were working in the barn, and Jean had Malcolm, her 4-year-old, with her. "I don't know what happened. He was playing over by the automatic feeder, and he knows not to touch anything, but anyway, he just about took his finger off. I thought he had at first. There was a lot of blood, and nobody was sure how bad it was." Tom, though accustomed to field-gutting deer and other bloody chores, was a bit squeamish about examining the wound, and Jean, normally calm, was in a panic. They finally mopped up some of the blood – "For once, I had a clean handkerchief in my pocket," says Jean – and had a look: Malcolm was missing a chunk of flesh from the end of the third finger on his right hand, a big enough chunk to include a piece of bone.

The working parts of the feeder – belts, augers and drive chains – are mainly enclosed. "We can't figure out what it was that got him. We don't think it could be the belt – the only thing might be an auger. There's the sprocket on the chain, but we can't figure how he could get at it, and Tom says if he had got down there, he would have lost a lot more than just the end of his finger." Jean rushed him to a hospital in Kingston – "I didn't know the old truck would go that fast" – where a doctor cleaned the wound and wrapped the hand. Malcolm fell asleep in Jean's arms before he was finished. "They can't do much except wait for it to heal over. He'll have full use of his finger. It'll be a little deformed, but that's no big deal." She says it without touching the scars on her lip.

On the way home from the hospital, Malcolm sat soberly with his hand taped up as big as a boxing glove, and Jean talked brightly about all the things he could still do with his left hand while the bandage stayed on his right.

"Mommy," he said as they approached a row of fast-food outlets, "I think my left hand could eat a doughnut."

"When he said that, I knew he was going to be all right," says Jean.

162

On Monday morning, with the rain still pouring down, Tom and Jean put what she calls "earrings" on the cows. These are triangular ear tags, each about the size of a small pie slice and made of insecticide-impregnated plastic that deters flies for an entire summer. Tom puts a tag in each cow's right ear with a tool similar to a pair of pliers that punctures the ear and locks the tag in place. With the older cows, he uses last year's ear hole, but the A-year cows, in their first lactation, are being treated for the first time, a process that seems no more painful than an injection. Still, none of the cows are eager to have Tom play with their ears, and they twitch them or shake their heads as he tries to get the pliers in position. It is an exasperating job – all the more so because he must remain outwardly calm to keep the cows relaxed. Jean accompanies him, ready to help and soothing the cows with her best teacher's voice. "Now remember your family heritage," she says to Seven's daughter Rave. And to Romona: "I can't say remember your family heritage because you haven't got any, but remember what a good cow you are and be proud of that."

The cows, tied in their stalls, have the full length of the tie chains. Some of them move their heads around so much that Tom cannot position the pliers, and he has to clamber in beside the cow and push her head to one side. Stidler is one of these, and by the time Tom has wrestled her head into position and inserted the tag, he is puffing from the exertion. When he releases her head, she swings around sharply and butts him in the chest hard enough to knock him back into the next cow.

"Got your hospitalization payments up to date, Tom?" Jean asks.

"Yeah, you bet," and he laughs, but three cows later, when he starts to climb in beside Arol, she throws a tantrum, kicking with her feet, charging back and forth and banging her head from one side to the other. Tom quickly retreats and pulls a pair of nose tongs from his back pocket. The tool also looks like a pair of pliers, but instead of regular jaws, it has rounded, heavy-duty calipers that can be locked in the closed position. He grabs Arol's nose with them, one caliper in each nostril, and locks them shut. The effect is like that of a nose ring on a bull – Arol is now securely held by a sensitive part of her anatomy but will not feel any pain unless she struggles. Tom secures the rope on the nose tongs over a beam, and Arol backs up hard, pulling her nose out of shape. She bawls but refuses to move forward. "Yeah, I bet that hurts," Tom mutters, with more satisfaction than sympathy.

Finally, they use a battery-powered cattle prod to move her forward where her head can be immobilized, and Tom puts on the ear tag and releases her. "We really should have a proper head gate for this kind of work," he says, referring to the kind of head-holding mechanism Twin L Hoof Trimming uses. "Doing ear tags isn't usually too bad, but if she had waited until I got in there beside her before she flipped out like that, I could have really got hurt." No question about it – Arol is not yet fully grown but already weighs as much as a small car, and if she had caught Tom against a stall rail, she could have easily broken an arm, a collarbone or several ribs.

They finish the rest of the cows by noon without incident, and Tom gets ready to leave. Today is his first wedding anniversary, and he is taking the afternoon off. His wife Audrey is a lively 40-year-old redhead with two children from a previous marriage. They make an odd combination – Tom young and strong and quiet; Audrey outgoing, with a soft English accent and equally soft peaches-and-cream complexion – but according to Eileen, they are well matched. "Well, Tom is kind of old for 24, and Audrey is young and full of life."

"They say the first year of marriage is the hardest," says Tom, "and I guess that's right. But I've learned you can't change the other person – not Audrey, anyway, she's too stubborn." He pauses. "You know, before I married a redhead, I always heard stories about them. Well, let me tell you, anything you ever heard about redheaded women is true."

"Now, we want you to have a good time on your anniversary," Jean teases, "but don't go out and stay up late. We want you to get your sleep, so you'll be able to work tomorrow."

Tom drops his eyes and all but blushes, then manages to mumble and drawl at the same time. "Oh, I might get a nap this afternoon."

———

Finally, on June 10, it does not rain. The sun shines and the wind blows – excellent drying conditions – and Bill makes plans to bale the next day. Hay in the field by the house, which was cut on June 1 and has been rained on every day since, is too poor to put into the silo, so Bill will bale it instead.

A baler is a wonderful machine, one of those mechanical marvels that replaces a half-dozen grateful workers. It picks up the hay that has been set in rows (called windrows), then compresses, shapes and ties it with twine in neat, convenient-to-handle packages, which it throws onto a wagon that trails behind it. All this commotion is controlled from the seat of a tractor – no pitchforks, no handling, no stacking, no walking. This is not to say that baling is easy. The heat from the sun and the tractor is oppressive, the noise and vibration fatiguing; the effort of looking behind, beside and ahead at the same time is hard on the back and neck; the constant readiness to jump on the clutch or the brake if something should go wrong is draining. Harvesting hay is not easy with modern equipment; it is just easier than it used to be.

All brands of balers are made much the same: a pickup reel, a set of spikes called needle teeth that feed the hay into a chamber, a plunger that cuts, shapes and compresses the hay, a pair of knotters that ties the bales, and a thrower or kicker that dispenses the finished product. A baler is all chains and gears and timing, a cacophony of several operations all happening at not quite the same time. The plunger plunges 75 times a minute – the needle teeth must push hay into the chamber in the split second the plunger draws back, then exit before it returns; the knotters must tie as quickly. A knotter is a small miracle of technology, a device that can reliably join two ends of twine together hundreds of times in a row while bouncing over a rough field. Each knotter has more moving parts than a human hand, and they cooperate to tie a simple overhand knot in a blur of motion that is easy to demonstrate but impossible to explain. Still, if someone turns the baler's flywheel by hand, it is possible to slow the blur and watch the knot being formed in something close to human speed.

Bill's baler is not an antique, but it is old. He bought it new in 1972 for $3,400, and it has made well over 100,000 bales. It is tired and worn. The precise movements of the knotters have been made clumsy by age, the weak parts having been welded, replaced and welded again. Last year, it broke down repeatedly – nothing major, but a string of minor complaints brought on by metal fatigue and the sloppy meshing of worn parts. At the end of the season, Bill put in his order for a new machine. Even with the trade-in for his old baler, the new one will cost him $9,600. "I could have got it for about $8,800, but I got a couple of options on it." But a labour dispute at the John Deere plant in Moline, Illinois, has held up delivery of the new machine, and Bill must begin the season with the old one.

He hooks on a hay wagon – it has four sides built in a loose framework to keep the bales from rolling off – and starts around the field. The baler shapes and compresses and knots in perfect rhythm and periodically flings a bale into the wagon. There are two types of bale throwers: one design uses a pair of constantly running belts to grab the top and bottom of the bales and spit them into the wagon; the other uses a sudden, mule-kick motion to knock them in. Bill has a kicker, a small platform on the back of the baler. When a bale is pushed onto the platform, it trips a lever, and a hydraulic ram jerks the platform up about three feet, kicking the bale up and back. Bill knows a farmer who carelessly pulled a bale onto the kicker when the baler was turning. The bale tripped the lever and rose up, hitting him in the chest. The next thing he knew, he was lying on his back in the wagon, sore but unhurt, with the bale on top of him. As Bill circles the field, the bales gracefully arc a dozen feet into the air at regular intervals, seeming to hang weightless at the apogee of their flight before nose-diving into the wagon.

On Bill's third trip around the field, Eileen comes out of the house and waits for him by the peony border. Her face is under tight control – something is wrong. Bill shuts off the tractor and baler before getting down. In a quiet voice, she tells him that Russell's youngest brother Art died of a heart attack while sitting in a chair at his home on Moreland Hill. Bill appears surprised and shaken. "My, my," he says, shaking his head. Uncle Art, at 71, was almost 10 years younger than Russell and in good health. Eileen's eyes have filled with tears, but she crosses her arms and holds her distance, and Bill does not offer an embrace. They briefly discuss plans for getting to the funeral on Saturday, then Eileen turns back to the house. She has to make some phone calls to family friends and neighbours who will want to know.

Bill checks over the baler, but before getting back on the tractor, he puts one foot on the wagon tongue and leans an elbow on the kicker. He stands there for a long moment, staring at a newborn bale. "It's been a long time since we were over for a visit," he says, finally. "You try to get away, but you just never do. We won't be able to go now, I guess, not to see Uncle Art, anyway." He sighs and looks up. "This is going to be hard on Dad. They were visiting each other a fair amount." He heaves himself back onto the tractor. There is no question of stopping the baling – clouds have moved in and rain threatens. Only a loss in the immediate family can stop a harvest, and sometimes even that won't do it. Hours after the bodies of the Conners boys had been removed from the silo where they died, neighbours – unasked – fired up the tractors and continued the corn harvest.

The hay is in remarkably good shape – brown and withered on top but green and fresh on the underside. According to Bill, it has been so consistently wet that the plants never knew they were cut. Had there been a day or two of dry weather between rains, the hay would have dried, then rotted. As it was, the crop just kept growing. So did the stubble, and now the second crop is growing up through the first.

Bill gets 800 bales on the wagons and is working on the last wind-row when a steel bar on the kicker snaps. He unhooks the wagon, flips a safety bar that locks the kicker and lets the last 25 bales drop gently to the ground. Later, he puts the tractor in low gear and lets Mark steer while he hops off and throws the bales on the wagon by hand. Mark is bursting with pride about helping his dad and proudly tells everyone except, with a 4-year-old's intuition, his mother.

While Bill and Mark are loading the wagons, Tom and Jean are unloading them into the barn loft. They park the wagons next to a bale elevator – a sort of portable conveyor belt – set up at the south end of the barn, facing the road. Jean drops the bales onto the elevator, which carries them up and through the barn-loft door, where they transfer to a permanent conveyor hanging from the peak of the roof. This runs the length of the barn but has a trolley that dislodges the bales and lets them fall 30 feet to the loft floor, where Tom stacks them in neat rows. Tom can move the trolley with a loop of rope and thereby adjust where the bales will fall. While still easier than forking loose hay by hand, unloading bales is a lot more like manual labour than baling is. The bales are wet and heavy, about 60 pounds each – Jean uses gravity as much as possible to let them fall on the elevator. But at least she is outside; Tom has the truly unpleasant job. Stuck in the poorly lit mow without a breath of fresh air, he must pick up each bale and carry it to its place, all the while walking on the uneven surface of the bales he has already stacked. In July, with the heat of the sun magnified by the steel barn roof, "mowing back" is torture, and even now, on a day so cool that Bill is wearing a jacket as he bales, Tom is sweating.

As if it had politely waited for Bill to finish, a light rain begins to fall seconds after the last of the hay is unloaded. Tom, hair stuck to his forehead and jacket under one arm, steps out of the barn and gratefully lifts his face to it.

"I hope that barn roof doesn't leak, Tom, and get that nice hay all wet," says Jean, making a straight-faced dig at both the weather and the wetness of the bales.

Having finally got something done, Bill is enthusiastic and animated at dinnertime. He tries to plan the weekend, which he and Eileen are supposed to have off. There is Uncle Art's wake to go to on Friday, the funeral on Saturday, and he'd like to spray the grain and cultivate the corn too, if the weather clears up again. In addition, they hope to attend a Sunday church service in Ottawa, where the teenage son of a family friend is being confirmed. But haylage is the first consideration – there are 50 acres of alfalfa cut and waiting at Bob Norris's. "If it stays overcast, we could start harvesting at 10 o'clock on Saturday morning. Let's see, 50 acres at about 3 acres an hour, that's 16 hours, better call it 20, we'd get done at 6 o'clock Sunday morning, and we might still get to Ottawa. Oh, but then there's the funeral to go to. Ahh, I don't know."

On Friday morning, Bill climbs into the mow to check the hay. It is like stepping into an Amazonian rain forest – warm, wet and so foggy, he cannot see the opposite wall. The wet hay, giving off moisture in the still air, has turned the whole place into a terrarium. Bill opens a door high in the north wall, giving a flow-through ventilation that begins to clear the fog. Even then, the air is so heavy with the scent of new hay, it is almost too thick to breathe. As it dries, wet hay gives off heat – enough to cause the bales to combust spontaneously. Many barns have burned down because of this phenomenon, and already, these bales are uncomfortably warm.

Bill is ready for this, however. In 1984, he installed a hay dryer, a plywood box on the floor of the mow, four feet wide by four feet high by the length of the barn. At one end of the box is a door to the outside and a fan. When Bill opens special slots in the box and turns on the fan, outside air is forced through the tightly packed bales – not between them but through them – carrying away the warmth and moisture. Once it is started, Bill leaves the fan on for a month, longer if necessary. It cost $2,000 to install the hay dryer, but he is satisfied that he has already recouped his investment by getting his hay in the barn sooner. This hay, for example, would have sat out in the rain again last night if he had not had the dryer. "This way, I can bring in hay when it's still a bit tough, a bit green. When I was thinking about building the dryer, a guy told me I wouldn't see as many leaves in the wagon, and that's true. If you let it dry completely in the field and then handle it, even with the baler, you're going to lose quite a few leaves. And leaves are nutrition – you really have to take care of those leaves."

Bill turns on the dryer – as it forces air through the bales, the 48-

inch fan sounds like an overloaded Cessna running out of runway – and climbs back into the mow. Heat is palpably being forced out of the bales, which now smell like boiled seaweed, but Bill is all smiles. "Feel this," he says, running his hand back and forth on the side of a bale squared by the plunger knife. The cut ends of the stalks are pliant, like the bristles of a new paintbrush. "Feel how soft that is? That's what the cows like." Bill's frustration over the past two weeks has dissolved into a happy enthusiasm spoiled only by his unrelenting perfectionism. "I really should have turned on the dryer last night," he chastises himself as he climbs down the ladder to the stable.

"I don't know why he didn't," says Tom later. "I would have, but then I'm not the boss." He speaks with an uncharacteristic petulance and is obviously tired and grumpy. He has reason to be. Yesterday, he lifted and carried and placed every one of the 800-plus bales, a total weight of almost 25 tons. Even for Tom, young and strong and used to hard work, it was a rude introduction to the haying season.

In the afternoon, he and Jean take Rolca and Vicky to dry-cow pasture. They load both cows into the trailer, intending to drop them off at different pastures, Vicky first. When they open the loading door at the first pasture, however, Vicky is facing the wrong way. Tom reaches in the door and tries unsuccessfully to turn her around, and the more he tries, the more stubbornly the cows refuse to cooperate. Impatient, he steps into the trailer, getting Jean to hold the door shut until he has turned Vicky around.

Trapped in a wood-and-steel box with a pair of unruly creatures that outweigh him 20 to 1, Tom reaches over their backs and tries to turn Vicky's head. The cows panic and throw themselves around while the trailer rocks on its wheels, and Tom barely avoids being crushed. In the confusion, Vicky slips and falls, with a hind leg stuck awkwardly out behind. Tom loses his temper. "Jesus Christ!" he says through clenched teeth and kicks her viciously. "Get the fuck up there." Jean pretends not to notice, but the effect on the cows is as though he has doubled their IQs. Vicky turns around and, when Jean opens the trailer door for her, steps regally down the ramp and into the pasture. Tom, breathing hard and embarrassed by his outburst, just shakes his head.

At dinner on Friday, Bill and Eileen try to plan their weekend again, taking into account Uncle Art's funeral on Saturday and the wake tonight, which they expect will be busy. "There's nothing worse than a busy wake," says Bill.

Eileen is scandalized. "Bill, what a thing to say."

"Well, you know what I mean – all those people and smoke and no place to sit down."

A wake is one of those old-country traditions that have survived in rural Canada. On the afternoon and evening of the two days between a death and a funeral, friends and relatives of the deceased gather at his or her home. In the old country, it was often an occasion for drinking bouts that sometimes deteriorated into brawls. Modern wakes, at least in Canada, are apt to be sedate affairs involving more food than alcohol, and they are upheld on the theory that the grieving are "kept busy" serving their guests. Bill, aware that some urbanites consider wakes in the home as either quaint or grotesque anachronisms, defends them on different grounds. "Well, I think they intensify the whole experience and help you get rid of all that emotion. Besides that, it makes you talk to people about it, and when you talk to people, you don't just talk about the fact that the person is dead. You remember things, and you can laugh about some stuff, even."

"And the other thing," Eileen interjects, "is you get it over with all at once. You're not afraid for the next month that when you go out, someone will come up and say how sorry they are – not that they don't mean it, you know, but it just gets to be an awful burden. This way you can get on with things."

"Yeah, you get it all over with in a couple of days and get on with living."

As if to prove his point, Bill launches into a story about Uncle Art attending a dairy-board meeting in Toronto. Art had a few drinks at dinner and went up to bed early. When the rest of the group came up to their rooms, Art's room was empty, but his clothes were there and the window was open. Before they had enough time to get really worried, a shriek from down the hall distracted them. Art, after sleep-walking to a different room, had been discovered by a female member of the party – he was asleep on her bed in his underwear.

The incident reminds them of Bill's school reunion and what for Bill and Eileen is the mystifying spectacle of people drinking all evening. "I don't know," says Bill, who has never been drunk in his life, "sometimes when I'm working in the hay on a hot day, somebody will hand me a beer, and it just tastes like ambrosia. But it doesn't make me feel like having another one."

In the end, they make it to the wake, which is busy but not unpleasantly so, and to the funeral at 2 o'clock on Saturday before driving to Ottawa. They attend a party that evening and are up early on Sunday to get to church, which is followed by a luncheon. Bill naps in the car on the way home, and they arrive at 6 p.m., just as Tom and Jean are finishing chores. There were a couple of rain showers on Sunday morning, but the evening is clear, and Bill decides to change out of his good clothes and get some haylage into the silo.

He starts on a section of alfalfa behind the barn and harvests three loads in the first hour. As each wagon is filled, Jean ferries it up the back lane to the big blue silo beside the barn. There, with the hay-dryer fan howling in the background, Tom has one of the John Deeres hooked up to a silage blower. The blower is a simple machine: a tray to receive the crop from the wagon, an auger to force it into the im-pellers and the actual blower – four impellers, each about two feet long and six inches wide, rotating like propeller blades. Clearance between the impellers and the drum that contains them is measured in thousandths of an inch. As the blower rotates, each pass of an im-peller knocks a handful of haylage out the top – hard enough to drive it 90 feet up a pipe to the top of the silo and often enough to move a half-ton of material every minute.

When he was young and careless, Bill once left a socket and ratchet on the blower after making an adjustment. The vibration of the ma-chine dislodged the ratchet, which fell into the blower. "Well, you know what a ratchet handle is like – it's a steel bar about a half-inch thick. It sheared the handle in half like a twig and, oh, I forget how far away we found it. Way out in the field, anyway."

After the past few days of relatively dry weather, the quality of the crop behind the barn has deteriorated rapidly, and Bill decides to wait to bale what is left there. He moves the operation to Bob Norris's, a mile down the road. The distance complicates the procedure, but a pattern soon develops. Bill, driving the big blue tractor, fills a wagon with the harvester. Bob's son Steve delivers an empty wagon with one of Bill's green John Deere tractors, then ferries the full one up to his house, where Jean waits with the old Mercury truck, the 700-gallon water tank still on the back. She hooks onto the wagon and drives it up the road to the farm, where she exchanges it for the third wagon, which Tom has just emptied into the blower. He uses the sec-ond John Deere to run the blower and the old Ford tractor to park the wagons and power their unloading mechanisms.

That's the way it's supposed to work, but things do not go smoothly. First, the old Ford tractor stalls and cannot be coaxed into starting. The tight schedule is thrown off, leaving Bill fuming in the field, unaware of the reason for the delay. Jean tows the tractor with the old water truck, and it starts for one load, then quits again. When news of this is passed on to Bill, he sends back instructions for Tom to get Tom Moreland to check the points. But Tom is away for the evening. Tom MacFarlane pulls off the distributor cap and rolls the engine over by hand, holding a flashlight to see if the points open and close properly. It's hard to tell. More delay. This time, Bill says to borrow a tractor from Dunc Robertson, a neighbour across the road who has a Ford tractor of similar vintage. But it is 10 o'clock now, and Dunc has gone to bed. Tom pounds on the door until he gets permission to borrow the tractor, promising to disconnect a trailer in the shed. The lights do not work on this tractor, so Tom backs the trailer into the shed by shining the flashlight over his shoulder. "This one doesn't have power steering, either," he mutters, grunting with the effort.

On the next load, Tom discovers that the PTO shaft on one of the wagons will not slide far enough onto the drive unit of the borrowed tractor to lock in place. He fiddles and fusses with it for a while, aware that Bill is waiting for the wagon at the other end and chafing over the delay, and finally decides to unload the wagon even though the shaft is not locked on. It is a potentially dangerous decision – Tom has to stand beside the spinning shaft to operate the blower and watch the wagon. If it flies off the tractor, it could hit him hard enough to break a bone or even knock him into the blower. He watches the shaft carefully, but it stays as tight as if it were glued in place and causes him no further trouble. Tom has, by now, worked the equivalent of a double shift, long enough to be more irritated than amused by the delays. "We just can't seem to get a flow going," he complains. "Once we get going, we almost look like we know what we're doing."

Things are not much smoother at Bill's end. On the outside row, which is the wettest, the harvester plugs four times. Each time, Bill has to stop the machine and clean off the cylinders with his jackknife, laboriously turning the mechanism over by hand to get it all. The wet haylage is greasy, almost slimy. "There's a lot of bejesus red clover in it along there," says Bob. "You get it where it's wet underneath like that, by Christ, and it's just like snot." After an hour of struggling with it, Bill decides to leave the outside row until later.

Even Jean, the perennial optimist, is unhappy. "I hate this," she says, taking care not to stall the old water truck, whose battery is unreliable. "I'm always afraid I'll be the one who does something wrong and holds everybody up." She backs up to a loaded wagon, with Bob holding the tongue for her and hollering, "Little more, c'mon, little more."

"I shouldn't be allowed to do this," she moans. "They know I'm not mechanical." Certainly, her expertise is in the barn with the cows, but with the wagon attached, she expertly double-clutches her way through the gears, babying the ancient truck up hills and using the throttle to smooth out bumps in the road.

By 11 o'clock, it looks as though all the kinks have been worked out, and Bill is obviously raring to keep at it. But he does not want to force Tom to work beyond his limit. He relays a message: "If Tom is tired and wants to stop, we'll quit." He means it, and if Tom says he is too tired to keep going, Bill will not hold it against him.

"No way," Tom says. "Hey, we're on a roll now."

"Yeah, a roll," says Jean dourly. "That's unloading one wagon with nothing going wrong." She goes home to bed, and I take over as truck driver.

The work continues without further problems. It takes Bill 20 minutes to fill a wagon. During that time, it takes me 12 minutes to run up the road with a full wagon and back down with an empty one, and it takes Bob's son Steve 4 minutes each way to ferry the wagons. That's 20 minutes too, so if everything goes well, Bill never has to wait for a fresh wagon: neither does he get a break between loads. I spend 8 out of every 20 minutes waiting, and Steve rests for 12. Tom can unload a wagon in 15 minutes, so he gets a 5-minute rest on every cycle – "enough time to get eaten by the mosquitoes."

The truck trundles noisily up and down the road, its unmuffled exhaust rapping off the darkened houses. A light cloud cover dapples the light from a three-quarter moon, and the sky looks like a painting by Monet. Bob is talkative during the breaks, and in his gruff, don't-mistake-me-for-a-nice-guy way, he can't decide whether to complain about the terrible state of farming or to express his pride in the farm. Bob is a part-time farmer, or at least is considered as such by Revenue Canada. He makes more money at his job than on his farm, so according to Section 31 of the tax law, he can deduct no more than a $5,000 farming loss from his other income in any one year. It's a regulation intended to stitch shut the kind of tax-law loophole that let professional people use a farm as a tax loss while it accumulated equity. But for Bob, who has taken over an unproductive farm that may never make enough money to exceed his income, it is an unwelcome restriction. He does not care about tax breaks or equity or any of that. He has a piece of land he feels attached to and responsible for, the way some people feel about a fragile family heirloom.

"When I get around to doing my income tax, it costs me bejesus about $8,000 or $9,000 to run this christly place, and they won't let me claim all of it. It's a goddamn shame." He shrugs his shoulders expressively. "But I like it." Bob is a natural worrier, though, the kind of person who is uncomfortable without something to complain about. "They say beef prices are up now, but I'm getting bejesus 85 to 90¢ [a pound live weight]. Well, I was getting that 10 years ago. But I could buy a good tractor for $5,000 then, and today it would cost bejesus $35,000. Oh, it's terrible.

"Things are bad all over, though. Now you take the farmers out west, that's really bad. But what are they going to do? There's more wheat than we know what to do with. Everybody's growing the fucking stuff. I don't know what they're going to do. And all them subsidies they give in the Common Market. The Europeans got no goddamn business growing wheat. Now I hear that India is exporting wheat too, and a couple of places in Africa. We shipped grain to those Third World countries for years to get them started, and then, bejesus, they turn around and stab you in the back."

Down in the field, Bill is pawing his way up and down the rows. The big blue tractor is lit up like Stalag 13, a bright intruder in the quiet night. High in the darkened cab, with bugs bouncing brainlessly off the windows, Bill can see the harvester and the maw of the wagon behind and about 50 feet of row ahead. This is Bill at his best – intense, with the kind of nervous energy one sees in athletes during the big game. He is half twisted around in his seat, paying more attention to the machines behind than the row ahead. At the back of the cab is a control box fitted with a dozen toggle switches labelled with international symbols, the effect of which is as confusing as a jetliner's cockpit. Bill pays no attention to the labels anyway, working the panel by feel, his eyes on the machines. In the harsh glare of the tractor lights, the rows look brown and lifeless, but this crop was cut later than the one at home, and the steady stream of haylage shooting from the harvester spout into the wagon is rich and green. "It doesn't look too good," Bill says, "but it's okay underneath."

Inside the cab, the terrifying howl of the harvester loses its edge, and the sense of isolation from the night is strong. The noise and vibration are numbing. Bill turns on the radio, but all he can get is an all-night country station, and he soon switches it off. "I prefer country music to pop, but it all sounds the same after a while." He alternates between silence and hurtin' music, putting up with each in turn for as long as he can. At 2 o'clock, Bill sends another message to Tom. "Ask him if he wants to work all night. It's up to him. Whatever he wants to do is fine with me."

Tom grins at this but is not going to be tricked into making the boss's decisions for him. "Tell him I don't care. Whatever he says."

"That's fine," Bill says, who obviously wants to keep going. "He's younger than me anyway. Of course, he's got the worst job." And so they continue, dividing the night into 20-minute intervals. Watches become irrelevant; time is measured in loads – by 2:20, 11 loads are in the silo.

Bob has exhausted the subject of farming and turns to his other hobby – auctions. He collects glass and on most weekends attends at least one auction to add to his assortment of bowls, dishes and vases. He now has 4,000 pieces, ranging from simple hobnail and swirl patterns to the bizarre colours of carnival and Depression glass, and some exquisite pieces of Royal Nippon. He has an enthusiast's pride in the collection, which fills two china cabinets, a sideboard and almost every horizontal surface in the house. The rest of the pieces are packed in crates and stored in the attic, but he has a photo album that details each one. Like most collectors, though, Bob is as fascinated by the process of acquisition as by the objects themselves, and he remembers the circumstance as well as the price of each piece. And like many auction-goers, he cannot resist a good deal.

"Look at this," he says between loads, indicating a pile of wood and canvas heaped on the backyard picnic table. "Know what it is? An iceboat. See, here's the mast and the boom, the sail and the jib or whatever they call it, and there's the skates. Now look at these wooden rings" – he holds up a solid-wood ring holding the sail to the mast. "Bejesus, they don't do it that way anymore. No, the way it was made, it's about 1900. Know what I paid for it? Two dollars. I don't think anyone else knew what it was."

Later, when Bob shows the iceboat to Bill, Bill nods his head politely, but at home he says, "What's he going to do with an iceboat? He's already got the house full of all that glass. Just can't pass up a bargain, I guess."

Eileen giggles. "Remember the bras, Bill? Bob was at a sale, and there was this box full of brassieres. Well, nobody wanted it, of course, so Bob bought it for, oh, I don't know, two or three dollars. Then he didn't know what to do with them, so he tried to give them away. For *months* afterwards, he'd dig around in this box until he found one he'd try to get you to take. They were just awful old things, but he'd hold one up and say, 'There, that's about your size,' but they were all just huge. Poor Bob, I don't think he ever understood why nobody wanted one."

By 3:30, the moon is obscured by an ever-thickening cloud cover, and everyone is getting tired. "Well, he's getting bejesus 3 or 3½ loads an hour. There's no christly way he'll be done in less than four hours."

In the field, Bill counts the remaining windrows and says, "About 10 more loads." He consults a pocket-sized notebook in which he has been checking off the loads. "Let's see, we've already got 14, so 24 loads in 28 acres, that's about right. Normal is a load per acre and 3 loads an hour. We might get done by 7." Bob sends a thermos of hot, strong coffee up to Tom, who is fading very quickly. The coffee gives him the boost he needs to get through the dark before the dawn. "It's wonderful what a cup of coffee will do for you at 4 in the morning," he says.

At this time of year, a week before the summer solstice, the sky turns grey at 4:15 and is light at 4:30, when Eileen appears with a package of ham sandwiches for everyone. At 5, Jean arrives for work, and the two women start milking, with help from Tom between loads. "Yeah, that's the problem with having cows," says Bill. "They slow you up. But they pay the bills, so I guess I can't complain." Bob has to leave for work at 6:30. Bill hears later that he napped on the seat of the truck while his crew put up road signs.

Working in the strangeness of the morning light, Bill finishes the field, including the troublesome outside row, at 8 o'clock. An hour later, he and Tom have all the equipment put away and can forget about harvesting haylage for another year. But the sky is clear and sunny, and if the haylage is done, the hay is not. While Tom sits down to breakfast – bacon and eggs and perked coffee – Bill grabs an apple and a glass of milk before fuelling and greasing the tractor so that Tom can begin raking as soon as he has eaten. Before he sits down, Bill starts his father cutting yet another field of hay.

By 8 o'clock that night, when Tom goes home, they have another 600 bales of hay in the barn. Tom has worked 39 hours straight, from Sunday morning to Monday night. "I haven't slept like that in years," he says the next day. "I woke up in the same position I laid down in. Audrey had to go downstairs 'cause she couldn't stand the snoring."

———————

On Tuesday, the weather is still sunny, so while Russell rakes hay and Bill gets ready to spray the grain at Ed Johnston's, Tom cultivates corn. The plants are about a foot high now – too high to be cultivated, really, but the weather has not cooperated. What was a green fuzz on the field two weeks ago has turned into weeds, grass and some sturdy stalks of alfalfa, now no more than a weed itself. Tom is driving up and down the rows on the old Ford, shiny new distributor prominent on its rusty side, carefully spaced cultivator teeth combing the earth behind like an overgrown garden hoe.

The tractor barely straddles two rows of corn; the cultivator works the centre space below the tractor seat, the two spaces the wheels ride in and half of the two spaces beyond that – four rows in all. And Tom follows the four-row groups left by Jim Greenlees' planter. The gaps between the teeth for the corn rows are only about eight inches wide, leaving little room for error. "The problem is if you hit one row of corn, you hit all four," Tom says. "If you're not paying attention, you're cultivating corn instead of weeds." He has his shirt off – the back strap of his red suspenders fits in the hollow between the long muscles of his back. He first leans on the right fender, trying to keep the front tractor wheel about four inches from the corn row. "When you first start, you can't take your eyes off the front wheel. If you try to look back at the cultivator, you're driving all over the corn. Now I'm more used to it, and I can glance back every once in a while."

It is a tiresome job, and Tom soon leans on the left fender to give his neck a break. After an hour, he is good enough at it to sit upright and squint along the radiator cap on the front of the tractor without going astray. In the few spots he does wander off course, he wipes out no more than a half-dozen plants from each row. It is hot, dusty, finicky, monotonous work, but it is better than working in the mow. "I don't mind this too much," he says, surveying the 20 acres he has yet to do. "But if there was another 100 acres of it, I think I'd be down the road."

Cultivating corn is a chore traditionally done by the hired man, and Russell explains why: "In the old days, we used to harrow the corn when it was the size it is now, about halfway to your knees. You pulled out quite a bit of corn, but you got all the weeds. But you see, in those days, corn seed was cheap and we put it on thick. So that was something you got the hired man to do, because if you did it yourself and ever looked over your shoulder, you'd quit 'cause you'd see all the corn you were pulling up."

The cultivator is set so that the wide shovels ride about an inch under the surface of the soil. They cause the dirt to explode in front of the tines, and it leaps into the air like a cheap special effect in a second-rate movie. As the teeth slice through the soil, they cut the weeds off at the ankles and leave them lying on the soil to wither and die. "You don't want to go too deep, or you'll lose too much moisture from the soil," Tom explains. It is a typical farmer's comment – two days of sunshine after weeks of rain, and he is already worried about a drought.

Bill has been complaining for weeks about not being able to spray his grain crop with herbicide. He has made long speeches about how wasteful and irresponsible it is to spray in windy conditions. Several times, he has stopped in front of the house to lift his hat and scratch his head and say, "Sometimes I wish I was the kind of guy who could just go out and spray the stuff and not worry about it. Lots of them do, you know, and don't give a darn about the drift." But every day has been too windy or too rainy. He has given up on the fields on the home farm – they will have to suffer the competition of a few weeds this year. The 40 acres on Ed Johnston's place, which were planted a few days later, have more weeds. They *have* to be sprayed, and this is the last week it can be done – already, the crop is too tall to be driven over without some damage, and soon, the grain heads will open and prevent the spray from reaching the weeds.

The air is calm on Tuesday morning, and Bill struggles to get things ready before the wind picks up, as he knows it will. Because of milking, he has no hope of getting started before 10 o'clock, and every delay is making him more irritable. The fact that he has had only one night's sleep since the all-night haylage harvest is probably having an effect too. "Aahhh," he growls in frustration when he sees he has to shuffle equipment around the undersized machine shed to get at the sprayer. "Everything takes so frigging long."

Agriculture Canada and the Ontario Ministry of the Environment agree that spray drift begins and field spraying operations should cease when wind speeds exceed 10 kilometres per hour. By the time Bill is ready to spray, wind speed is almost twice that, with gusts that threaten to blow off his hat. But Bill can wait no longer; he sets his jaw and begins spraying. Ed Johnston, digging one of his interminable ditches on the other side of the field, wrinkles his nose. "That stuff stinks, don't it?" he asks.

Still in a bad mood, Bill shakes his head. "I don't know. This barley is so tall, maybe we'll have to rely on the spray drift to get down to the weeds. Maybe it'll kind of swirl down there." He doesn't sound convinced.

Back at the house for lunch, he tells Tom they are going to start baling in the field behind the barn after lunch and will haul the wagonloads of hay down the road to repay Bob Norris.

"Have you heard a weather forecast?" Tom asks.

"The last one I heard said good till Thursday. I don't want to listen again in case they change their minds."

But as Bill steps out of the house after lunch, raindrops stop him in his tracks. His shoulders sag. "Somebody get me a gun," he says, cocking an index finger at his temple. "On second thought, never mind. I'd probably shoot myself in the foot."

Fortunately, it is only a sun shower and will not stop Russell from baling or Bill from finishing the spraying – *nothing* could stop Bill from finishing the spraying. Tom will have to finish cultivating the corn tomorrow and the next day.

But first, they have to set up the bale elevator. Bob's barn is small, with room to stanchion only 20 cows, but it has a full-sized mow. At the top of the front wall is the mow door, hinged on the bottom to flop down and pointed at the top to fit under the peak of the barn roof. Last summer, after filling the mow, Bob pulled the door up and wired it shut. Now, a dozen bales remain in the mow, and the wire, which has to be undone before the elevator can be set up, is more than 20 feet above the bare boards of the mow floor. Bob is not around, and Bill's irritation is once again evident. "C'mon, Bob, where are you? This should have been done."

He climbs into the mow and, without hesitation, shinnies a dozen feet up a barn beam with the grace and agility of a cat. Standing on a narrow cross beam, he shuffles sideways, jamming the ends of his fingers into gaps between the barn boards, until he reaches a smaller elevator (used to carry bales the length of the mow) that hangs from the peak at one end and rests on the cross beam under the door. Bill climbs onto it, one foot on each rail, and reaches for the wire. He is a couple of feet short.

"See if you can find a ladder, Tom," he calls down. Tom finds a wooden ladder in the drive shed, but it offers no height advantage.

As he is putting it away again, Bob arrives with Tom Payne, a friend from work whose family owns a farm a couple of concessions over.

Bob is also tired, and he looks harried. He stumps around the barnyard and climbs into the mow a couple of times without accomplishing anything beyond entertaining his guests with a demonstration of imaginative invective. Finally, he produces an aluminum ladder, but it, too, is short. "This asshole of a thing is no good," he hollers, this time starting with body parts. "It's nothing but a pain in the nuts." Bill and Tom wink at each other, grinning hugely at each new outburst. Tom makes a couple of trips up the aluminum ladder with a bale of hay, which Bill sets crosswise on the elevator, then stands on them. It is a caricature of folly, as dangerous as stacking books on a kitchen chair, but by standing on tiptoe, Bill is just able to reach the wire.

"Jesus Christ, you be goddamn careful up there, Bill," says Bob, turning religious. "That christly thing isn't wired down." Nevertheless, Bill gets the door unwired, and Bob lowers it with a rope. Together, they align the elevator in front of it. The door is higher than Bill's, and the angle of the elevator is steep—last year, when Bob was unloading a wagon, a bale curled back at the top of the elevator, cartwheeled down the length of the elevator and caught him in the back of the head as he turned for another bale, knocking him unconscious. "Nearly broke my christly neck," he says. "Had trouble with it all winter, bejesus, and it's still not right."

When Bill and Tom leave—Bill to finish the spraying, Tom to get a full wagon from Russell, who has already started baling—Tom Payne starts razzing Bob about his habit of tying the cows in the barn every night. "Why don't you leave these cows out, Bob? I don't enjoy shovelling shit enough to do it all year long." The answer is that since Bob drained his fields and cleaned up the fencerows, he has no pasture left. He has refenced a section of land around the barn, but the drainage is still poor there, and despite the 18 tandem dumptruckloads of crushed gravel Bob put in the area last year, it is a quagmire of mud and manure. Bob tries to deflect Tom's merciless sarcasm by asking his advice about a calf standing in the yard.

"Do you think I can breed that heifer this fall, Tom? Think she's big enough?"

"I dunno, Bob. She'd look a lot taller if she wasn't up to her knees in shit."

By 8 o'clock that night, when the dew forces them to quit and go home for supper, there are seven wagonloads – 1,000 bales in all – in Bob's mow, Bill has finished the spraying, and Eileen was once again needed in the barn to help Jean with the milking. After the last load, Tom takes the elevator back home. The hay they will bale tomorrow has not been rained on, and Bill is going to keep it for himself.

On Wednesday, Bill puts the last 1,000 bales from Bob's place in his barn, and on Thursday, after Tom finishes cultivating the corn, he puts in another 1,600 from his own place. Bill, who described the hay he gave to Bob as "not bad," grabs a handful of the stuff going into his own barn and says, "Now that's real hay – green as the day it was cut, but dry."

––––––––

Audrey, Tom's wife, works day and evening shifts at a nursing home for senior citizens, and because of her schedule, combined with Tom's 12-hour days, they see very little of each other for several days at a time. Lately, with Tom working extra hours, they have become almost strangers. So on Wednesday and Thursday, Audrey comes out to the farm to lend a hand and spend some time with her husband. "The bales were light, so we could really pack them in tight," Tom grins. "But Audrey thought they were heavy enough."

"God, the first load just about killed me," Audrey admits. "I haven't done this in 10 years. But after the third load, it got a lot easier." Today she climbs into the mow to help Tom stack.

"I don't know," Bill mumbles, just loud enough for them to hear, "a young couple like that up in the mow." He shakes his head with exaggerated disapproval, then says more loudly, "You keep your mind on your work, Tom."

He needn't have worried – Audrey comes down before the first wagon is unloaded. "God, there's no air up there," she gasps and climbs on the wagon to throw bales for Bill. He calls her "Slinger" Mac-Farlane and teases her about her throwing arm.

"Yeah, well, when I went to work last night, I could really throw those patients around. Of course," she adds, struggling to get her fingers under the baler twine, "that was easier because you could get a better grip on them."

Shortly before supper, the bale kicker breaks again – the same part as the last time. "Judas Priest!" Bill exclaims. "Son of a perch." He is really irked. The part can't be welded again, so he calls Oakley Clow at the John Deere dealership. "They already had it on order, but now they've got it on special order, and they're going to courier it up. It'll be here in the morning. Hmph," he snorts. "It had better be here in the morning. Oh well, I can't complain. I've already got more hay off today than I expected to. A fellow shouldn't complain too hard."

For the first time this week, Tom and Jean do not have to work late. On his way home, Tom says, "Bill's got another 70 acres of his own hay to get in, plus another 100 acres he rented when the hay looked short. He's got more hay now than he knows what to do with. I don't know where he's going to put it."

And so it goes. Day after day through the last half of June, another thousand bales or so each day. Tom cuts the field behind the cow pasture and finds it full of thistles as tall as the hay. "I don't know where they came from," Bill says. "There's never been thistles there before." For a while, he calls that field the Christmas tree patch because of the weeds' shape and regular spacing. Tom makes another discovery in that field and reports it when he comes up for lunch.

"I was cutting along and just got a glimpse of something down by the wheel of the tractor. At first I thought it was a nest of skunks, but then I realized it was three baby hawks. I managed to miss them" — a complicated feat, requiring enough reflexes and coordination to jump on the brake and clutch, turn the steering wheel and pull a lever to raise the mower-conditioner all at the same time — "and they kind of waddled off and hid under a windrow.

"At first, I kind of ducked my head, thinking I might get it from the mother. She was flying around, all right, but she didn't bother me. By the time I came around the field the next time, I was hoping one of those sea gulls that are always hanging around would go over to look at them and get its head pulled off by the mother hawk."

"Tom," Eileen says, "you sadist."

"Oh, I hate those things. They're nothing but scavengers."

They consider what to do about the baby hawks. Nobody knows if the mother will abandon them if they are handled by humans, but it is plain that they will die if nothing is done. Bill hasn't got time to do anything about them himself, but he asks me to look after them. The hawks are large and gangly but very young, and only a few dark feathers poke out of white down, as if escaping from a pillow. When approached, they spread their wings and open their mouths menacingly. But it is only a gape reflex — they are hungry and scared, and they allow themselves to be carried to the nearest fence line without protest. A parent, with the telltale white rump of a marsh hawk, circles overhead but does not attack, and when the babies are placed in the shade of some long grass, she floats away. A severed leg found near the nest indicates there was a fourth chick that was never found, and Russell uncovered the body of one of the other three when ploughing in the fall. It was right next to where it was moved and was almost fully feathered, suggesting that it had survived several weeks after the move. Of the other two, there was no trace, except perhaps among the indistinguishable predators that coast above the fields with hungry grace.

––––––

The days now join together seamlessly, blurred less by the overlapping cycles of cutting, raking and baling than by the merciless oppression of a sudden late-June heat wave. The workdays are long, with barely enough time after morning milking to get the equipment fuelled, greased and adjusted before the dew has dried and it is time to roll into the fields. The sun is relentless – high and blindingly pale in a humid blue sky. There is no shade and no respite from the heat, for although the blue tractor has air-conditioning, Bill will not use it. "It's not bad when you're in the cab," he says, "but when you have to get out, it's like getting punched in the stomach."

Late one afternoon, tired from a grinding day's work and made careless by the numbing heat of the sun, Russell takes a fall. Getting off the tractor to make an adjustment to the baler, he swings himself down off the wrong side; that is, the right-hand side, where the platform is cluttered with pedals and levers. His trousers catch on the brake pedal, and he topples from the three-foot-high platform onto the concrete-hard ground, scraping his shin in the process. For an 80-year-old man, it is a serious fall, but Russell gets to his feet and, after wrapping his shin in a clumsy bandage, carries on. With the stubbornness that often comes when people hurt themselves through their own clumsiness, he does not want to stop what he is doing or let the others make a fuss.

Later, though, he is more forthcoming. "When something like that happens, I just let myself go – I just try to relax completely. Still, that's quite a fall, y'know. But I'm pretty hard to kill." This last is said with a grin and a wink, but he soon turns sombre. "Not like my brother Art – it didn't take him long to die. He was only 70 years old, so nobody thought he'd be the next to go. My other brother Paul, he was 84 when he had a stroke. But 70, now, that's three score and ten, so I guess you can't complain about that.

"I used to see Art quite a bit. Sometimes he'd be over at my place in the morning before I got back from the barn. Oh, he wouldn't stay too long and off he'd go, but we'd have time for a chat. He was pretty much retired. They've got a lot of young people over there, and they like to drive the tractors. 'Course, that's about all I do here is drive the tractor, but there's always a job for me. They didn't have much for him to do over there."

Started on this line of thought, he carries it through to the end, his age giving a weight to the words that no young person could achieve. "Well, I guess I'm going to die soon too. I don't mind. I'm not afraid to die. I've had a long life and a good one. I've done a lot, and I've got nothing to worry about. It'd just be fine anytime they're ready to take me." He mulls this over for a moment, perhaps surprised that he could say it and mean it. "Only I would sort of hate to leave Ruth, the way she is now. You know, she could never stay alone. So maybe they'll keep me hanging on for a while to look after her." Love comes to this, eventually: a willingness to outlive your partner, so it is you who endures a lonely, perhaps institutionalized, old age while the one you love finds release in the grave.

The next morning, when Russell is ready to start baling, Bill says to him, "Now be sure you get off on the right side of the tractor."

"Yeah. Well, I knew I shouldn't have." But within half an hour, Russell is clambering off on the wrong side again, saving himself a few steps at the risk of another fall.

Bill, waiting for the first wagon to be filled, watches him and shakes his head. But when Russell gets off to adjust the bale tension and leaves the baler in gear, Bill tears across the field and hollers at him over the noise of the machinery. "Father, shut the baler off whenever you get off the tractor." It is an elementary safety rule, but Russell is of a generation that did not invent the safe workplace, and there is more exasperation in Bill's tirade than any expectation of change. Russell usually tries to keep the peace by obeying Bill's safety rules – at least when Bill is around – but today, he forgot.

These bales are going into the barn at Pearl's. Except for a pocket at the back that will hold about 1,000 bales – needed for the second cut in July – the home barn is full. The peak of the roof, once so impossibly high, is now too low to stand up under. And the mow at Pearl's is already starting to bulge.

Bill shakes his head. "Holy baldhead. You walk these fields in May, and they're all like this" – he holds a hand halfway to his knees – "and you wouldn't think there was anything in them. Now look at this." The field they are baling today belongs to Ed Johnston's daughter and her husband, and Bill rents it only if he figures hay will be short. This year, the grass was chest-high and so thick that Tom had to gear back to half speed to cut it without plugging the mower-conditioner. Now that it is raked for baling, the windrows are waist-high – Bill has to jump them to walk across the field – and so close, he can touch adjoining rows with his outstretched hands.

In the shade, the heat is withering; in the sun, it is breathtaking. Russell, with red forearms and a peeling nose, carries on, relentlessly forcing the clanking, whirling baler around the field in its ever-tightening spiral. In machine years, the baler is as old as he is, and each round is a contest of will against metal fatigue. Bill keeps his head down, sparing no energy for the garish colours of summer. As hot as it is in the field, the heat in the mow is multiplied to the nth power – the barn at Pearl's is an airless steel box set under the blazing sun, which is a reasonable definition of a solar cooker. Stacking bales in the mow is like doing an aerobic workout in a sauna. Between loads, Tom drags himself across the barnyard to an outside water tap on the back of Pearl's house. He is wearing torn jeans – it is impossible to work with hay in shorts – but no shirt under the red suspenders, and the engineer's cap has been replaced by a red bandanna headband. The torrents of sweat float pieces of chaff from his shoulders to his waist. When he reaches the tap, he carefully removes the headband, rinses it in the cold water and wipes his face, neck and arms before taking a drink.

The heat and dust are starting to take their toll on Tom, who felt ill on the weekend and is still not quite right. "I don't know, I just don't feel like my usual self. I tried to treat it with some, uh, liquid medication on the weekend, but it didn't help much. I just went to bed."

Later, Bill says, "Look at this, it's only 2 o'clock, and I feel like quitting." He feeds 5,000 bales of hay in an average year, maybe 6,000 at the most. By day's end, the counter on the baler will top 8,000, and he has not even started the second cut. He is understandably sick of baling, but he has hay amounting to about 1,000 bales ready to be brought in tomorrow and another 50 acres of hayfield that hasn't been cut yet. "I'm not going to cut any hay on the weekend," he announces. "I'm sick of it, and I think Tom needs a break too. But I wonder if I dare phone Mangans and ask them to take that front field at Pearl's tomorrow." He rinses his mouth with a bubble of air, as he does when he can't make up his mind, and goes back to work.

Mangans – never "the Mangans" – are a local farm family whose name is synonymous with size and efficiency. "When they start in the hay," says Bill, "they really go at it. They have a big crew of guys, and they don't stop until they're done." Mangans have a round baler, a machine that rolls the hay into 1,200-pound spools that are moved with tractors – no wagons, no elevators, no mows, no manhandling the bales. "It's not a bad system," says Bill, "if you're set up for it. I'm not." Mangans have a large, almost military operation that seems dedicated to the notion that growth is as important as profit. As well as milking cows, they do a lot of buying and selling, and they specialize in buying up truckloads of Holsteins that they ship to customers in the southern United States, a business that is long on organization, risk and profit.

The empire began with two brothers, Neil and Arnold, who married girls who were cousins. According to Russell, they were both aggressive women, "the kind that help a man get ahead if he wants to but maybe make life tough for him if he doesn't want to." Arnold and Neil wanted to, and they both built prosperous farms. Neil sired five boys and two girls; Arnold, five girls and two boys. These boys, Tom and Eddie, run the farm with Arnold. On the "Mangan Team Farms" calendar hanging in Tom Moreland's workshop – that's the kind of farm they run: one that gives out calendars to its business associates, like a bank – are two pictures. The first, with a neat brick house and farmstead, is labelled "The Home Farm," and the other, dominated by a huge dairy barn, "The Udder Place." Bill went to school with Ed Mangan, a muscular man with close-cropped hair and a military bearing. Bill calls him about the hay that evening. "It turns out Eddie's going to have an extra man tomorrow, and he'd be glad to have it."

———

The heat, so hard on those who have to work in it, is a boon to the crops, especially the corn. It is growing daily, the long, narrow leaves arched gracefully toward the dark earth as if flung back by the thrust of the stalks leaping out of the ground to clutch the sun. There are farmers who claim they can stand in their fields and hear the corn growing, the tissues forming and changing so rapidly it is audible. In one 3-week period in late June and early July, the corn is in danger of achieving lift-off: it springs from something less than knee height to over Bill's head.

BARLEY STALK

It is too late to cultivate the weeds a second time, but it doesn't matter. The corn is now like a primeval rain forest in its greed for sunshine, the leaves having crisscrossed themselves into a canopy—no weeds will prosper in their shade. Indeed, squatting in a grove of cornstalks with the rustle of leaves arm wrestling for more sunlight overhead and the cool moistness of the bare earth underneath, one can even find a measure of relief from the heat.

The barley is less appreciative of the sun than the corn is, but it, too, has filled out enough to shade the ground. No longer the whisker bristles of May or the unkempt lawn Bill was reluctant to drive over with his spraying equipment, the barley is now knee-high. The topmost node of the stalks, about the fourth or fifth one formed, is a hollow vortex, a swirl of leaves disappearing down its own drain hole. Over the course of a week or so, little topknots of stiff green hairs sprout through the drainpipes of all the barley stalks in one field. By the time they are a couple of inches high, the whole field has taken on a fuzzy look, like an out-of-focus photograph.

The hairs are the plant's sex organs— 50 or 60 of them, each ending at the tip of an unformed seed grain. As the hairs, themselves four or five inches long, push up through the drain hole, it splits open and falls away, exposing the whole grain head. The stalks, all planted at the same time, perform this last step in sudden unison. The whole field appears to "head out" overnight—one day, it looks like fuzzy grass; the next, it has burst into a swath of grain that will soon need to be harvested.

Now, in the first week of July, the bright

green grain hairs are fading in the hot sun, and the first tinge of brown is starting to appear. The individual grains, empty on the day they burst from the stalk, have filled with a watery white germ, and the swelling has pushed the hairs apart and given the heads a bourgeois plumpness. By the end of the week, the grains have firmed up enough to be chewable, and Bill pops a few into his mouth as he pulls more thistles out of the field in front of the barn. He is happy with the look of the crop and expects to harvest it in three or four weeks.

"Hope there aren't too many weeds in it, though," he says.

For all the difference the blast-furnace heat of July makes to the lives of the other living things on the farm, it has the most effect on the cows.

"The heat is a lot harder on them than the cold," Bill says, then reflects on the corollary to that statement. "And it's a lot easier to keep them warm than it is to keep them cool." Because they carry around in their rumens the equivalent of a 40-gallon self-perpetuating hot spring, cattle need never fear even the fiercest cold. They may lose the tips of their ears to frostbite, and they are as susceptible as any creature to drafts and freezing rain or the debilitations of hunger and thirst, but even newborn calves, once suckled and licked dry by their mothers, can be safely exposed to minus-20-degree temperatures.

But they are less well equipped to rid themselves of unwanted heat, and high-producing cows such as Bill's have their thermostats turned up already. Their internal furnaces are well stoked with high-protein, high-energy feed, and when the air temperature exceeds 80 degrees F, they start to suffer. Milk production is always the first to go, the first sign that some microchip has shorted out in the finely tuned bovine circuit board. This is soon followed by a loss of appetite, then stress weakens the immune system, leading to an increase in mastitis and other infections. The cows respond to this stimulus like a supportive community to a grieving family: they draw closer. Instead of spreading out across the paddock to stretch out on the cool earth, they herd together, mirroring each other's heat and blocking out whatever languid breeze may disturb the viscous air.

When Ridout calves in early July, she develops milk fever, or hypocalcemia, a shortage of calcium in the blood caused by the sudden filling of the udder with calcium-rich milk after parturition. It causes paralysis – typically, the cows lie down with their heads curled back to their tails – and death occurs within hours. Milk fever affects about 1 cow out of 15, almost always the best and most productive ones in the herd, those with the genetic potential to drain themselves of calcium in one filling of an udder. James Herriot, the English veterinarian who has charmed readers worldwide with his stories of life in the Yorkshire Dales, writes eloquently about his feelings of helplessness as he watched a struggling young farmer's prize animal die; and later, when the condition's cause and cure (a few hundred cc's of a calcium solution given intravenously) were established, of his wonder and pride that cows so close to death would rise within minutes of being treated and carry on as if nothing had happened. When Paul O'Neill comes out to repeat this miracle for Ridout, he mentions that he is treating a lot of milk fever this summer, probably because of the heat.

"Yeah," says Jean, "their bodies just aren't supplying them with the stuff they need."

On the second day of the heat wave, Bill says, "I feel like I've died and gone to hell." He watches the cows, who are standing in their stalls with their heads down, panting. He knows he can ease their discomfort by reducing the amount of high-energy feed they eat. "By rights, we should cut back on their feed a little bit and give them a break — not work them so hard." He shrugs helplessly. "But that doesn't pay the bills. The milk is still up, but once you let it get down, it's really hard to get it back up again. We'll just have to assume the heat won't last too long."

A couple of days later, he is taking the cows' temperatures morning, noon and night. From a normal of 101 degrees, some of them are up to 105, and even after being outside all night, they still top 102. He treats the worst ones with acetylsalicylic acid, one whopping tablet three times a day. "But you can only do that for about three days," he says. "Aspirin's hard on their stomachs." At the end of that regimen, he begins spraying them with water to lower their temperatures. Morning and afternoon, as the cows are let out of the barn, he catches the most affected cows in a jury-rigged chute formed by a pair of gates. While Tom holds the gates shut on them, Jean hoses them down by holding her thumb on the end of a garden hose. The treatment works twice: the cold water cools them, then the evaporation of their wet coats continues the process. "I figure you have to get their heads," Jean says, "because if your head is cool, so are you." It's hard to tell if the cows enjoy being sprayed, but they shake their heads like dogs after a swim and seem in better spirits — at least for a while.

After a week of temperatures in the 90s, Bill is spraying *all* the cows. Each session takes an hour, two more hours out of a day already crammed full of chores and mowing and baling and sweat. Tom, who hasn't quit work on time for a month or more, is starting to grumble. "These cows aren't getting enough forage, that's why they're so hot. You know, we're putting some nice hay in the barn, but it's still pretty hot stuff." He means it is rich in alfalfa. "You've got to have some grass hay for these cows."

Bill is concerned too. Despite his efforts, milk production is starting to fall off, and he is doubting the wisdom of his earlier decision not to reduce their feed. "It's easy to say now with hindsight that we should have cut back on their feed, but it gets hot and you give them some aspirin or you spray a few, then it gets hotter, so you do a few more, and that's what happens. Pretty soon you're spraying them all."

And their temperatures are still high. "Heat stress is a cumulative sort of thing." Bill glances around the barn for a metaphor, and his eye falls on a light bulb. "It's like an electrical wire. It's so heavy, and it's made to take so much current, so much amperage, so much heat. You can put a little overload on it, then a little more and a little more, then pretty soon, it just starts to overheat and burn out. That's the way it is with the cows. The way we feed them, they're close to the limit already. You get weather like this, and they can take it for a day or two or three, but then they start to overload and they get too hot and their bodies can't get rid of the heat, and that's it. The vet says that when it gets to be too much, they start panting and working to cool down, but after a while, even that starts to work against them. They reach a point where they're working so hard to get rid of the heat, they're actually making themselves hotter.

"Some people will stay out in the sun and get heatstroke, but most of us have enough sense to jump in a lake when it gets too hot. These guys, well, maybe they would if they could." He laughs. "I remember we went over to Pykes' on Wolfe Island in one of these hot, muggy periods. We got over there, and they were milking 110 cows, and they were all out in the St. Lawrence River up to their necks. You looked out, and it seemed as though the water was full of floating cow heads. It was strange, but they just got too hot and went in the water till they cooled off. If we had a lake here, I suppose our cows would do the same. But we don't."

After 10 days, the vicious heat wave finally breaks, but as Bill predicted, it is weeks before milk production returns to normal.

————

The second cut of hay fits seamlessly into the first. One day, Bill is baling "a little corner across the road, about 400 or 500 bales," and the next, he is back in front of the house, where he started on June 1, five weeks ago. There have been several such "little corners," and Tom's enthusiasm drops to a new low with each one. "Yeah," he says sardonically, "we've got to piddle around at it till we get to the second cut. We don't like to stop because we might lose momentum."

"Goodness gracious," says Russell with a slow shake of his head, "it just goes on and on and on. We should be thankful, y'know" – he looks over at a field braided in windrows – "but, boy, it's hard."

One day, Bill does a little work for Dunc Robertson, his neighbour across the road. Dunc broke a part on his field mower, and he asked Bill to come over with his mower-conditioner to give him a hand. A lot of Dunc's land is pretty rocky, so Bill is not enthusiastic, but he goes anyway. "Well, I could hardly refuse, especially after waking him up in the middle of the night to borrow his tractor." It takes him about an hour to cut Dunc's field, and he finishes without breaking anything. "That's the other side of having neighbours," Bill says. "It's nice to have them around when you need something, but when they need something, you pretty much have to do it for them. I mean, I don't mind, but sometimes it's a pain." For all his generosity, Bill can be self-centred when it comes to his farm. As much as he has grown up with and understands in the pit of his stomach the concept of neighbourliness, it is always a bit of a surprise to him that his neighbours sometimes don't realize that Bill's farm is more important than theirs.

To some extent, the same can be said of his relationships with his employees. He doesn't ask Tom or Jean to do anything he won't do, but he occasionally forgets that they don't have as much at stake in the success of the farm as he does. Bill pays Tom a salary of $1,300 a month, which works out to minimum wage if broken down to an hourly rate. Tom's benefits amount to two meals a day, the use of Bill's truck to drive back and forth to work and as much milk as he can drink. "So we figure that, realistically, Tom's wages amount to $18,360," says Eileen, who makes out his paycheque every two weeks. "Plus, he gets a side of beef every year." For this kind of work in this part of Canada, it is a fair wage.

In return, Tom works 12 hours a day and gets every second weekend off. He is also supposed to get every second Wednesday off, but he seldom takes it, preferring to work on the farm instead of sitting around his rented row house in Gananoque. He is allowed an hour to eat lunch, but he always gets up from the table with Bill, who goes back to work as soon as he has eaten. The extra hours he works are reimbursed in one way or another – perhaps some extra cash or an occasional long weekend to go hunting or camping with his family.

Jean, who serves as record keeper as well as worker, earns $1,600 a month plus the use of the truck, and Russell takes a token $400 a month – enough to pay his bills, but a pittance, considering the work he does. In addition, he receives $2,500 every six months as a payment on the $45,000 no-interest mortgage Bill agreed to when he took over the farm. Eileen takes $1,000 a month for her work, and it costs Bill about $4,000 a year for payroll expenses: pension, unemployment insurance and workers' compensation payments.

Last year, he paid out almost $55,000 in wages and benefits. He sees himself as a fair employer, someone who treats his workers with respect and who offers them good working conditions, responsibility and a wage that is at the upper end of the normal range. As self-assessments go, this one is quite reasonable, and for most of the year, Tom and Jean would probably agree. Lately, though, there have been too many days that have finished late, too many extra hours that interfered with their families' plans, too many assumptions that the needs of Bill's cows and crops must come before their own. In the sweat and ache of hard work in the hot sun, small issues become big ones. While other people are playing at the beach or relaxing in the shade because it is too hot to do anything else, Tom and Jean are working harder than ever. At a time of year when most people are taking vacations and feeling laid-back, Tom and Jean are working until dark every evening and giving up their days off.

It is no consolation to them that Bill is right there beside them – it is, after all, his farm. As 80-degree days climb into the 90s and the first cut becomes the second, Tom and Jean grow restive. They are both under pressure from their families to spend more time at home, and although they do not say anything to Bill, they grumble to each other about the long hours. Still, they both know that the workload on any farm is heaviest in summer, and despite their complaints about the long hours, they *do* care about the farm in a proprietary way. So they become irritable at home as well as at work, but they do not talk to Bill about their concerns.

One day, Audrey stops by to visit Tom and gets talked into ferrying an empty wagon back to the field where Russell is baling. The second-cut hay is dry and dusty, and it rolls off the back of the baler in a black cloud that makes it look as if the baler is on fire. "Isn't that something?" she says, watching as Russell fills the last corner of the wagon. "Eighty years old and still going like that." When he comes over to change wagons, Russell pulls his jug of water from underneath the tractor seat and offers her a drink.

"I don't want that," she scoffs.

"Don't want that?" Russell says, all round-eyed and offended.

"It hasn't got any rum in it, has it?"

"No," Russell admits, shaking his head and grinning.

"Well, it's no use to me."

Russell tips back the jug, watching Audrey out of the corner of his eye. "Ah, that's good stuff," he says, lowering the jug. "That's Adam's ale. You can't beat that."

"You've got a hole in your hat, Russell."

"Yes, the bugs get in there, and I've got a sunburn on the top of my head too."

"Well, why don't you get a new one? They're right down at the Co-op."

"Yes, but they cost money."

"Why, the wages you're getting here, you can afford a dozen of them."

"Oh no, I'm just doing this for the love of it."

On the way back to the barn with the full wagon, Audrey stops to glance back at Russell. She spends her workdays with people who are lingering over their last months, wasting them away in solitude and boredom. "When his time comes," she says fondly, "I hope this is what he's doing. He loves it so much. I hope he just drops one day out here on his tractor."

———————

The next morning, a Monday in mid-July, the area representative for Boumatic, the company that makes Bill's milkers, stops by for a regular service call. He is a blond-haired, red-skinned fellow named Bill. It is early – before the magic hour of 10 a.m., when the sun is high enough to remove the last of the morning dew and baling can begin. Russell is in a talkative, reminiscent mood, and as Boumatic Bill replaces the teat cups on the milkers at the milk-house sink, Russell bends his ear about the old days. "One time, a farm equipment dealer came by and said, 'Your grain binder is shot. Do you want me to order you a new one?' Well, I only had $100, so I said, 'Would you take that and order me one?' After a while, he came by again and said, 'Your grain binder's in. Come and get it.' All word of mouth, no contracts or anything. I mind once I owed a fellow $1,000, and that was a lot of money in those days. I had a bunch of pigs that were ready to go, so I sold them and paid him off, but, d'ye see, he knew I had the pigs and was good for it. Of course, a lot of that was my Dad. He established that for me."

It was a different world then, when one man lent another money based on the reputation of his father, when deals were made on a handshake and moneylenders knew better than to pester a man for payment before his pigs were fat. In the way of many elderly people, Russell clearly misses those days, misses the a-man's-word-is-his-bond approach to business and the small world in which he dealt only with people he knew — not just them but their fathers and grand-fathers, and besides, my sister-in-law's niece is married to your second cousin. Russell is not comfortable with the chain-store mentality in which prices and policies are set by head offices in Toronto and the department managers are fresh-out-of-high-school kids responsible for little more than keeping the shelves stocked.

"You can't dicker like you used to. They're just kids who can't change the price, and the boss, the guy who can, he's never there. It used to be you went to the store and you knew the guy who owned it, and you could dicker with him and get a little better deal for yourself. I used to know an old fellow, and he'd go to buy a suit, maybe a $25 suit, and he'd talk the guy down to $20, then just as he was about to hand over the money, he'd say, 'Well, I have to have a tie to go with it,' and he'd get that thrown in. Then they'd talk for a while, and he'd say, 'Well, I really need a new belt too,' and he'd walk out of there with the whole thing, suit and tie and belt for $20. Now it's all changed."

Boumatic Bill has listened patiently through this monologue, nodding his head in recognition of the reality of what Russell says. He finishes his work, gathering up the old teat cups as Russell finishes the story, and manages to squeeze in a few words. "Well, that's good if you're a real talker and if you're an aggressive person, but if you're kind of timid, you get left behind. That's not right, either." He looks as if he would like to be a timid person.

"Yes, you're right," says Russell, and it is plain that this possibility has never occurred to him. "That's true." Unfazed, though, he continues with his stories. "I mind my brother Les had to have an operation for appendicitis, and afterwards, Dad said to the doctor, 'How much do I owe you for that operation?' and the doc said, 'We usually charge $150 for that.' Dad had the $150 in his wallet, but he said, 'Well, I've got $100 here. If I give that to you now, is that okay?' And the doc said that was fine."

At this point, Bill Moreland sticks his head in the milk-house door and asks his father for help adjusting the bale elevator. Boumatic Bill follows them out of the milk house to his truck, a small cab-and-box affair with a definite import look about it. The word "FORWARD" is written in chrome on each front door, and Russell can't pass it up. With a sly glance at Bill, he indicates the name. "Is that the end that goes forward, or do you have to label the forward end so you know which end to get in?"

"Yeah," Bill chuckles, "you're liable to get in the back and wonder who stole your steering wheel."

"I don't know why that's there," says Boumatic Bill. He tries to extricate himself from the centre of attention by changing the subject. "It's a GMC, but it's made in Japan. They call them Isuzu in the States."

"Well, it's a diesel. I imagine it's a pretty good little truck." Bill hopes that people will buy his Canadian-grown food, so he buys Canadian too, but he recognizes the quality of imports.

"Say, maybe you can answer this for me, then," says Russell. "Somebody told me that Mitsubishi is making Chrysler products. Do you know if that's true?" Russell drives a Chrysler.

"No, I don't know anything about that. All I know is that if they're small, they're from somewhere else."

Russell never skips a beat. "Well, what does that say about Eileen? She's small. Does she come from somewhere else?" Although Eileen grew up only 50 miles away, she is not, in Russell's eyes, a "local girl."

Boumatic Bill starts to say that he doesn't even want to know about that, but Bill interrupts him. "Well, if she comes from far away, is she going to be good? That's what I want to know. Is this truck well-behaved?"

Bill takes a step back and holds up his hands. "I'm not going to say *anything* about that. Besides, I've gotta get going. I'm not like you dairy farmers—I can't stand around and talk all day." He opens the truck door and gets one leg up. "Don't you fellows work too hard."

"That's good advice," Russell says, "but we don't need it."

"Not going already?" Bill adds. "We were just getting ready to put in some hay. We can always use a good man."

"How much do you pay?"

"The same as I get. About 75¢ an hour."

"Well, maybe I'll come back later."

"We'll be here."

BOOK VI

HARVESTING GRAIN

It is Thursday, July 23, before the last of the hay is finished. Bob Norris's barn is now full to the peak, and where Bill had reached up precariously to open the mow door, Bob has to crouch to close it. The mow at Pearl's is literally full to overflowing: Tom had to throw half a wagonload of bales on the barn floor. The home barn is practically bulging, and the excess has been stuffed into the second-storey mow of an old barn on the other side of Tom Moreland's shop. The excess from that was piled on the building's dirt floor. And the 2,000 or 3,000 bales that Bill didn't have room for or couldn't stand the thought of baling were taken by Mangans.

"We should have known," says Russell. "Things didn't look too good there in the spring, but Bob Norris knows all these old sayings, and one of them is that if you have a good crop of dandelions in May, you'll have a good crop of hay. And, man, we sure had a bunch of dandelions this year."

The past two weeks have made quite a difference in the barley. Fields that were once green with a graceful tinge of brown at the temples have turned gradually to brown with remnants of green. Heads of grain that reached for the sun are now heavy with seed and nod toward the ground. The once dense hairs, spread by the swelling of the kernels, appear thin and sparse. Brown has matured through gold and yellow, and the fields around the barn are now a bright, astonishingly pale amber – the colour of candlelight reflected in white wine. When the sun shines on the fields, the effect is blinding, and the grain glows like the sun itself.

"This grain here by the barn is down to about 12 percent moisture, and that's about right. I probably should start combining now, but holy baldhead, we just finished haying, and I don't feel like starting today. It won't hurt to wait till next week." One reason for this decision is the Kingston Exhibition, which is being held this week. As president of the Frontenac County Holstein Association, Bill is expected to preside over the cattle judging on Saturday. Besides, it is his weekend off, an opportunity to spend time with Mark and Eileen that he does not want to miss.

Saturday morning, the fairgrounds are all but empty. A few vehicles, many of them pickup trucks, are huddled on the black pavement near some single-storey buildings that house the dairy and beef cattle, as well as some sheep and goats.

Inside, the buildings are bustling with activity. The first events, starting at 9 a.m., are the Senior and Junior Holstein Heifer Classes, in which half the marks are given for the conformation of the heifers in the ring and the other half for the showmanship ability of the youngsters who lead them. The junior class includes children aged 7 to 11, showing calves born this calendar year; the seniors are up to age 18, showing yearlings. All are dressed in white pants and shirts with numbered white cardboard hats. There is tension in the holding area outside the ring, and several youngsters are infecting their animals with their own skittishness.

"Should I let this halter out a notch?"

"Oh jeez, are we going in already?"

"They're going in the other door? Oh, excuse me, please."

In the ring, they walk – slow, fast, slow – in a big circle, then stand. The judge, a stern-faced, middle-aged man who might be a high school math teacher except for his farmer's tan, makes them line up in a row and walk their heifers individually while the others stand still. He appears to be watching the calves, not their handlers, but at the end of each class, when he announces his placings to the crowd of parents and grandparents, he mentions only the youngsters' showmanship.

With varying degrees of enthusiasm, regularity and parental nagging, these kids have been working with their chosen heifers for months, breaking them to halter, letting them get accustomed to being brushed and handled, training them – well, cows can't actually be trained; the best to be hoped for is that they will become used to something by repetition – to hold a flattering pose: erect, back legs a bit farther back than normal, leaning slightly forward, head up. In the ring, two things become apparent: how much or how little work has gone into preparation and how discreetly the animals are handled. Ideally, the heifers are effortlessly guided around the ring with only one hand on the halter, they stop and start when the handler does, and their feet are perfectly placed every time they stop. In reality, of course, some heifers lock their knees and refuse to move, others will not stop, and all of them prefer a head-down, feet-under stance.

The seniors, led by Bob Norris's oldest son Steve, do better. When the judge is watching, they are models of relaxed competence. When his back is turned, they are maelstroms of activity. Misbehaving animals are settled down with a discreet but authoritative punch in the ribs, front feet are picked up and set down in the right place, back feet are stepped on until they are moved far enough back, tail heads are tickled until the backs arch, and halters are heaved on with both hands until the heads rise. The judge knows his role in this duplicity and carefully turns his back on each contestant for just long enough. When he turns around, the animals are standing pretty, and the perspiring contestants are calmly scratching them behind their ears.

Steve Norris and a pretty, dark-haired girl are clearly better than the rest of the senior class. Each of their yearlings is well-behaved – Steve's a trifle more so – well built (in a leggy, adolescent way), pristinely clean and well groomed. Steve's heifer, in fact, is borrowed from Morley Curtis, his next-door neighbour, which explains both its breeding and its cleanliness. Steve takes the blue ribbon, winning an opportunity to compete in Ottawa, and as they parade out of the ring, the judge approaches the microphone and explains why.

"Well, these are a fine bunch of competitors" – he says this about every class – "but the boy in first had a little better control than the girl in second." As he says this, the second-place heifer, perhaps startled by the amplified voice, begins hopping and bucking, drawing a chuckle from the crowd.

Bill, Eileen and Mark, having slept in, arrive late, just in time to see the junior class receive its awards. Each child gets a little cash and a new rope halter; the winner gets a ribbon as well. Bill looks sideways at Mark and rolls his eyes. "Well, I guess I've got a couple of years anyway." The breed judging includes classes for 6-to-12-month-old heifers, 12-to-18-month-olds, 18-to-24-month-olds, 2-year-olds, 3-year-olds, 4-year-olds, 5-year-olds and mature cows, as well as grand and reserve champions and best group of four animals. There are no marks for showmanship here, but all the handlers use the same tricks as the youngsters, discreetly stepping on toes when the judge is not looking. The adult animals were only partially milked this morning, so their udders look full and firm, although a couple that were not milked enough are swollen and misshapen.

Bill, as president, welcomes the crowd, most of which arrived well before he did, and stays in the ring to hand out ribbons and congratulations, but his heart is not in it. "I have a lot of respect for someone who shows," he says later. "It's not just the time they spend here but all the time at home too, working with the cows and grooming them – all that. I guess you need to love it to have that kind of dedication. I don't have the time for it, but if I did, I'd just as soon go in the house and read a book." The entrants are serious about the competition – serious enough that there is some grumbling afterwards about the judging – but between classes, there is a lot of kibitzing and kidding.

"The 4-H Club is having a 50/50 draw, Bill. It's one dollar a ticket, but I know you're a bargain hunter, so how about five for $5?"

"Darcy, you got your barley off yet?"

"Hah. What do you think I am, anyway?"

"Oh, I figured you'd have the barley off and the first cut on the seeding in the barn."

"Look out, Pete, there's some calves coming through here. We wouldn't want to get a farm boy run over." Pete is in his 50s. "It's bad enough with the city people."

Bill steps out of the building between classes to get a drink of milk from the canteen, but the heat soon drives him back inside. "I'd almost rather be back in the hayfield," he says glumly. "I don't like hot pavement."

After a while, Eileen takes Mark outside. The midway is not yet open, and the fairground seems oddly quiet, but there is a horse pull in progress on the racetrack, and they wander over there for a change of pace. A dozen teams of workhorses are taking turns pulling a stoneboat; that is, a platform of the kind once used to load stones onto when clearing a field. This one is loaded with 100-pound blocks of concrete, and each team pulls it 25 feet down the dirt track. A tractor pulls it back after each attempt, and when every team has had a try, it loads on more concrete. The horses are plainly eager to pull the weight but less willing to back up to it to be hooked on – they want to go forward. The harness of each team culminates in a single hook, and as the driver carefully guides his prancing, snorting team backward – "Back, back, easy now, back" – an assistant carries the hook so they don't step on their harness, and when they get back far enough, he drops the hook into an eye on the stoneboat. The sound of metal on metal is the horses' signal. They throw themselves into the load, almost as if they were trying to jump through their collars, and their mighty haunches bunch and flex as they heave themselves forward. The drivers are not allowed to touch the horses during the pull, but there are sound effects aplenty, with "Hyah! Giddap!" and "Whoa!" when the pull is done. With the hollering, the palpable desire of the horses, their smell, the creak and shine of their harnesses and the tension of the contest, it is quite a show.

"I like to watch them when they can pull it," says Eileen. "But, oh, it just breaks my heart when they can't. The poor things." Indeed, as the weight is increased, the teams that are forced out are not nearly as pretty to watch. They fall to their knees, drawing a gasp from the crowd, or they strain at the load, like dogs at the end of a chain, until the driver can make them stop. If the horses do not stop pulling or, rarely, even if they do, they can injure themselves, sometimes fatally, by twisting an intestine.

When the load is up to 8,050 pounds, only four teams are left. The second team, a jittery black and brown pair weighing 3,150 pounds, stamp their feet and chew on their bits as they are unwillingly backed up to the stoneboat. The assistant drops the hook, hitting the eye with a metallic clang but missing the hole. The horses throw themselves against their harness and, not meeting any resistance, quickly break into a gallop. The driver tries to hold them but can't and, when he loses his footing and falls forward, lets go of the reins to avoid being dragged. The runaway team careens up the track, and the moment of otherwise frozen silence is broken by the announcer's helper, a woman who grabs the microphone and screams, "Grab your children! Grab your children!" Runaway teams are almost literally in a blind panic, and horses that normally would not harm humans will trample anyone or anything that gets in their way – and there is no telling which way they will go. Eileen pulls Mark into the safety of the stands.

This team narrowly misses a pickup truck on the track, then veers through a gate on the first turn, where it is confronted by a concrete abutment from which a pair of calves has just been loaded into a truck. The right horse jumps onto the abutment; the left one tries to jump the truck. It clears the truck proper but cleans off an aluminum cap housing the calves, which are sent rolling across the lot, uninjured. The man who has just loaded them, unaware of the ton and a half of horseflesh bearing down on him, is not quite so lucky. The impact of the cap knocks him out of the path of the horses, perhaps saving his life, but it also gives him a severe gash on his forehead and all but severs the middle finger of his left hand. The horses then run into the side of a building, where they are caught, shivering and foaming but unhurt.

Bill, Eileen and Mark stay at the fair all day, a rare family outing that they all enjoy. In the evening, Eileen goes to the old-time fiddling contest, and Bill, who is not keen on fiddle music, takes Mark to the demolition derby. Later, he makes a face and says, "I should have gone with Eileen."

On the last Monday in July, Bill turns his attention to getting ready for combining. The first item is to sweep out the remaining few hundred pounds of last year's crop from the grain bin. The bin has a capacity of 4,000 bushels and is a type familiar to anyone who has taken a drive in the country: round, covering about the same amount of floor space as a single-car garage and about 20 feet high – a shiny, squat silo made of corrugated steel. It has a lid about a foot wide at the peak of the roof to put the grain in, and a submarine-type door – for a very small submarine – on one side for access. It stands beside the old-fashioned wooden granary that Russell built, which is now used to store shovels, rakes, loose boards and all the other items on a farm that don't belong somewhere else. The only grain in the old granary is a few bags of calf ration, protected from rats and insects in an old chest-type deep freezer.

"I really love these steel granaries," says Bill. "The rats used to get in the old wood one, and the grain would be leaking out the corners and the bottom. The rats would be crapping all over the top of it and making a mess." As Tom cleans off the floor, he reveals an X of screens that cover trenches in the concrete. The trenches lead to an outside fan, which is turned on for a week or two after harvest to pull cool, drying air through the barley and prevent it from overheating. It is on now to keep the dust down as Tom works inside the structure.

"One year," Bill remembers, "I could hear barley being sucked into the fan, a 'ping, ping, ping.' When we got it cleaned out, we found that some rats had got in, and there was a hole in the screen where the barley was falling through. I hadn't been able to get the right mesh to cover the fan outlet, and the stuff I got looked pretty small, but I guess rats can get through a pretty small hole. Anyway, we pulled up the screen and started chasing them, and a couple ran out into the fan. That thing's going around at 1,750 rpm, and it's pretty hard on the old cranium. One of them it just turned into a rag, but the other must have been really going, because he got about halfway through before it caught him."

The next job is to line up the silage blower and erect enough pipe to blow the grain into the granary lid. Bill would prefer to use a grain auger (a kind of spiralled drill bit in a pipe) instead of the blower, which is powerful enough to shatter some of the kernels, but, he says, "an auger costs money, and it's another thing that you keep around all year and use for only three or four days. I've already got the blower, and this is another way to use it." But in the cramped quarters around the granary, an auger would be easier and quicker to put into place. It takes almost two hours to set up the blower – the kind of fiddly work that is easy to discount when planning a day.

First, they park the blower – after several tries – just so. They find it impossible to position it where incoming wagons will miss both the old granary and Eileen's garden.

"Tom, you go in the house and tell Eileen we're going to have to run over her cucumbers."

"Unh-hunh," says Tom, without looking up. "I enjoy breathing too much." He grins. "Maybe if you don't tell her, she won't notice."

They turn to securing the blower pipes. One rope to the old granary is not enough; Bill wants to drive in a stake over by the garden to give more support, but he can't find the sledgehammer in either the old granary or the trailer. Bill is pushed for time – "I should have had all this done last week," he says. "It's a sign of poor management" – and Tom suggests pounding in the stake with the back of an axe. Most people in Bill's position would agree, but using the wrong tool is not Bill's way, and he sends Tom over to his brother's shop to borrow a sledge.

With the pipes in place, it is plain that one of the joints is not grain-proof and will leak barley under pressure from the blower. Bill and Tom dig an old binder canvas out of the old granary and, working from a ladder and the roof of the granary, tie it around the joint like a bandage. In Russell's day, a binder – the first models were horse-drawn and wheel-driven; later models were pulled and powered by a tractor – cut the stalks of grain when they were not quite dry and tied them in sheaves that it laid on the ground six at a time. The sheaves were stooked to dry, then forked onto a wagon and stored in a mow until the threshing machine came around and separated the grain from the straw. The binder's canvas worked like a short, wide conveyor belt, carrying the stalks from the cutting bar to the knotters. The machine this canvas once served is long gone for scrap, but like an ageing ball player still called in to make a sacrifice bunt in the big game, the canvas sits in the dark in case it is needed. Its job is not as prestigious as before, but it still takes part in the harvest.

It is almost milking time, and Bill heads over to Tom's shop to tighten a few bolts on the combine. When he is gone, Russell, who has been ploughing the Christmas tree patch behind the paddock, pulls up on the blue tractor and hollers at Tom, "What's going on here? I've been looking for the combine, and looking and looking – and nothing. What are you fellows waiting for?" He is equal parts good humour and bad temper.

"Bill's over at Tom's making some last-minute adjustments."

Russell snorts, now more annoyed than amused. "Oh, Bill will be wanting to put a new engine in it or something. He never just goes out and does something – he's got to fool around with things first."

When Bill drives the combine back over to the barn, he is late for milking, and Eileen has already come out to help Tom and Jean. He decides to take a couple of turns around the field in front of the barn to make sure everything is working well. Bill is intense, even grim. He has the same aura of pent-up tension he did when harvesting haylage – now, as then, the next few days are among the most crucial of the season. If things go well, the crop may be worth $10,000; if not, it will be next to worthless. Of course, those are paper figures – Bill will never get a cent for the grain. It will all be stored in the steel granary and fed to his cows. But if the harvest is a failure, he will have to buy $10,000 worth of feed next year.

COMBINE

The combine is an International Harvester product, red and white and, like much of what Bill owns, neither bottom nor top of the line. It has a cab that gives the operator some protection from the sun, dust and noise, but it is not air-conditioned, as many of the more expensive models are. The floor is about six feet off the ground, and the full-length windshield in front slopes in toward Bill's feet to help him look down at the 12-foot-wide "head" of the combine – the part that cuts the grain and feeds it into the threshing part of the machine. The head consists of the reel, those familiar rotating bars that bend the stalks so they can be cut, the cutter bar and the auger, which has replaced the old canvas.

The rest of the machine is considerably more complex. It takes the whole plant and scrubs off the grain in the "concaves" (another sort of wringer-washer affair), then lets the kernels fall through a series of screens to the bottom, where an auger spirals them up to a hopper. The straw, too large to fall through the screens, is carried by a series of "straw walkers" to the back and dumped on the ground. A fan blows away any chaff small enough to fall through the screens with the grain. Each part of the process is individually adjustable and affects the quality of the crop. For example, if the fan is turning too slowly, the grain will have too much chaff; too quickly, and it will blow away part of the crop. The success of the crop is largely dependent on Bill's ability to make the right adjustments when they are needed.

All the components are driven by one engine, set directly behind the cab, and it seems they are all powered by rubber drive belts. Behind access panels on each side of the machine is a bewildering array of belts and pulleys: narrow belts, wide belts, single belts, gangs of belts on one pulley, short belts, belts that travel 20 feet in one revolution. The machine seems to be made as much of rubber as of steel. Bill makes a few casual adjustments – "That looks about right" – and heads off around the field. He wants to keep the head high enough to avoid cutting much of the alfalfa seeding, but from his perspective, looking almost straight down on it, it is difficult to judge its height. So he looks sideways, at the ends of the cutter bar, and this additional angle gives him a better view.

At first, though, the cutting height is the least of his worries. Grain stalks repeatedly bunch up in front of the concaves, and he has to stop and wait for them to go through. And when they do, the flow of grain and straw seems anything but smooth. Bill mutters to himself for a while but finally declares, "Well, it's working better now. I think we've got the rust worn off." As for the plugging, he guesses the problem is a loose header drive belt – a simple adjustment should fix it. He struggles around the field once, half filling the 80-bushel hopper, and quits for the night, too late to help with milking. Tomorrow morning, he will make the required adjustments, give the machine a final greasing, and when the dew has burned off at 10 a.m., he will tear into the crop. When things are going well, he can combine about 3 acres an hour, or, working from dew to dew, about 30 acres a day. He has 118 acres in barley, so he should be done in four days.

When he sits down for dinner, he is confident of a good crop and a smooth harvest. It is a good feeling.

While Bill is washing up for dinner, Mark shows him the scrapes he got when Duchess, the family dog, sent him sprawling in the gravel in front of the barn. Mark enjoys playing with Duchess but is too small to control her yet, and she has knocked him down several times. Bill is not very sympathetic, and Mark responds by pouting. When they sit at the table and bow their heads for grace, Bill intones, "Thank you, Lord, for this food and the day we have had. Give us the strength to get along with our friends and our doggies. Amen." Mark grins, his good humour restored, and gets a wink from Eileen.

While they eat, a couple of sun showers settle the dust and take some heat off the day. One storm splits the house – they can look out the south window at rain and out the east window at sunshine. Another drops a rainbow behind the barn, apparently in the barley, a good omen for tomorrow if Bill abided by such things. Eileen asks Mark what causes a rainbow. "Sun shining through the rain," he says with his mouth full of potatoes.

Bill tells Eileen how good he feels about getting everything ready ahead of time. "We're not going to have to fool around in the morning getting the machinery ready. We can just get started."

Mark lets this sink in for a moment. "Why are you going to combine on Mommy's birthday?" he asks. There is a brief silence as Bill's face goes blank, then sags. He has forgotten Eileen's birthday – again.

Eileen laughs out loud at the expression on Bill's face, but she is not going to let him off the hook too easily. "Well, I wasn't going to say anything, Bill, but I suppose you'd better run off to the store and get me something."

Bill glances at his watch – 8 o'clock on a Monday night. "Yeah, well I imagine the only thing open is the truck stop down on the 401. Maybe I can get you a belt buckle with a picture of a truck on it."

Later, Eileen says she doesn't think Bill has ever remembered her birthday. "He just never thinks of it, and I don't expect him to, not anymore anyway. The first couple of years when he forgot, I was a little hurt, but now I just don't worry about it. I go out and buy myself something, and that's my present. I know he doesn't expect anything on his birthday, either. It's just not something he thinks about."

The next morning, after the milking and a hurried breakfast, Bill leaves the house to begin combining. He is still keyed up but happily so, whistling aimlessly and enjoying the less intense heat of the early hours. It is one of those perfect summer days that make office workers wish they were at the beach and farmers glad they are not office workers. Yesterday, the Monday after his weekend off, Bill said, "I can imagine being away from things here for a month and being really anxious to get back at it. But not after two days." This morning, though, he is fresh and eager.

By 10 o'clock, when the grain is dry enough to combine, he has the machine adjusted, greased, fuelled and ready to go. He bounds up the ladder and pulls into the field, still whistling. He doesn't get 10 feet before something in the back of the combine goes bang, and he comes to a halt. He spills out of the cab like a guard dog after an intruder, swings open an inspection panel and, fortunately, spots the problem right away — a locknut has come loose, and the ground drive pulley, which supplies power to the wheels, is off its shaft. Nothing is actually broken, so the problem is not serious, but Bill is purple with frustration. Uncharacteristically, he breaks loose with a string of invectives. "Damn," he says, rocking back on his heels. "Damn, damn, damn." This is the worst language Bill has used all summer. He takes off his hat and scratches his head. "If that isn't enough to make a preacher curse, I don't know what would be." His outburst seems to calm him down again. "Cursing," said Mark Twain, "often brings a relief that prayer cannot afford." Bill grabs the nut — it is too big to fit in his pocket — and drives over to get some tools and help from his brother Tom.

Compared with Bill, Tom is relaxed, almost lethargic. He turns his face to the breeze and draws a breath. "This is just the kind of weather I wish I could get away and go on a car trip for three or four days." But Bill has no time for that. He slams the pulley in place, twirls the locknut onto its threads and tightens it with an enormous wrench. Together, they slip the belt over the pulleys in what seems the obvious configuration. When they step back, though, it is just as obviously wrong. "Hunh, isn't that interesting," says Tom. "I wonder why it's like that." He touches the belt with his fingers, following the flow of energy with his hands. He has a mechanic's patience, and his hands want to know how this thing works before they go about fixing it.

Bill, at least for the moment, couldn't care less how the thing works. It's wrong this way, and there's only one other way for it to go, so that must be the right way. Together, they peel the belt off the pulleys and rearrange it, Tom still muttering, "This one turns this way, so this one goes that way. Hunh, I wonder why they did that." Reaching into the machine, their four hands are equally strong, equally scarred, equally greasy on the knuckles and under the fingernails. They grasp and pull and change positions for a better purchase, like con men running a shell game – Which hand belongs to whom?

Back in the cab and under way again, Bill's good cheer returns. The combine is working well – cutting and rolling and blowing and sifting and augering a steady stream of grain into the hopper. The colour of the grain has changed again, from amber to bright gold. As Bill rounds the corner by the road and heads west, into the prevailing wind, the heads of all the grain stalks are bent toward him, like loyal subjects bowed in submission before being sacrificed to their lord. The rows are indistinguishable until the reel combs the stalks against the cutter bar. There, just before the chattering knives cut them off at the ankles, the planter's straight lines are briefly visible, a moment of spring relived before the finality of harvest.

Combining reminds Bill of a trip to the midwestern United States, where he saw the corn belt of the American heartland. "It's amazing. You go down there and see thousands of acres of corn in one spot – whole counties in nothing but corn. You'd see 2,000 acres of corn in one field, then look across the road and there's another one just as big. It's the kind of thing where you head off down one row, and you take your lunch with you because you won't be back in time. And the equipment! We saw a 12-row combine head for corn. Up here, you hardly ever see a 6-row head.

"We watched one guy going down his field, and he stepped out of the combine cab and walked back to check the grain bin – while the combine was still going down the field. I thought, 'What's going on here?' but he had automatic steering – little sensors on each side of the corn row that bump against the row and make little adjustments in the direction. They do a better job of steering than you could ever do. The big problem they have down there is getting the corn away fast enough. Here, with a 4-row head, a fellow can fill a 200-bushel bin in 15 minutes, so multiply that times three, and it's not hard to see how long it takes those guys to fill a hopper. They draw away with great big buggies that have those big flotation tires and carry 20 or 25 tons at a time.

"But it's kind of sad. They have these great big farms, and they're getting tremendous yields, but they're just about broke. And these guys are good farmers too – they're not dummies. They're cabbaging up these rigs that do four or five things at once, spraying and working the land and smoothing it out all in one pass. They're bright and they're working hard at it, but they're just not getting enough for their corn."

In addition to low prices – corn sells for no more now than it did 20 years ago – part of the problem is the high cost of farming. Yields have doubled, redoubled and doubled again, but so have the costs of seed, machinery and overhead. Bill's combine is an under-$20,000 bargain off the used-machinery lot that he will make last 10 years or more, but he knows other farmers with a taste for newer equipment. One man spent $60,000 for a new combine with an air-conditioned cab and automatic height controls on the header. "Two years later, when he traded it in," says Bill, "it had 40 hours on it. That's a big investment to have sitting around like that. Can you imagine spending $60,000 on a Mercedes or something and driving it only 1,000 miles a year?"

It takes about 35 minutes to fill the hopper with barley, and two hoppers to fill the wagon. Once it is full, Tom drives up to the blower and unloads. The first load he drives over a hill of cucumbers on the corner of Eileen's garden. "I told her last night about running over the garden," says Bill. "She was very understanding." He rolls his eyes.

"Yes," Eileen agrees, "Bill came in and told me he was going to run over my cucumbers." She sighs. "Well, at least he told me. A lot of men would have just run over them."

At lunch, Eileen announces that she has to go into town to renew the licence plates on the car – it is in her name, the truck in Bill's. "He's 42 years old, and he's never owned a car in his life. Isn't that something?" Before she leaves, Bill calls Mark into his office and closes the door. When Mark comes back out, he is holding tightly onto something in his pocket and grinning hugely. Eileen may get a birthday present after all.

Bill moves into the field beside the barn after lunch. The sun is filling the world with that special quality of light that defines a summer's day from one's childhood, and the afternoon's work creates a beautiful pastoral scene. Bill drives the combine away from the barn with his unloading auger sticking out to one side. Tree swallows perform hammerhead stalls in his slipstream as they dive for the insects he disturbs. The breeze-ruffled grain is transformed into a dust of chaff and a pick-up-sticks of golden straw. Across the ditch, Russell is ploughing up an old hayfield, burying the green grass under row upon row of black earth. In the next farm stands a field of tall corn, and beyond that, a wooded hillside rising to meet the clear sky.

Bill soon falls into a rhythm, driving up and down the field until the hopper is full. Then, as the auger is unloading into the corn wagon, he steps out onto the combine head and wipes the black dust from the cab windshield with his handkerchief, shakes it out, wipes his glasses and then steps back into the cab to shut off the auger. Tom, who is ferrying the corn wagon back and forth, is relaxed but wary of the morrow. "Yeah, this is pretty easy today, but tomorrow we'll have to bale the straw too. That'll keep us going, unloading the wagons and keeping an eye on the combine and all."

Later, when Russell returns in the blue tractor, Tom is unloading the wagon, but it is parked just a little off-line. A trickle of grain is leaking from the edge of the blower. By the time Russell gets there, the wagon is half empty and there is a cone of grain on the grass beside the garden – perhaps a shovelful. Russell stoops by the edge of the wagon and catches the grain in his hands so that he can throw it in the blower. They are harvesting thousands of bushels of grain, but he is concerned about the wasting – no, the falling on the ground – of a few handfuls of grain. Every kernel matters, not because they can't afford to lose it but because caring has no threshold – no minimum acceptable level at which it kicks into action. Russell is like a master carpenter appraising the fit of a joint: there is no "good enough," only "good" and "needs more work."

Eileen passes the afternoon and evening of her 42nd birthday milking cows and preparing a dinner for herself and Mark. When Bill comes in at 9 o'clock, she reheats it for him and thanks him for her present. With a 4-year-old's tastes, Mark has chosen a box of Smarties and a package of gingerbread men for her.

On Wednesday, while Bill is combining at Ed Johnston's, he hits a rock and breaks a tooth on the cutter bar. He pulls the big machine into Ed's backyard and asks to borrow some wrenches so he can remove the bar and replace the tooth.

"Shit," Ed bellows at him. "The highway man never takes the cutter bar off to fix it. Show me where it is."

So Bill stands meekly out of the way while Ed hunches under the reel. After a career of cutting grass on highway verges, Ed is as good as his word and replaces the tooth with little help and no disassembly.

In the meantime, Russell is baling straw, and Tom and Jean are packing it away in a reserved space in the mow. This is familiar work – it has hardly been a week since they were baling hay. Mercifully, the heat is less intense and the bales of straw are lighter than hay, but the old baler still goes "chompah, chompah, chompah, ka-chunk" as it spirals its geriatric way around the field, and the wagons creak under their loads, and the bale elevator rattles, and the mow is just as airless and cloying and maybe even dustier than before. The dust devils that blow in the gravel in front of the barn pick up pieces of chaff and twirl them around and around in a crazed Viennese waltz before they collapse, exhausted, on the ground.

The next day, Bill is back home trying to finish off the stuff in 14-inch rows behind Tom's – the last of the harvest. But the forecast is for showers, and the sky is cloudy and dark. "I want it to rain," Bill says, wiping the windshield with his handkerchief. "The corn is starting to look awfully dry. But I want to get this grain in too. I don't know which to hope for." He pockets his handkerchief and steps back into the cab. "I guess I come out ahead either way, so it doesn't really matter."

Optimism aside – many in Bill's situation would see it as a losing proposition no matter what happens – he would very much like to finish combining today. Eileen's family is having a reunion on Sunday, and it is Bill and Eileen's weekend to work. They have arranged for Tom and Jean not to work on Friday – tomorrow – and to cover for them on Sunday. But Tom has said that if the straw is not finished, he will likely work on Friday anyway. "I wouldn't be happy at home knowing this straw is sitting here and might get rained on. I don't know, it'd just bother me."

Jean has no such compunction and is miffed at Tom for even thinking about it. "Everybody who works here for a while gets the feeling that this place is more important than their family." She is cleaning the cows' water bowls, using a brush to scoop out the bits of hay and grain that have washed off the cows' noses. She straightens up and punctures the air with the brush. This is something that has been bothering her for a while. Jean works long hours and misses the time spent with her 4-year-old, her husband and her stepchildren. "I'm gone in the morning before they get up, and then I don't get home till almost 6:30. Well, the older kids have got stuff to do in the evening, so they've already eaten, and you can't ask Malcolm to wait that long for his dinner. There are times when we don't sit down to a meal as a family for a week.

"I have some extra time off now, but I still work an average of 54 hours a week. Maybe if my family lived right across the road and I could go home at lunch and see them at mealtimes, it wouldn't be so bad. And Tom is the same. Audrey was over the other night, and she said, 'Oh, I better get home, Tom might be there now.' I looked at my watch and just laughed. 'Audrey, are you out of your mind? It's only 6:30.' And she said, 'I suppose I know what you mean.' Sure enough, Tom wasn't home that night till well after 7. And he's supposed to be off at 6.

"I don't know if Bill and Eileen can understand. Bill's never lived anywhere else but here. Good grief, eight months after they were married, he asked Eileen to quit her teaching job because he was lonely. He wanted someone here to have lunch with. I don't know if he can transfer that feeling to his employees or not. I probably should say something. I'm usually a pretty nervy person but – I don't know – maybe because it's family."

Instead, she has taken more direct action. She has put herself on the job market. "I put my name in at a few places, and I'm going to apply at the A&P this weekend. It's good money – I could work fewer hours, make more money and have all the benefits. Of course, I'd have to work weekends, but I'm doing that anyway. Ed says I'm working too hard here. He says he doesn't know any other 40-year-old woman who carries on like I do." She moves down the barn and starts cleaning the next water bowl. "Oh dear," she sighs. "If I knew at 25 what I know now, things would be a lot different. But I guess we'll survive. I don't know, maybe I should just keep on farming. It's what I always wanted to do. And in 25 years, I'll retire, and Ed and I can go someplace together."

Of the weekend, Eileen says, "Tom says he's going to work on Friday, but Bill thinks he needs a day off. Really, he needs a vacation. He's been working too hard. You have to take some time for yourself."

Bill finishes the last of the combining that night – it does not rain, after all – and when Tom shows up on Friday, they get the rest of the straw in too.

———

A preg check at the end of July reveals seven of the eight cows that were bred since mid-June are pregnant. This confirms for Bill the success of the dietary changes he made in the spring, but he's disappointed at the failure of the eighth, Peggoty, who has not shown any benefit from having most of her vagina sewn shut. "Look at her BCA, there," he says, waving his arm at the card over her stall. "Almost a triple 200." He shakes his head. "It just breaks your heart."

Peggoty is not the only cow on her way out. The medial ligament in Teasel's udder is shot, and her teats stick out to the sides so much they will hardly accept the milker. "She's a good cow, but you'd have to milk her by hand," Bill says. He looks over the top of his glasses for emphasis. "We don't do that. We're going to have to beef her." And Quest, a cow whose poor tailbone structure makes the mounds of her hipbones stick up unnaturally – "She looks like Dolly Parton lying on her back," says Tom – has developed abscesses in her back feet. "The vet told us it's like what they used to call putrid blood in people," Jean says. "They can cure it in one place, but it would crop up in another."

But not all the news in the barn is bad. Milk production is up to 2,500 litres every two days from a low of 2,300 during the heat wave. And a pair of certificates arrive in the mail to verify the lifetime production records of Lulu (70,000 kilograms) and Seven (80,000 kilograms). Lulu's total, of course, will never get any larger, but Seven is waiting in dry-cow pasture to bear another calf in late September, and she could conceivably break 90,000. As it is, her record merits an article in the *Holstein Journal*. The story appears in the September issue, next to a photograph with a businesslike caption headed RUSTOWIL KRAVE SEVEN (V.G): "A daughter of A. Clinton-Camp Majesty (VG-Extra), she is reported this month with 12,966 kg milk, 3.8%, 496 kg fat, 3.2%, 414 kg protein (245-258-262) in 305 days at 10 years. Bred and owned by William Moreland, Joyceville, Ont., she has lifetime totals to date of 81,754 kg of 4.2% milk in eight lactations."

The day after the magazine calls to gather this information, though, a neighbour phones to say that one of Bill's cows is on the railroad tracks. "Sure enough," says Jean, "there was Seven. She'd escaped from the pasture and was standing there in the middle of the tracks. If a train had come along," she shakes her head rather than complete the thought. "So we'll have to put in the paper that she likes to travel by train. I told them everything about her, and I tried to tell them all the positive things. The only bad thing is that she's had six daughters and none of them have turned out well, except for Rave. And, of course, her son is down the road." Marcus, Seven's Marlin offspring the previous year, is servicing cows for an elderly farmer a couple of miles away.

"The guy who has him is 88 years old," says Jean. "I went to his 60th wedding anniversary in the spring. He said he has only ever missed two milkings in the barn, and he can still wear the suit he was married in. In fact," she confides, "he wears it all the time – it was a real good suit. He just got a certificate from the Leeds County Holstein Association for having a 20th-generation cow." She means that he has milked an unbroken string of 20 descendants – daughter, granddaughter, great-granddaughter, and so on – from a cow he bought decades ago. "I don't know if we'll ever do that," says Jean admiringly.

———

With both cuts of hay in the barn, a successful crop of barley in the grain bin and its straw safely in the mow – all before the first of August – it should be time to relax a little. Oh, there is still some ploughing to be done, but Russell will take care of that. And the corn has to be harvested, but that's not until October, and Bill hires it out anyway – his combine is not suited for that kind of rugged work. But before everyone can lie back a little, there's the Twilight Meeting to contend with. Less than a week away, the Twilight Meeting is the responsibility of each year's president of the county Holstein Association, who invites all the members for a tour of his farm, followed by a barbecue put on by the association. Like having one's prospective in-laws over for dinner, it is a matter of some pride to have the place spruced up and presentable for the occasion.

Jean has been plugging away at one corner or another of the barn and has already managed to repaint the inside walls – "I thought about painting a mural of some palm trees to make the cows feel cool, but then I thought, no, if all they see is white, it'll make them think of milk. Maybe we'll get our production back up where it belongs." Bill hired a crew to whitewash the stable ceiling, but there is still a list of cleanup chores that threatens to swamp everybody. The week is spent frantically scrubbing parts of the barn, cleaning the feed room, mowing lawns, trimming the grass around the buildings and fences, tidying the milk house, updating the signs over the cows, spreading fresh straw under the calf hutches, scraping the exercise yard, and so on. Bill even puts the loader on the small Deere and tidies up around the manure pile. "You never know where people are going to want to go," he says. "Usually, they're crawling around everywhere." It is not hard to imagine some farmer investigating the enclosed manure pad in his good shoes, and Bill wants to make sure he doesn't step into an ankle-deep soft spot.

Thursday, the day of the Twilight Meeting, is sunny and busy. Bill is off doing some custom combining for a fellow on the next concession. Before he leaves, he says, "I'll try to get back at 4:30." The meeting starts at 7:00.

When he is gone, Jean says, "You watch, I'll bet he doesn't get home till 6:30."

Russell snorts. "More like 7:30."

With Bill gone, Eileen gets Tom to change the mailbox, exchanging the rusty old one that still says Russell Moreland for a nicely painted black one with "Bill and Eileen Moreland" that is mounted in an old stainless steel milk pail full of rocks. Tom grumbles about the weight as he loads it in the back of the truck. "Here it is the first week of August, and we're just going to have to change it back again before Halloween." But on the way back up the driveway, he notices the potholes as if for the first time. He grabs a shovel from the old granary and backs up to a pile of gravel behind Tom Moreland's shop. "Who cares how nice the barn looks if your car falls apart coming up the lane?"

He is still filling potholes when Russell comes back from feeding the calves at Pearl's. "What are you doing?" he asks, although it is perfectly plain.

Tom grins his slow grin, knowing he is in for a hard time. "Just making it nice."

"My, my, my, they're only a bunch of farmers, you know. They've all got big cars anyway – they're not going to notice." Later, Russell shakes his head and says, "Bill is just too fussy, too fussy."

People start to arrive in the afternoon. The first visitor is Chris English, a big, soft-spoken young man whose father hosted the Twilight Meeting last year. "I know what it must be like for you guys today," he says shyly. "Is there anything I can do?" Jean puts him to work cleaning the glass on the pipeline.

Soon after, Bill Bracken pulls in with an eight-foot-long barbecue, which he sets up downwind of the lawn where the guests will eat. He lights it and, squinting through the smoke of a cigarette that waggles from his lips, organizes his equipment, which includes a cooler full of pork chops. He is getting beyond middle age, with thick hands and a posture that speaks of a lifetime of hard work. He inherited a prosperous dairy farm north of Kingston from his father and will pass it on to his two sons fully modernized and just as prosperous. His sons are each operating a combine today, trying to get in the last of the grain. "I guess I'm still the boss," he says, "but the boys are doing all the work. I told them when I turned 50 that I wasn't going to milk cows anymore. I started when I was 8 years old, and 40 years of that is enough."

Russell looks up from refuelling the lawn mower to watch Bracken work at the barbecue. "I'm the same age as his dad, Norm," he says, meaning they were born the same year – Norm has been dead for several years. "There was a bunch of us there the same age. We used to tease each other about who was going to die last." The question is settled now, but there is no one to congratulate the victor.

When Bill gets back – about 5:30 – Mark expresses concern about "that man" who has been working in the sun all afternoon. He offers to take a glass of lemonade out to him. Bill and Eileen exchange glances. "Somehow, I don't think a glass of lemonade is Bill's speed," says Bill. Indeed, Bracken has the remains of a 12-pack of beer buried among the pork chops and does not appear to be at all bothered by the heat.

Visitors start to pull in at about 6:40, parking their cars on the barley stubble in front of the barn. The stragglers, those who milk late, arrive about 7:30. A few come in half-tons, but most drive midsize to large North American-made cars. There are no small cars and few foreign models. Most are fairly new, and some are expensive. Among them, the 135 people gathered on the Morelands' lawn and poking around the grain bin and the feed room control assets worth at least $100 million. But although these people are tanned (at least on the exposed parts) and, for the most part, fit, there is no country-club atmosphere. They are presentably dressed in casual attire, but farmers do not spend a lot of money on clothes. The men all have large, strong hands, and some are creased with the kind of dirt that doesn't come out even after a hard scrub. The women's hands, too, are strong and sometimes leathery.

During the meal – pork chops, coleslaw, potato salad, beans, buttered rolls, ice-cream sundaes with little wooden spoons, milk and coffee – several youngsters noisily take over Mark's sandbox and get absolutely filthy. Everybody is too busy chatting and laughing and calling out to people three tables over to take much notice. Then, over coffee, they listen to the speeches of the two contestants for the title of Frontenac County Dairy Princess. The first girl, the prettier, has come with her boyfriend and speaks on the importance of education, pointedly mentioning how she would like to address high school students on the wonders of farming. The second girl, who has come with her parents, speaks on free trade but does not take a clear stand. Following this, Bill, freshly showered and changed, gives a brief synopsis of the farm operation, while Eileen, radiant in a sundress that shows her freckled shoulders, looks on. Then, still chatting, everyone troops out to the barn for the "entertainment."

There, in the coolness of the stable with most of the cows let out for the night, the gathering takes on the sound and atmosphere of a cocktail party – the same background chatter punctuated by laughter and the odd phrase that rises above to be heard clearly. Knots of two or three people stand in stalls, and larger clusters in the centre aisle, chatting animatedly while individuals carrying foam cups of coffee try to slip by them without spilling. In conversation, people lean forward to hear each other better. Most of the conversation is about cows and crops:

"You still working away at those round bales?"

"Oh God, I'll be at them all summer."

Child: "There's a spider on your dress."

Woman, calmly: "Well, take it off, but don't kill it."

Man, smiling: "Unless it's a daddy longlegs. If you kill one of them, it's supposed to make it rain."

Another man yawns. "Must be past my bedtime. What time is it, anyway?"

"Nine-fifteen."

"Oh golly, it *is* past my bedtime." He is not joking.

Finally, someone from the entertainment committee is roped into being master of ceremonies and clears a space in the aisle for himself. He thanks everyone for coming, thanks the Morelands for hosting the event and apologizes for not being prepared. As papers and pencils are passed out, he announces that the entertainment will consist of several guessing contests. "First," he says, "we want you to guess the projected BCA of this heifer." He gestures at Atticus, one of seven cows that have been left in the barn. "Now, where's Jean? Come on out here, and give us some information on this nice-looking heifer."

Jean has not had a chance to change clothes, but she put earrings on this morning and has washed up, so she is clean as high as her elbows anyway. She has stayed in the barn all evening, earnestly talking cows and breeding and conformation with visitors who plainly respect her opinion. She is positively glowing as she steps forward.

"This is Atticus," she says, "and she's a Mars Knight daughter out of a good plus dam that was born here on the farm. She's one of five sisters – one was sold to Argentina, and another was sent to Pennsylvania. That was a good-looking one, but she wouldn't work. This heifer was born out in the exercise yard in February 1985. She kind of caught us by surprise because we just found her in a snowbank one day, but it doesn't seem to have bothered her. She's in her first lactation, and she's had only three tests, but we think she's got some potential."

"When did she calve?" asks a man in the front.

"The middle of May."

"So that's almost five months into her lactation," announces the emcee.

"No," says Jean, "that's almost three months into her lactation. What calendar are you using?"

Grins turn to chuckles when a voice from the back of the crowd calls out, "He said he was going to stumble through this."

Chastised, the emcee asks Jean for a hint. "Well," she says, "her total BCA is over 600."

"Whoa," says the emcee, "that's quite a hint. We don't want to give it all away." BCA is impossible to guess right to the number. Atticus has a projected 226-233-244, and few guess she is that high.

The emcee moves the crowd down the aisle until they are gathered around Treasure. This is the cow Jean paid $6,700 for, and her BCA is 164-170-167 – not a smart buy. The contestants are invited to guess her height and weight. The emcee gets a man of medium height to stand next to the cow for comparison and, as he walks away, says, "Now I'd say that fellow is six-foot-four, so judge for yourself how tall the cow is." Several men and a couple of women approach Treasure and place an outstretched arm on her withers, then examine the angle of their arms. Breeders look for tall cows now, and Holsteins are several inches taller than they were a few decades ago because of it. Most breeders are sensitive to a cow's height, but some, before they go to buy a cow, will eliminate the guesswork by measuring the exact height of a button on their shirt. Treasure is 59 inches high – there are several correct guesses – and she weighs 1,920 pounds – several are close, but more people guess too low than too high.

Next, people are invited to guess how many calves Olivier has had. Since cows calve once a year starting at age 2, this is a simple age-guessing contest, and the assembled farmers are very good at it.

There is a fair sprinkling of "five" and "seven," but most guess "six." But it is a trick question. Yes, Olivier is going on 8 years old and has calved six times, as the majority surmised, but she has had two sets of twins, eight calves in all. There are raised eyebrows as the correct answer is announced, and good-natured groans as the trick is revealed.

For the final game, there is no correct answer. Jean has Connie, Lily, Squida and Stidler tied side by side – the idea is to place them as if they were in a show ring. Jean is called forward again to give the details, and she speaks about each animal without using notes. Of Lily: "This one's sire is A. Puget Sound Sheik" – A. for American – "and we bought her from Murray Jackson. He's bred a lot of good animals, and we liked the look of her, but we don't have any family history on her. She arrived on March 28 and calved on March 29. What else? Oh, her BCA is 195-183-198."

Of Stidler: "Our first daughter out of Shore Stylist, the bull known as Mr. Consistency. He's stayed around a long time." Later, she recounts the story of Stylist's 14th birthday at the semen collection facility. "They threw a big party for him. There was a cake, and they brought him out and walked him around and made quite a fuss. Then he died the next week."

Of Connie: "Her sire is A. Marshfield Elevation Tony, and her BCA is 211-189-187."

And Squida: "She's a Matador daughter. He's a superior bull for type. As a 2-year-old, she had an unbalanced udder – as all Matadors do – but it evened out toward the end of her first lactation, and her BCA is 187-187-172." Squida is universally given top marks, which Jean finds amusing. "She's on our cull list. She's got a little mastitis, but she looks great when she's not milked." Lily is second – "She'd be worth showing" – followed by Connie and Stidler.

The crowd reassembles on the lawn for the crowning of the dairy princess – they are judged on public speaking and suitability rather than appearance, but the prettier girl wins anyway – then chats for a while longer and breaks up around 10 o'clock. It has been a lot of work and worry for a short three hours, and even before Bill and Eileen have said goodnight to the last of the guests, Jean is back in the barn, milking the four cows that were judged. "There," she says, throwing her hands into the air when she is done. "We never have to have another one of those."

———

With the Twilight Meeting out of the way and no pressing fieldwork to be done, Bill and Eileen take a break: a four-day weekend at a church-sponsored adult retreat near Ottawa. They are looking forward to renewing old friendships and having a few days together with no responsibilities. They phone back to say they are having a wonderful time and some nonfarming friends have talked them into staying an extra day. In their absence, Tom and Jean talk about their working conditions. Neither is very happy about them.

"We have to do something about these hours," Tom says. "I've had one day off in the last month. I don't feel pressured to work on my days off, it's not that. I like to work, especially when we're living in town – there's nothing to do except twiddle your thumbs anyway. No, I don't mind that so much, but we're supposed to be off at 6 o'clock, and that hasn't happened since we let the cows out in the spring. I don't mind during cropping or planting or whatever – you know, when something has to get done – but a lot of it there's just no reason for.

"And another thing. We're supposed to have an hour and a half for breakfast and dinner, but there's a lot of days that breakfast and dinner *together* don't add up to half an hour. Sometimes, it's just five minutes. I know guys that work on other farms – good, big, well-run farms too – and they get coffee breaks in the morning and afternoon. I don't think Bill knows what a coffee break is. And when they get an hour for dinner, it's a real hour – by the watch. They sit down at noon and they don't go back to work until 1, so if they finish eating at 12:30, that's their time, and they can have a nap or read a book or go home or whatever. I mean, they work real hard when they're working. I'm not saying they have it easy or anything – they really go at it – but when it's dinnertime, they sit down for an hour, and that's that. It doesn't have to be like this.

"I don't have a farm of my own, and I don't have to make these decisions, but I think Bill was wrong not to hire someone for the summer. You take Jean, now. I've worked with her long enough to know when she's really tired, and she's beat. You can see it in her eyes. Of course, she's family, and I don't want to get in the middle of that, but you're not going to find anybody else with her experience around these cows. I mean, it's her family farm too, and she's got a knowledge of these cows and a, I don't know, a *dedication* to them. Bill's not going to find someone else like that. And she's thinking of quitting. I'm afraid he's really blown it. He's going to end up running the place by himself."

While Jean was putting her name in at the A&P, Tom was asking at the Farm Labour Pool if other dairy farmers in the area needed some help. "There's a couple of guys who need a man," he says. "I don't know what I'm going to do.

"I don't want to say that Bill is taking advantage of me, but"–he pauses, compressing his lips–"well, it's just not right. You take this weekend, for instance. I understood Bill was going to be back on Tuesday night, Wednesday morning at the latest. Well, now I hear they're not going to get back till Thursday at noon. It's not right. I'm going to have to have a talk with Bill. It's possible he doesn't realize. I can hardly believe that, but I suppose it's possible. Bill's kind of wrapped up in all this, and maybe he doesn't see what's going on. I don't know. Jean feels the same way, so we're going to have to sit down and work something out."

––––––––

Since the 10 days when Bill cut the first of the hay in early June, there has been very little rain–a few days of scattered showers, but none have fallen on Bill's fields. Now, in late August, it is not yet a drought, but it is getting close. When George, the blond-haired football-player driver from the Co-op, comes out to spread a load of fertilizer on Bill's new seeding, Bill mentions the dry spell and George agrees. "Yes, my dad's on holidays in British Columbia now, so I'm getting the green chop for him while he's gone." He means that his father's beef cows are kept in a paddock, and every day, he drives out into a hay-field and cuts a day's worth of grass for the cows with a forage harvester. The harvester blows the grass into an open-bottomed hopper on a feed rack, called a zero-graze wagon. When the hopper is full of fresh-cut grass, he parks the wagon in the paddock so that the cows can eat out of it. "It usually takes about 45 minutes to fill the wagon," George continues, "but now it takes an hour and a half because, even though it's green, it's so dry that the wind just blows it away."

With all the crops gone, the home farm has a clean look about it, like just-vacuumed broadloom. The barley stubble is the colour of a corn broom, hard and bristly looking but softened by the fuzz of green seeding underneath. Back at Pearl's, the fields of stubble and still-standing corn are a study in contrasts: gold versus green, short versus tall, tidy versus fecund, finished versus waiting. But even the corn is starting to look brown on top. The long, narrow leaves that fold up in the midday heat are shrivelled on the ends, and the cobs droop on their stalks. When Tom Moreland tells his brother he's heard that some farmers are going to start combining their corn next week because of the dry weather, Bill decides he'd better have a close look at his own crop.

He and Mark drive back to Pearl's, park the truck at the gate and walk into the field. Bill is happy with the absence of weeds – the spray did its job and so did the single cultivation. He is less happy about the crop. The cobs are only 6 to 8 inches long – he was hoping for 10-to-12-inch cobs. And they are not completely filled out; that is, the kernels on the ends did not mature. Bill and Mark walk about 20 rows into the field, where Bill peels back the husk and breaks a cob in half. He chews on a kernel, holding the broken end of the cob up to the light. It is quite moist in the middle. "Corn is supposed to mature and dry from the inside out," Bill explains. "Because of the dry weather, this is drying from the outside in. It's not drying out, it's drying up. Much more of this, and it will just turn to mush." Still, he decides the kernels are too moist yet to harvest. This is enough of a surprise that he wonders if Pearl's got more rain than the home farm, a mile to the south.

Mark brings a cob with him to the truck, and Bill teases him about taking food from the cows. "Somebody's going to go hungry tonight because you stole her food." Mark punches him in the shoulder.

As August matures, Bill starts to think about the fall chores, the largest being the removal of the manure at Pearl's. The calves that were raised in the barn there have been outside most of the summer, but the manure from last winter is still packed in the barn – two feet of shit, straw, spilled hay and urine tromped into an adobelike consistency by the sharp hooves of ever active calves. Bill breaks it up with the front-end loader on the small Deere, and Russell and Tom take turns enriching the barley stubble across the road with a pair of manure spreaders. The warm sun and cool breeze combine to create a truly pleasant fall day. In the field, the tractors drive through a green mat of boot-top-high red clover, flinging bits of brown manure against the blue sky.

For Russell and Tom, this is easy going. It is all tractor work, and the field is close enough to the barn that they can keep ahead of Bill, giving each of them a pleasant break while their spreaders are being loaded. Bill is having less fun. He must duck under the door every time he drives into the barn, and the manure pack is hard enough to make every bucketful a struggle. The ammonia from the disturbed manure stings his eyes, and the tractor exhaust is just as bad or perhaps worse. The work is a tricky balance between charging and bulling to get somewhere and holding back in the cramped quarters to preserve the building. But he remembers worse.

"We used to have calves over in that old barn behind Tom's shop, and we had to do the pens there by hand. The stuff would be tromped down just about solid, and oh, it was an awful job. Then after a while, we got an old tractor and loader in there, but it didn't have power steering, so it was easier on your back, but your arms would hang down to your knees after a day of that."

Russell, of course, remembers even further back. "You know, it's a lot better than it used to be. We used to have to do all this by hand — pitch it on and pitch it off. We'd throw it out of the barn and onto a sled, then fork it off the sled as the horses pulled it down the field. Mind you, there was a lot more of us and a lot fewer cows to do it for. But hydraulics have been a wonderful thing for the farmer," he adds, not for the first time. "Yessir, a wonderful thing."

Once, when Russell returns from the field with an empty spreader, Tom is using a pitchfork to return some small clumps of spilled manure to his spreader. Russell smiles. "Careful you don't break the handle on that," he says, and Tom grins his slow grin.

"Well, it's a grand day," Russell continues, stepping down from the tractor. "You know, I like to live where they have four seasons, not someplace where it's the same all the time. I like change. I know a fellow who worked in the aluminum plant in town. He and another guy took pieces of aluminum from one machine to another, one of them on each side of these big sheets, d'ye see. That was their job, and that's what they did all day. He told me that after a while, they ran out of things to say to each other. It drove him crazy — he couldn't stand the job. That's why I like farming — you're out in the sunshine, and you have a chance to do something different all the time. Of course, there's such a thing as too much sunshine. I see there's a lot of fellows putting in corn silage. That's the first time in my life I can remember corn going into the silos in August." He glances over at the brown tops of Bill's corn and shakes his head.

As 12 o'clock comes and goes, Russell looks at his watch. "The thing about Bill," he says, "is you never know when he's going to quit. It used to be when it was dinnertime, it was dinnertime, and you went and had your dinner. With Bill, now, you never know. Of course, this new time doesn't help anything, either." Daylight saving time is a favourite hobbyhorse for Russell, and he likes to give it a ride at every opportunity. DST is nice for office workers, he says, who enjoy the extra hour of light in the evening without missing it in the morning, but it is no boon to farmers, who must get up in the dark almost every day of the year but are still driven to work until it is dark again. "You're out there in a field, and it's quitting time, and the sun is still up in the sky. I just can't get along with this new time – it doesn't work out for farmers."

Having exhausted the weather and his eating and working habits, Russell turns to current events. The Liberals have just swept to power in a decisive provincial election. "I'm not sure it's a good thing to have a big majority like that. I think we're better off with a strong opposition. But I hear on the news that there were more women elected this time than ever before. That's good to see. There are a lot of good women out there, and they should be running things. Look at all the work women do in the church – there are a lot of churches that would fall apart without their work." Russell would hardly categorize himself as a feminist, and he certainly doesn't hold with such things as abortion on demand, but he has seen too many farm wives working alongside their husbands to have doubts about the equality of the sexes. Russell's hard-bitten practicality leads him to conclude that women can "run things" as well as men – therefore they ought to. "There are a lot of women pretty upset by what the Pope said about birth control too. And they're right to be upset. We're past all that now."

Also in the news is labour trouble at Via Rail and the post office: "Oh, this labour thing is just getting out of hand. But then, you think about these corporation presidents or whatever that they're working for. They're making big money – far too big. You can't blame the unions for wanting a little more when they see that."

And finally Pearl, who has announced that she is going to move out and live with a relative: "Oh, I'm glad she's moving. Now we don't have to worry about her all alone up here in the winter and maybe finding her frozen someday."

Ironically, Pearl told Eileen of her decision to move on the same day that Tom and Audrey moved into *their* new house. "I'm real glad I've got this new place and I'm not moving into Pearl's," says Tom. "And Audrey is glad too." He and Bill have had enough of a chat to agree on new hours. Tom now comes to work at 8 a.m. instead of 5, but he is still not entirely happy. "I really like coming in at 8 – I get to see the kids in the morning – but, I don't know, Bill may have to hire another person. Look at all the work Russell does around here. There's going to come a day when he can't do that. And Bill and Eileen are gone every second weekend. Oh, I know Bill stays home during planting and cropping, but he usually gets every second weekend off. There's not many farmers – not many dairy farmers, anyway – who can do that."

If the truth were told, though, working alternate weekends is not a problem for Tom, and neither is working late during the busy times. He is irritated by the extra hours that seem unnecessary to him, but it is only after grumbling about some of the small irritants that he gets around to his major complaint. "I don't like all this working in the barn. I want to work outside more. I know it doesn't make any money, but I'd like to get out in the bush." Tom grew up cutting wood and building things, and those are the jobs he likes. If he had his way, he would spend all his days outside, perhaps building log houses for a living.

Bill is not happy with the new arrangement either. "Tom wants to come in at 8, and I can understand that – I see his point – but it's not when I need him. I need him here early. What I need is to have someone here early in the morning, and then, as far as I'm concerned, he could turn around and go home at 9 till noon, after we get the day set up. He comes in at 8, and that's almost the time I don't need him. It's costing me almost $40,000 a year for labour, and I'm not getting enough for it. For a 50-cow operation, I'm doing too much work for having to pay out that amount.

"It's not the money so much – we're fairly well off financially, and according to the Farm Labour Pool, we're in the upper end of what people pay – it's not that. It's that I'm not getting enough work done – I'm still working too hard myself. You know, I have to think about my back, and I have to rest it. A couple of short rests are better for it than one long one. I'd like to be able to get someone to come and milk in the morning once in the middle of the week.

"Now with Jean, that's not too bad. I'd like to keep her as a sort of full-time relief person, keep her working all the time and on salary but just relieving everybody. And maybe coming one day a week to do all the cow registrations and all that – that takes a lot of time.

"So we'll wait till things get settled down. Tom can get in his new place, and we can get the manure out and the ploughing finished and all that. Then we might have to get someone new. I'm certainly not happy with this new setup. I like Tom and I'd like to keep him. I certainly don't want to just drop him and see him stuck, you know, just after his move and everything. But I'm not getting what I need. Sometimes you have to look out for number one." Bill is so uncomfortable with this last thought, he squirms as he says it.

"What I'd really like is to have someone live back here at Pearl's. Now she's moving out, and that's fine – I'm glad we don't have to worry about finding her frozen to death some morning this winter – but I think I'll just leave this place empty for a few months and see what happens. If I had a man who lived here, he could go home for lunch if he wanted to. You know, you can't work someone to death. You have to give them time off too. That's something I have to remember. If I could get someone a little older – 35, 40, maybe even 45 – someone with a little experience," the sentence trails off with a shrug. "We don't do too much bull work here, so someone who can milk cows and drive a tractor is all we need. I used to think I wanted a young fellow so I could get some work out of him, but now, well, maybe I should get someone I can keep up with."

––––––––

Toward the end of August, Bill agrees to give a tour of the farm to a group of visitors attending a science conference at Queen's University at Kingston. Bill believes that such public relations efforts pay dividends in consumer acceptance of dairy products – and their prices. He believes his cause is just, and if people could have a glimpse of things from his side, then they would agree. And besides, the barn and grounds are still spiffy from the Twilight Meeting.

On the appointed day, everybody gives the place a little spit and polish, and it positively glows. Two items have been prepared differently for this event than for the Twilight Meeting: the cows have been left in their tie stalls; and the manure gutters behind them have been filled with fresh sawdust from a couple of bags Bill bought for the occasion. It's nice to let city people see the country, but some things are best hidden. After lunch, Bill, Eileen, Tom, Jean and Russell stand around in the milk house waiting for the bus to arrive. Under their nonchalant, no-big-deal attitude is a strum of tension. After all, this is open house on their lives, like having 40 strangers peek into their bedroom closets.

Twenty minutes late, the bus finally pulls into the barnyard, and 12 or 15 families gratefully spill out. They are from all over North America – Texas, California, British Columbia, Pennsylvania – and this stop is a welcome break from the endless seminars and hotel coffee-shop breakfasts. Bill asks the tour director, an improbably blonde woman, what the group is interested in.

"The high-tech aspect of modern dairy farming," she replies without hesitation.

So Bill gets their attention and starts by introducing himself and his crew, who are all standing around, leaning on walls. "This is my father, Russell Moreland. He's retired now, but he helps us milk every morning and still does a lot of tractor work. My sister Jean, here, is our herdsperson, but she does a lot of work too. Tom Mac-Farlane is our hired man. And this is my wife Eileen. She helps out in the barn when she's needed" – Eileen and Bill share their private joke in front of strangers – "and our son Mark." He then launches into an ad lib about high-tech farming. "When my Dad started farming, they milked the cows in the summer and dried them up in the winter. All the calves were born in April and May, and the cows were out on grass all summer. Then in the winter, they fixed up the machinery and got everything ready for the next summer. Now, of course, it's a year-round proposition."

This is a group that has heard lectures for four days straight, and several pairs of eyes are starting to glaze over when the tour director steps ahead. "Maybe we could have a look in the barn now, and people can ask about the equipment as they see it." It soon becomes apparent, though, as the group straggles into the barn, that they want nothing more than to look at the cows and stretch their legs. Nobody asks any questions about the equipment, high-tech or otherwise.

As people wander through the barn, Bill leans close to Tom and whispers, "Lily just crapped. Grab a fork and cover it up, will you?" The cows are nervous, so this happens quite a lot, and the visitors go home with the impression that covering cow flaps is a full-time job. A 15-year-old girl, in the throes of adolescent intensity and wearing a pair of pristinely white shorts, can hardly bear to enter the barn. The country air, the whitewashed ceiling, the freshly painted walls, the immaculate milking equipment that Jean is so proud of mean nothing to this girl. All she can absorb is the *disgusting* smell of that *yucky* stuff. Holding her nose and waving her other hand in front of her face, she bravely ventures into the barn. Just then, Chrissy arches her back and urinates onto the concrete behind her. It is too much for the girl – she flees.

A middle-aged woman has a stronger stomach. "Oh, I haven't been in a barn for 40 years," she says, looking around with a smile. Meanwhile, her companion has spotted a calf at the back of the barn. "Ohhh, it's so cute," she says to Russell. "Tell me, what is a calf like that worth?" From the tone of her voice, she might be considering buying one for a pet, but she has asked the wrong person about the wrong calf. Russell is enjoying his role as old codger, and the calf is a bull that Bill will sell to a veal farmer in a few days.

"Well, that calf is worth over a hundred dollars, but of course, that's now. I remember back in The Dirty Thirties, when I was farming here, that what you did with a bull calf like that was you skinned it because then you could get 25¢ for the hide." The women gasp in horror and move on.

Two men walk slowly up and down the centre aisle, stopping to look at the back end of every cow. Like art critics in a gallery, they take turns nodding sagely, rubbing a chin in consideration or stepping back with crossed arms for a different angle. When they come to Tom, standing in the aisle to the milk house, they examine him as closely as they have the cows. Tom is leaning on a pitchfork, dressed in his work boots, with jeans and freshly washed red suspenders over a plaid work shirt. Shocks of hair stick out from under his dilapidated railroad engineer's cap. After a while, one man nods and says to the other, "Hired man." The second man nods in agreement, and they move on to the next cow.

This pleasant interlude is interrupted by shrieks from outside the barn. When everyone rushes outside, they find the 15-year-old girl in tears beside the calf hutches. "It tried to eat my shorts," she wails, pointing to one of the calves, which had latched onto her shorts and all but inhaled them. One saliva-sodden corner – which the girl will not touch – is twisted into the shape of a teat.

The tour director takes this opportunity to finish up the event with a few hurried words of thanks to Bill, then harries her charges onto the bus. The woman who last visited a farm 40 years ago straggles behind and is obviously reluctant to leave. With one hand on the door of the bus, she takes a final look around, then smiles at the idyllic beauty of it all.

"It's so quiet in the country," she says. "So peaceful."

EPILOGUE

When Bill can't get a part he needs for his chain saw, he borrows Ed Johnston's saw for a couple of days, but a plastic piece breaks when Tom is using it, and the handle comes off in his hand. The next day, Ed pulls up in front of the barn. Using the car door for support, he pulls himself to his feet and straightens up. "Aarrgghh," he hollers, loud enough to make the cows jump to their feet in alarm. Bill comes out of the milk house with the broken saw.

"Well, Ed, we had a little trouble with it. I'm sorry, I hope it doesn't put you out." He explains how it happened. "I'll certainly get you a new piece."

Tom steps out of the barn. "Sorry about the saw, Ed. Is there still a warranty on it?"

"Haw, haw, haw. Why, that saw's older than you are."

"Well, Tom," says Bill, with a wink at Ed, "do you come with a warranty?"

"I don't know." Slow grin. "I never had any defective parts."

"Haw, haw, haw. Well, this has been a pretty good saw, but it's not like that old John Deere saw I used to have. I put 147 gallons of gas through that old saw." Ed smiles at his memories, and Bill mumbles something appropriate. It is obvious that Ed wants to reminisce. "Yessir, that's a lot of gas when you put it in one pint at a time. I cut wood with that saw for 10 years – went through 14 chains. And when I'm done with a chain, it's done."

"Yeah," says Bill, "that chain looks like it's about beat." The teeth, about three-eighths inch long when new, have been reduced to nubs.

"That? Why, that's just getting broke in. Oh, Christ, yes. I can hardly wait till they get like this. When a chain is new, you have to sharpen it every couple of hours, but I can cut all day with this chain if I don't hit anything with it, and it'll still be sharp." Once started, Ed moves even farther back in time and talks about the days when he cut wood with a crosscut saw. In one story, he remembers working for someone who had a contract to supply firewood for the local schoolhouse. On the last day of the contract, the wood was cut but not split, and it had to be stacked in the school by 3 p.m. "We was cutting hard maple, we was, with a crosscut saw, and we had it all cut in 22-inch-long blocks for the school. I remember this one tree was 22 inches across the butt, and we cut 22 blocks out of it, so you can figure out how much wood was in it. Anyway, we got it all split and put in the school on time, and he gave us $5 each. That was really something."

Bill smiles. "It doesn't seem like much money now, does it?"

"Yeah, but that was back when you worked 10 hours a day and got $1.50 – 15¢ an hour. So that $5 was really something."

In all, Ed rambles on for about 45 minutes. Bill has not stood in one place for this long all summer, and he frets about the lost time. Later, when Ed is gone, Bill says, "Well, it seemed like he wanted to talk, and you can't really say, 'Here's your saw, sorry I broke it, now excuse me, I'm kind of busy.' Besides," he spreads his hands, "he had time for me when I hit that rock with the combine, and he helped me get it fixed."

So Bill stands in his yard listening to Ed's stories about the old days. Finally, Ed looks at his watch and says, "Well, I can't stand around here and talk all day, by the Jesus. I've got things to do."

"A fellow goes for a walk with this girl, d'ye see." It is a rainy September Saturday, and Russell is driving down to the county ploughing match. Ruth, who has taken another fall, is unable to walk on rough ground, so she stays home. "After a while, the fellow sits down on the ground. He puts his hand on the grass beside him, and he says to the girl, 'Some dew.' 'Yep,' she says, 'and some don't. I'm going home.' "

On his way, Russell drives across a bridge over Highway 401 – "I never thought I'd live to see a highway like this go through here" – and passes the church his father used to attend. "I mind when the churches joined." He means when the United Church was formed from the union of Presbyterian, Methodist and Congregational churches in 1925. "The people at this church were pretty upset. When they were supposed to join, some of the men came in on Saturday night and drilled two holes in the church doors. Then they looped a big chain through them and put a lock on it so no one could get in on Sunday morning. My dad said, 'If that's what religion is, people fighting each other like that, I don't want any part of it,' and he never went to church again. But I keep going. Oh, yes, I like it."

Russell knows everybody at the ploughing match, which consists of a few equipment displays, a tent with a doughnut concession and a field divided into sections being ploughed by competitors driving tractors or horses. The sections will be judged on the straightness and even spacing of the furrows. Both of the newly elected MPPs from the area are here, and Russell asks after their parents by their first names. Somebody complains about the wet weather to him, and

Russell commiserates. "Well, it's like my dad used to say. It's too bad dry weather causes any harm. We need the rain, but every day we get some is a day you get behind.

"Say," he says, brightening, "did you hear about the three little boys who were talking? The first fellow says, 'My dad is so fast, he can shoot an arrow and then run and catch it.' The second little fellow says, 'My dad can shoot a gun and then get to the target before the bullet.' And the third boy says, 'Yeah, well, my dad works for the government. He gets off work at 4:30, but he's so fast, he's home every day at 3 o'clock.' "

Later, looking at the row of farm equipment on display, Russell finds the John Deere baler Bill ordered last fall. It arrived in time to sit out in the rain here before being dropped off at the farm a month after all the baling was finished. "We were lucky the old one held together as well as it did," says Russell. "Damn lucky."

Also in September, Bob Norris tells Bill and Eileen about an adventure he had the previous weekend when he went out for dinner with his wife and another couple. Eileen tells the expurgated version: "Well, Bob dropped everyone else off at the door and went and parked the car. As he was walking back up to the restaurant through this little park area, a woman asked Bob to take her photograph with a Polaroid camera. She was wearing one of those sweater dresses, and Bob didn't think she had too much on underneath it. Anyway, she places Bob and goes over and stands by this low wall and says 'Okay.' But when Bob looks through the viewfinder, she's got her dress pulled up over her head – not a stitch on underneath – and one leg cocked up on the wall. Can you imagine? 'Take it,' she says to Bob, so he does. Then she wants *another* one, but Bob can't wind the film ahead, so she comes over and shows him how the camera works. This time, the dress comes off entirely, but she's got this wide-brimmed hat that covers her face. Four pictures in all, and when they're done, she offers one to Bob. Well, he figures he'd better take one or no one will ever believe him."

"Sure enough," Bill says, "he pulled the picture out of his wallet, and there she was." He grins and shakes his head. "It could only happen to Bob."

"Well, I think he missed a real opportunity," says Eileen. "He could have gone back and gotten one of his brassieres for her."

Jean gets a job offer from the A&P but decides not to quit the farm after all. Instead, she reduces her hours, working only until noon – a mere seven hours a day – so she can have lunch, dinner and a full evening with her family. Her major disappointment in the fall is Seven, who, after what was thought to be her last pregnancy, delivers twins, both bulls. "She's given us lots of heifers already," Jean says. "We could just never find the right bull for her." Despite a bout of milk fever, though, Seven is in astonishingly good health heading into her 12th year, and Jean decides they will try to breed her once again.

Tom, however, does take a new job on a dairy farm just down the road from his new house. He and Bill part company amicably at the end of September. Tom's new boss, George Horton, "isn't quite as particular as Bill," he says, "so everything isn't maybe quite as spick-and-span as it is at Bill's, but he's a good farmer just the same." More important, he has a different philosophy, preferring to give a lower-quality feed to lower-quality cows, thus producing less milk at less expense. Compared with the Ferraris in Bill's barn, George's Volkswagens chug along at the speed limit with considerably less care, allowing Tom to spend fewer working hours in the barn. Also, George has a large woodlot that includes a substantial sugar bush. Tom is looking forward to cutting wood all winter and boiling off maple syrup in the spring. "I like Bill and Eileen," he says, "and I learned a lot from Bill. But I think this is going to work out better for me."

Bill and Eileen take their time looking for Tom's replacement and end up doing without anyone for more than a month, during which Eileen spends a lot of time in the barn. "I don't know how people can farm and not get a weekend off every once in a while," she says. "I just don't know how they can get along like that, 365 days a year." Eventually, though, they hire Murray Geekie, a young man with a family and a hope that he will have a dairy farm of his own someday. Murray moves into Pearl's house, where it is convenient for him to come to work at 5 a.m. and to take care of the calves in the afternoon. "We really like him," says Eileen. "He seems to fit in well."

In October, Tutu, one of Lulu's daughters, bears a fine-looking heifer calf. It is a C-year – Cool, Corey, Carol – but Bill asks Jean if they can make an exception. She agrees, and thus Lulu is reincarnated. Mark is thrilled and immediately claims her as his new favourite cow.

Looking back over the summer, Bill's attention is drawn to his year's milk production. He filled all his Group 1 quota but fell short of his MSQ – 190,431 litres, only 92.5 percent of his allowable total. Bill usually ships about 99 percent, and this is his poorest showing yet, but it is more than the 80 percent he needs to avoid being assessed a penalty. "Well," he explains, "we were down a bit last fall, but I figured we could make it up in the spring. But then we had a little bout of mastitis. I mean, Emy Q gives 128 pounds of milk a day, and she had mastitis off and on all spring. That really adds up. Then as soon as we got over that, we had all that hot weather, so we never did make it up." The shortfall would have been worth 43¢ a litre had Bill filled it, more than enough to buy and feed a cow to make up the difference.

"It cost us about $6,400, and I guess you could say that's poor management." Bill has been gesturing with his right hand, but now he drops it and uses his left. "On the other hand, we only missed by 15,000 litres. Our monthly production is over 40,000 litres, so 15,000 is only about 10 days' worth of milk. Over a year, that's not that bad. So it's good management that we came as close as we did.

"And besides, it gives us something to improve on next year."

AFTERWORD

Careful readers will be able to piece together enough clues to determine exactly where Bill and Eileen live. If you wish to hop in your car and drive past the farm, I encourage you to do so. Slow down as you go by, and wave if you see someone in the yard or working around the barn. They are polite people, and they will wave back. But please, leave it at that. Do not pull in the driveway to say hello or to get a closer look at the barn. The Morelands are too nice to be rude to you, but they have no time to entertain unexpected visitors. The farm comes first.

CREDITS

Marta Scythes: illustrations on pages 32, 36, 40, 57, 85, 93, 105, 107, 108, 139, 142, 149, 159, 187, 205

Eric Hayes: photographs on pages 129-135

J.A. Kraulis: photograph on page 136